C000018331

Management
Consulting
in practice

Management Consulting
in practice

Award-winning International Case Studies

Fiona Czerniawska & Paul May

M·C·A
MANAGEMENT
CONSULTANCIES
ASSOCIATION

**KOGAN
PAGE**

London and Sterling, VA

Publisher's note

Every possible effort has been made to ensure that the information contained in this book is accurate at the time of going to press, and the publishers and authors cannot accept responsibility for any errors or omissions, however caused. No responsibility for loss or damage occasioned to any person acting, or refraining from action, as a result of the material in this publication can be accepted by the editor, the publisher or any of the authors.

First published in Great Britain and the United States in 2004 by Kogan Page Limited

120 Pentonville Road
London N1 9JN
United Kingdom
www.kogan-page.co.uk

22883 Quicksilver Drive
Sterling VA 20166-2012
USA

© Management Consultancies Association, 2004

ISBN 0 7494 4281 6

British Library Cataloguing-in-Publication Data

A CIP record for this book is available from the British Library.

Library of Congress Cataloging-in-Publication Data

Czerniawska, Fiona.
    Management consulting in practice: case studies in international best practice/
Fiona Czerniawska & Pual May.
        p. cm.
    Includes bibliographical references and index.
    ISBN 0-7494-4281-6
    1. Business consultants--Case studies. I. May, Paul, 1963- II. Title.
    HD69.C6C9235 2004
    001'.068--dc22

                                        2004013741

Typeset by Datamatics Technologies Ltd, Mumbai, India
Printed and bound in Great Britain by Thanet Press Ltd, Margate

Contents

About the Management Consultancies Association

The Management Consultancies Association (MCA) was formed in 1956 to represent the consultancy industry to clients, the media and government. Today, the Association's members employ around 60 per cent of the UK consulting sector, which is worth approximately £10 billion, contributing £1 billion to the balance of payments. MCA members work with FTSE 100 companies and all government departments.

A principal objective of the MCA is to maintain high standards within the UK management consultancy sector by ensuring that member firms meet stringent entry criteria and adhere to a code of professional conduct. MCA members must also comply with professional and ethical standards, which provide reassurance to purchasers of consultancy.

As well as setting and maintaining standards in the consulting industry, the MCA supports its member firms with a range of services including events, publications, interest groups and PR. The MCA works with its members to recruit and retain the top talent, provides advice to purchasers of consultancy on the selection and use of management consultants and is the main source of data on the UK market.

Management consultancy is the creation of value for organizations, through the application of knowledge, techniques and assets, to improve performance. This is achieved through the rendering of objective advice and/or the implementation of business solutions.

About the authors

Fiona Czerniawska is one of the world's leading commentators on the consulting industry. Since publishing her first book on consulting five years ago, she has become an internationally regarded authority on future trends in the industry whose ideas have shaped the boardroom agenda of major consulting firms. Fiona is the Director of the UK Management Consultancies Association's Think Tank and the founder and managing director of Arkimeda (www.arkimeda.com), a firm that specializes in researching and consulting on strategic issues in the consulting industry. Fiona speaks and writes extensively on the consulting industry and related issues. Recent books include *Management Consulting: What Next?* (Macmillan, 2002), *Value-based Consulting* (Macmillan, 2002) and *The Intelligent Client* (Hodder & Stoughton, 2002). Fiona is also the author of many commercial reports on consulting including *White Space: Who are the Real Thought Leaders in Management Consulting?* (Arkimeda, 2004).

Paul May is a business technology author, consultant, systems architect and business development executive. In October 1998, he formed the independent e-commerce consulting practice Verista (www.verista.com), and has since undertaken strategy and implementation projects with well-known global companies such as BP and Siemens, and with business-to-consumer and business-to-business e-commerce startups in the UK and USA. He is a co-founder of the software development company Avenida (www.avenida.co.uk), and of RioBrand (www.riobrand.com), the global brand information repository. Paul is also the author of *Mobile Commerce: Opportunities, Applications and Technologies of Wireless Business* (Cambridge University Press, 2001) and *The Business of Ecommerce: from Corporate Strategy to Technology* (Cambridge University Press, 2000).

Foreword

How many management consultancy projects can claim to have made significant improvements to the lives of millions of people? The case studies in this book contain practical solutions to monstrously complicated problems requiring not only clever, innovative thinking and broad international experience, but tact and diplomacy qualities which would challenge the UN.

Claims are often made for the impact of consultancy projects, but all too often this is at best piecemeal and at worst anecdotal. The majority of projects described in this book employed rigorous and extensive measurement techniques to assess the effectiveness of the initiatives and policies undertaken.

Management consultants – or at least the benefits they bring – are regarded with a good deal of scepticism by big business (as measured in MORI's Captains of Industry surveys for example), and the media delight in telling us of big government project failures. This book does a great job of redressing the balance.

Professor Robert Worcester
Chairman
MORI

Acknowledgements

Books such as this are never possible without the help and cooperation of a large number of people. The authors would particularly like to thank Sarah Taylor and Joy Hewgill at the Management Consultancies Association, and the team at Kogan Page, for their energy and commitment to the project. We are also grateful to the numerous individuals in the PR and marketing departments of the firms included in this book for their help in pulling together the case study material.

Chapter 1 makes use of some material first published in the MCA report 'The UK Consulting Industry 2003/2004'; this material is reprinted here with kind permission of the MCA. All other trademarks that appear in the text are recognized as the property of their owners.

Introduction

What is 'best practice' in management consulting? Can it be recognized, measured, and replicated?

The Management Consultancies Association's Awards for Best Management Practice are designed to highlight the very best standards in all areas of management consulting, from business strategy, through operational performance improvement to outsourcing. Consulting firms entering for an award have to present case studies of their work with clients for evaluation by a distinguished panel drawn from industry and academia. The awards are given for real projects that make a genuine difference to clients' businesses.

This book collects case studies from the most recent MCA award winners to show just how these firms and their clients succeeded in ensuring high-quality consulting. Each case study explores a unique business situation and the way it was tackled by the team. The case studies also examine how teams responded to the challenges that arose during their projects and the sometimes unexpected lessons they learned.

The first part of the book introduces the themes that occur repeatedly throughout the book. Using data gathered from clients and consultants as part of the MCA's awards process, Chapter 1 argues that, in a world where project-based work is increasingly the norm, collaboration is the key to success. The key obstacle to genuine collaboration – as opposed to lip-service about working in partnership – is obtaining the buy-in from stakeholders on all sides of the relationship. Effective relationships are characterized by openness, honesty and trust. Trust can only be built up by individuals working together over a period of time; it's not something that can be transmitted by a consulting brand. Chapter 2 introduces three overall winning entries from the MCA Awards: the International Olympic Committee's work with Atos Origin; PA Consulting Group's work with Westminster City Council; and Edengene's work with BT Business.

The remaining case studies are divided into seven sections, reflecting the original award categories:

- change management;
- human resources;
- operational performance;
- business strategy;
- technology exploitation;
- outsourcing;
- electronic trading.

Management consulting is a broad and mature industry that plays an integral role in the development of successful businesses. The MCA is dedicated to articulating the professionalism, diversity and value-add of management consulting organizations. Its annual awards are a key part of that mission. We hope this book will form a powerful and unique resource for consultants, managers and business students looking for real-world insights into the sharp end of contemporary management consulting.

The power of working together

Business is not what it used to be.

It used to be that a manager got up, arrived at (invariably) his office, managed the same processes, ticked the same boxes, talked to the same staff, day in day out. A consultant, when he (again, invariably) was called in – which was not very often – was present purely as an adviser, a sounding board for the manager's concerns, a person whose business school education gave him superior techniques for solving the problems his client faced.

Today's client is just as likely to have an MBA as a consultant; indeed, he or she may be an ex-consultant. The consultant is just as likely to have had line responsibilities as the manager. Clients expect consultants to be committed to their opinions and accountable for the results, to be doers as much as advisers. Consultants want to be able to share the credit if things go well; they also know that they will have to share the risk of failure, too. According to Derek Turner, the Managing Director of Street Management at Transport for London, and one of the clients featured in this book: 'The days are gone when a consultant borrows the client's watch to tell him the time.'

In the last 10 years and despite a significant downturn in 2001–02, the revenues of the world's top 40 consulting firms have grown from US $17 billion to more than US $82 billion. Alongside these firms is an immeasurable number of medium-sized and small-sized firms, and independent consultants. Nor is the significance of the consulting industry confined to its size. As the case studies in this book illustrate, consultants are now used in a wide variety of capabilities in every sector of the economy, from working with hardware manufacturer Sun Microsystems to improve its problem-handling processes, to helping

Sainsbury's Supermarkets outsource its massive IT function. And it is not just business that is affected – the consultants in this book have done things as varied as improving the way in which doctors can order drugs to making public transport safer.

What is driving this is a gradual shift away from thinking about organizations as permanent structures, which have to have all the facilities, resources and skills they need in-house, to treating them as portfolios – of opportunities to be exploited, threats to be minimized, problems to be solved, resources to be deployed. As a greater proportion of work in organizations becomes project-based, it makes sense to turn to organizations that are accustomed to working in this way and have specialist knowledge of particular fields – consulting firms. Why insist that everyone on a project has to come from your own organization when consulting firms may have the specific know-how you need, experience of solving the same issues before, and new tools and techniques?

However, the fact that consultants can add value in this project-based environment does not mean that they always do so. Inept consultants, overselling, lack of innovation, ambiguous scope and conflicting aims are just some of the reasons for poor-quality consulting.

The case studies in this book (see Table 1.1) illustrate how both consulting firms and their clients are working to improve the contribution consultants make and the effectiveness of management overall.

If these lessons could be summed up in one word, it would be partnership. As the firms profiled here have recognized, neither clients nor consultants benefit from a confrontational environment in which each side is seeking to promote its own interest at the expense of the other. Of course, partnership is a dangerous word to use in this context, abused as it has been by a generation of marketing literature from consulting firms that paid lip-service to an idea that was rarely realized in practice. During 2000–02 the term was jilted in favour of a heavy reliance on rigid contractual arrangements. A genuine partnership, however, involves a combination of the two.

At a corporate level, it is clear that the aims of each side need to be closely matched. Each party needs an incentive to behave and contribute in a way that supports the collective effort, not self-interest. In most of the projects described in this book, the consulting firms are not being remunerated according to time spent, but to objectives met. Most clients are sharing, not just the risks of a project going badly, but the rewards of it going well.

At an individual level, people simply have to get along. A close working relationship, mutual respect and openness among the people involved will carry a project through the bad times as well as the good far more effectively than a contract will.

Table 1.1 *Projects, organizations and consulting firms featured in this book*

Case study	Title	Client	Consulting firm
2.1	Customers driving local services	Westminster City Council	PA Consulting Group
2.2	Reinventing a core offer	BT Business	Edengene
2.3	How to build a new digital city every two years	International Olympic Committee	Atos Origin
3.1	Living the brand — for real	Tesco	Trilogy
3.2	Delivering safer buses	Transport for London	PA Consulting Group
3.3	Electronic payments for 13 million citizens	Department for Work and Pensions	PA Consulting Group
4.1	Protecting the benefits of staff in transition	Apache Corporation	Mercer Human Resource Consulting
4.2	Diagnosing and treating workforce ailments	Evotec OAI	Penna Consulting
4.3	Standing down, moving forward	Ministry of Defence	Right Management Consultants
5.1	Blue skies, blue bills and online breakthroughs	BT Retail	Edengene
5.2	Smarter methods to beat constraints	Norwich Community Hospital	Ashridge Consulting Ltd
5.3	Relocating the organization and redesigning its mind	Government Communications Headquarters (GCHQ)	PA Consulting Group
5.4	Bringing rationality to bear	Sun Microsystems	Kepner-Tregoe
6.1	Changing people for a change	Harrogate Healthcare NHS Trust	RightCoutts
6.2	Releasing the future from the present	The Duke of Edinburgh's Award International Foundation	Capgemini
7.1	Closing the net on persistent offenders	Home Office	PA Consulting Group
7.2	Great journeys and small steps	Transport for London	Deloitte

(Continued)

Table 1.1 *Continued*

7.3	Mobile technology as enabler and enforcer	Bradford Hospitals NHS Trust	Atos Origin
7.4	When small businesses go global	All England Lawn Tennis Club	IBM
8.1	Evolving the outsourcing market	Medicines and Healthcare products Regulatory Agency	PA Consulting Group
8.2	Outsourcing for outcomes	Vehicle and Operator Services Agency	Atos Origin
8.3	Gearing up for renewed battle	Sainsbury's Supermarkets Ltd	Accenture
9.1	Pioneering multi-channel voting	The Office of the Deputy Prime Minister	Unisys
9.2	Collaborating systems drive down costs	BAE Systems Customer Services	CSC Computer Sciences Corporation
9.3	A knowledge portal helps close the deprivation gap	Neighbourhood Renewal Unit	PA Consulting Group
9.4	Flow, streams and the erosion of resistance	Aon	Impact Plus

Put these two things together and you can – as the case studies show – achieve extraordinary things. 'What's the key lesson?' asked one client. 'The power of working together.'

But there are other lessons, too.

The first years of the new millennium have been difficult ones for the consulting industry. Client cynicism – the result of frustration with a succession of management fads that have failed to deliver – combined with economic downturn have put the consulting industry under unprecedented pressure to defend the contribution it makes to clients. In place of the implementation of large-scale IT systems, clients have focused on a better use of their existing assets; instead of developing visionary strategies for emerging markets, they have concentrated on cost-reduction closer to home. There was something of an improvement during 2003 and the first half of 2004 (as this book went to press), with consulting firms' order books filling up and key sectors, such as financial services, starting to use consultants again.

Every year, as part of the awards process, the MCA carries out a survey (the MCA Awards Survey) of the projects submitted for consideration. Clients and consultants are separately asked to discuss:

■   the factors that led to the consulting firm winning the work;
■   the challenges faced;
■   the client-consultant relationship;
■   the aims of the project and the extent to which these were achieved.

This material provides some important insights into the consulting industry as it moves into a more buoyant market.

REASONS FOR SELECTING A PARTICULAR CONSULTING FIRM

Both clients and consultants agree that the ability to deliver is the most important reason why clients chose a particular consulting firm (see Table 1.2). Clients do not want consultants who fall into the conventional trap of writing a report, then walking away from its unfeasible recommendations. They want consultants who are committed, who can roll up their sleeves and make things happen, and who are accountable. Consultants, too – as the case studies in this book demonstrate – are keen to slough off their hit-and-run image.

Table 1.2   *Factors leading clients to select a particular consulting firm, ranked by importance*

Rank	Attribute
1	Ability to deliver
2	Experienced consulting team
3	Specialist expertise
4	Originality of approach
5	Experience of client sector/market
6	Reputation
7	Existing relationship with individual
8	Technological resources
9	Recommendation from client networks
10	Existing relationship with firm
11	Price competitiveness
12	Size of firm/team
13	Geographical representation

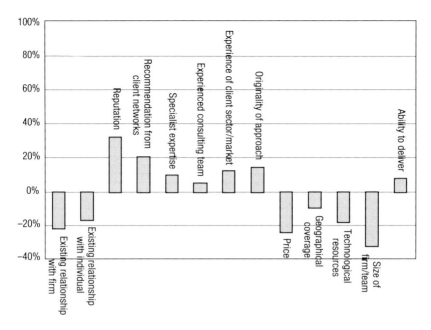

Figure 1.1   *Consulting firms' perceptions of the evaluation criteria used by clients when hiring strategy consulting firms, compared to the other types of consulting*

Given the focus on delivery, it is not surprising that the next most important factors in choosing a consulting firm are specialist knowledge (the consultants know what to do) and an experienced consulting team (they have done it before). Perhaps more surprising is the importance of originality. Surprising in the sense that innovation does not often sit comfortably with experience and track record. The former implies doing something differently; the latter, doing something the same way. But research has repeatedly suggested that this combination of the new and the tried-and-tested is exactly what clients want. They want, in effect, to have their cake and eat it.

For consulting firms, this poses a real challenge, as the people, process and systems that encourage innovation are not necessarily those that guarantee results. Another challenge is the relatively low level of importance accorded to some of the traditional tools of competition – geographical coverage, a firm's reputation, word-of-mouth referrals, existing relationships, even price. These factors are important, but, when it comes to choosing consultants, nowhere near as important as being able to deliver.

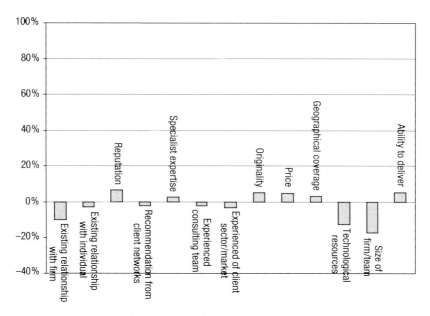

Figure 1.2 *Clients' actual evaluation criteria when hiring strategy consulting firms, compared to the other types of consulting*

Of course, no two consulting projects are alike. To what extent is it possible to draw conclusions across an industry where the work undertaken varies from strategy to systems integration? Segmenting the MCA Awards Survey data reveals differences, not just between types of consulting projects, but between the attitudes of clients and consultants.

Firms involved in strategy consulting tend to think that clients rely more on traditional selection criteria – a firm's reputation, word-of-mouth referral and original thinking – than they do when purchasing other types of consulting (see Figure 1.1). In practice, strategy clients' attitudes are close to the overall average (see Figure 1.2).

In HR consulting, clients' and consultants' views of selection criteria are closer, although consultants appear to underestimate the importance attached by clients to a firm's knowledge of a particular sector. HR clients are also less likely than other kinds of client to rely on existing relationships and word-of-mouth referral. The factors involved in selecting IT-related consultants differ from those used elsewhere: both clients and consultants agree that technology resources, geographical coverage and size of firm are all more important.

Given the growth of offshore outsourcing, it is perhaps surprising that geographical coverage is less important to outsourcing-related consulting. In fact, this probably reflects the fact that the MCA Awards focus on consulting around outsourcing deals – sourcing strategy, supplier selection, negotiation, change management – all of which activities are likely to happen close to the client's site, rather than overseas. Word-of-mouth recommendation is more important for out-sourcing-related consulting – and is certainly more important than consultants seem to realize. By contrast, change management clients agree with consultants that existing relationships are particularly important for this type of work.

THE CHALLENGE OF CONSULTING PROJECTS

While clients and consultants mostly agree on the factors taken into account in selecting a consulting firm, there is more variation in their perceptions of the hurdles that have to be overcome. Both sides recognize that timescales and complexity are often significant problems (see Tables 1.3 and 1.4): after all, no one's going to call consultants in to do something easy.

Both sides also realize that buy-in is important. For clients, ensuring the commitment of the consulting firm is perceived to be a significant challenge. For consultants, getting the support of stakeholders is vitally important. Indeed, many of the case studies in this book involve situations where there are multiple stakeholders, public and private sector, many of whom have not worked together before. Small wonder, then, that an increasing number of contracts for consulting projects now involve some degree of shared risks and rewards.

Clients, however, attach more significance to the cultural challenges than consultants do, suggesting that clients remain more sensitive to the impact consultants can have – as outsiders – on internal politics. Clients also rate limitations – of resources, budgets and skills – slightly more seriously than consultants do, again suggesting that consultants may sometimes downplay the constraints that clients are under.

Understanding a client's business is significantly more of a challenge for consultants doing strategy work than in other types of consulting. This may have something to do with the changes in personnel on the client side which clients highlight as a problem themselves. And it is no surprise that cultural challenges are rated as more serious by clients and consultants when it comes to HR consulting. By contrast, the

Table 1.3   *Consulting firms' perceptions of the challenges to be overcome in consulting projects, ranked by importance*

Rank	Attribute
1	Stakeholder buy-in
2	Complexity of project
3	Time frame
4	Cultural challenges
5	Expectations of client
6	Scale of project
7	Communication with client
8	Consultancy firm's understanding of the business
9	Changing requirements
10	Budget limitations
11	Skill limitations
12	Changing deadlines
13	Changing personnel (client)
14	Changing personnel (consulting firm)

obstacles faced in change management consulting projects seem more logistical – changes to requirements, deadlines and people. The fact that clients rather than consultants draw attention to these issues suggests that change management projects can be frustrating – perhaps a

Table 1.4   *Clients' perceptions of the challenges to be overcome in consulting projects, ranked by importance*

Rank	Attribute
1	Cultural challenges
2	Time frame
3	Complexity of project
4	Scale of project
5	Consultancy buy-in
6	Resource limitations
7	Budget limitations
8	Skill limitations
9	Consulting firm's understanding of the client's business
10	Expectations of consultants
11	Changing requirements
12	Changing deadlines
13	Changing personnel (client)
14	Changing personnel (consulting firm)

function of their largely intangible outputs and the fact that they have to adapt to changing circumstances.

Buy-in and culture were considered to present fewer problems by both clients and consultants when it came to IT-related consulting, but client expectations and communications were thought to be more of an issue. Interestingly, outsourcing was almost the mirror image of this, which may reflect the fact that outsourcing projects tend to be longer-term. Cultural issues and buy-in were more important here, but changes to requirements and people were seen to be less of a challenge.

THE CLIENT–CONSULTANT RELATIONSHIP

The MCA Awards Survey allows us to compare and contrast the attitudes of clients and consultants. We have to be cautious here. Human nature (and some of the responses) suggests that there may have been a degree of collusion between the two sides when it came to commenting on this most sensitive issue. There remain, however, some points worth drawing attention to. Both sides make much of the level of collaboration and openness achieved in the practical, everyday running of the projects: 'Our relationship was characterized by close communication and understanding. It was very open and honest.' 'There was complete openness and honesty around how we need to work together in order to handle the delivery issues.' 'Our relationship was open, constructive, mutually supportive and open to change.'

However, it is also clear that even the best relationships go through rocky patches, particularly in the early stages of a project, primarily caused by individuals failing to get on: 'There were a few minor hiccups during the early phases due to individual personalities.'

Trust, of course, is a word which occurs frequently: 'Our relationship involved a high degree of mutual trust and respect.' It clearly took time to develop trust, and the most effective way of building it was for the clients and consultants to work together: 'The building of trust took around six months, but we worked together exceedingly well thereafter. A very high degree of trust grew between our organizations; this developed into a strong partnership as the workload increased.'

While trust is clearly important glue at all levels in a relationship, a significant difference emerges when we look at the way in which the client and consulting organizations view each other. From this it appears that consulting firms are more likely to focus on high-level sponsorship, suggesting that they tend to view the relationship top-down. Clients, by contrast, seem to have a more bottom-up perspective and are more likely to highlight issues that affect day-to-day interaction – the transfer of skills from the consultant to client, and the professionalism and flexibility of the consultants. Clients also tend to see the benefits of working with consultants in practical, indeed personal, terms: 'They rolled their sleeves up and behaved like true partners. It felt as though we were in it together.'

There is an important message here for consultants, who often invest most of their time in building relationships at high levels (the buyers) within organizations. Clients see trust being developed and reinforced at other, middle-management levels – and consulting firms would do well to learn the lesson of one particular consulting firm:

> The commitment of the executive team from the very early phases proved to be vital as the operations team had support in their decisions and targets. Of equal importance, however, was the time spent at the coal-face. Many consulting organizations focus their attention on strategic and executive level work. But we learned quickly that the place to make a difference was 2.00 am on cold winter nights. The trust built through this level of hands-on consulting confirmed our approach that commitments must exist through the ranks of an organization to ensure success.

What did those involved learn about building effective relationships? The comments divide into three categories as follows:

- Discipline and accountability:
  - 'A good project manager is essential.'
  - 'You need a clearly understood structure: governance is vital.'
  - 'We need to ensure that the client understands how the project will operate.'
  - 'If you sell a long-term benefit, you must be ready to measure the long-term benefit, and not get sucked into short-term meddling.'
- Leadership:
  - 'We now appreciate the effect of a strong leader on a major initiative.'
  - 'Senior management sponsorship and decisiveness is critical.'
  - 'Keep things simple; do not try and take on too much; ensure senior management buy-in throughout the life cycle of the project.'
- Flexibility:
  - 'Projects of this size and complexity need more, not less, flexibility.'

- – 'The solution must be owned by the client staff, as they are responsible and accountable for it. As a consultant, you need to be able to advise and challenge where appropriate .... You also need to be able to back off at times.'
- – 'Maintaining a flexible approach throughout this project helped us to exceed our clients' expectations.'

MEETING CLIENT EXPECTATIONS

Being able to measure the impact of consulting has become something of a holy grail for clients and consultants alike. Clients want the reassurance that, in bringing in consultants, they have made the right decision and that their selection of a particular firm will stand up to scrutiny. Consultants want to be able to demonstrate a track record of quantifiable results to an increasingly sceptical client base. However, no two consulting projects are alike and measuring them against a single standard would be highly misleading.

The MCA Awards Survey therefore asked clients to rate the extent to which the consulting firm had exceeded, met, partially met, or not met their expectations in the following categories:

- motivational (eg improvements in staff satisfaction);
- ability to finish a project on time;
- greater management capability;
- improved customer satisfaction;
- increased productivity;
- reduced costs;
- changes to headcount;
- increased revenue;
- acquisition of new customers;
- increased market share;
- better share price performance.

Although clients are obviously concerned that a consulting project should be completed on time and within budget, they otherwise tend to judge the success of consulting projects in terms of 'softer' issues such as motivational impact, customer satisfaction and management capability (see Figure 1.3). They are also more likely to be concerned about productivity and cost-reduction issues than revenue-generation ones.

Figure 1.3 looks at what proportion of clients said that their expectations had been either met or exceeded in projects where these critical success factors were judged to be important. Almost all the projects

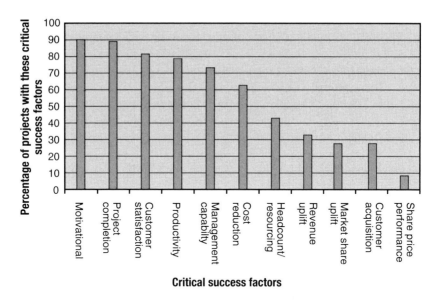

Figure 1.3   *The critical success factors used by clients to measure the impact of consultants*

were completed as planned and almost 90 per cent of clients believed that consultants had met or exceeded their expectations in motivational terms. Trilogy's work with Tesco (Case study 3.1) and Penna Consulting's work with Evotec OAI (Case study 4.2) both involved gauging and implementing ways of improving staff engagement. The consulting firms performed well, too, in those softer areas important to most projects, such as improving management capability. The work of RightCoutts with the Harrogate Healthcare NHS Trust (Case study 6.1) was not designed to tell the Trust's senior managers the answers to all their problems, but to improve their ability to take the right decisions more quickly. Similarly, the success of Edengene's work with two different areas of BT (Case studies 2.2 and 5.1) depended on improving BT's ability to generate and evaluate new ideas. Consultants also do well when it comes to helping clients improve productivity – almost three quarters of the projects entered for an award met or exceeded clients' expectations when it came to this area, and many of the following case studies illustrate this: Kepner-Tregoe's work with Sun–Microsystems (Case study 5.4); Atos Origin's work with the Bradford Hospitals NHS Trust (Case study 7.3); and Impact Plus's work with Aon (Case study 9.4).

But the consulting industry can not afford to rest on these laurels: when it comes to harder, more quantifiable measures – and particularly

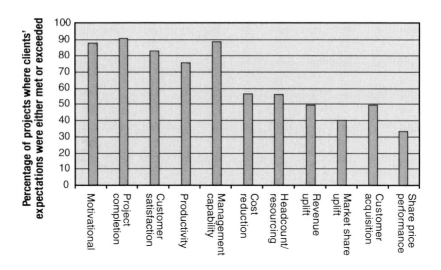

Figure 1.4   *Comparing client satisfaction levels*

to those relating to growing the revenues of a business, rather than cutting its costs – there is significant room for improvement.

Analysing client satisfaction in different types of consulting suggests that:

▨   Clients of outsourcing-related consulting projects were more likely to be satisfied across the board than clients of other types of consulting. In particular, their expectations for increasing market share, increasing revenue and improving customer satisfaction were more likely to be met. The growth of the outsourcing market, which has accelerated since the millennium, is often attributed to macro-economic factors – falling share prices, a focus on costs. However, these findings suggest a more positive reason: many clients are simply pleased with the results.

▨   By contrast, clients of IT-related consulting are more likely to be dissatisfied. These were the clients who, across all the different categories of expectations, consistently rated consultants as less likely than average to exceed expectations. Disappointment was most apparent when it came to rating the impact of projects in broad business terms (increased revenue and market share, improved share price performance). Of course, it may be that technology consulting clients simply had higher expectations than outsourcing clients, but it does suggest that clients continue to find it difficult to relate the immediate increases in productivity that come from using IT with business performance overall.

- HR consulting clients are more positive than others when it comes to cost reduction and headcount issues – not surprisingly. Perhaps more worryingly from the consulting firms' point of view, they are less likely to be satisfied when it comes to improving productivity or management capability.

- The surprise in change management consulting lies in the extent to which projects exceeded clients' expectations when it comes to the financial impact. Increased revenue and market share, and improved share price performance are all areas which we do not particularly associate with something as traditionally 'soft' as change management. Like outsourcing-related consulting, change management consulting may be benefiting from low expectations – neither clients nor consulting firms have historically found it easy to correlate its 'soft' process with 'hard' economic facts. That expectations are being exceeded here may indicate that this is now changing, that clients can see a connection between changing people's behaviour and overall performance.

- Strategy consulting was one of the principal casualties of the 2001–02 downturn in the consulting market and, although this type of consulting may now be picking up speed, it still appears one of the more vulnerable areas of consulting. There are only two areas in which strategy clients' aims are more likely to be met, compared to other types of consulting – headcount and cost reduction. Those measures that reflect growth rather than retrenchment – increased revenue and market share, improved customer acquisition rates and satisfaction – all scored particularly badly, suggesting that clients still see strategy consultants as delivering less than they promise.

The overall scorecard is therefore good, but consultants can do even better. And that is the challenge for the consulting industry. As Anne Bennett, a consultant at ER Consultants, puts it:

> We need to reframe how clients see consultants. Compared to the amount of money auditors and lawyers take out of a business, consulting should be a net gain. Hiring consultants shouldn't be seen as an admission of management failure or a smack in the face to your own staff. Consultants aren't there to take over a client's business but to supplement in-house skills. We need to overcome the predominately transactional nature of consulting at present, and move to a more transformational agenda.

SUMMARY – KEY LESSONS FOR MANAGERS AND CONSULTANTS

- More and more work is being done on a project, rather than permanent, basis. Organizations are becoming portfolios of opportunities and resources: some of those resources will come from outside suppliers, such as consulting firms, who offer experience and specialist knowledge.
- In this environment, collaboration – across internal divisions, with external partners – will be key. As the case studies in this book show, genuine collaboration is best secured at two levels: the corporate (shared risks and rewards) and the individual (personal chemistry).
- The most important reasons for choosing a particular consulting firm are that firm's ability to deliver, experience and specialist knowledge. Clients are also more interested in originality than in a firm's size, geographical coverage, or even its reputation.
- Both clients and consultants recognize that getting buy-in from all those involved is perhaps the most serious obstacle to effective collaboration. However, consultants appear to underestimate the cultural challenges they face and the constraints their clients may be operating under.
- Effective relationships are characterized by openness, honesty and trust. Trust can only be built up by individuals working together over a period of time; it's not something that can be transmitted by a consulting brand.
- Clients believe relationships are forged at middle management levels, whereas consultants tend to think in terms of building top-level relationships only.
- The keys to building effective relationships are: focus and accountability; leadership; and flexibility.
- Consultants are very likely to meet or exceed client expectations in terms of increased productivity, revenue growth and improved management capability. However, outsourcing and change management clients appear to be more satisfied than IT and strategy consulting clients.

2

What sets excellent consulting apart?

FOUNDATIONS OF GOOD CONSULTING

The factors that distinguish good consulting probably have not changed since the early 1980s, when the era of the independent adviser gave way to that of the large-scale, complex projects that dominate today's skyline. That these factors have not changed is certainly a testimony to their fundamental importance to the consulting process, and may also indicate that – even 20 years on – clients continue to be frustrated by the number of projects that fall short of this standard.

Project, time and cost management

Clients want consultants to play by the rules. Once a project has been agreed, clients want consultants to do what they have said they would, when they have said they would do it. They also want to be charged an agreed amount of money, not write a blank cheque. When consultants step outside the parameters of a project, they can erode the benefits of a project perhaps to a point where the costs exceed the return, and embarrass a client internally (who has to defend the choice and management of the consulting team). Above all else, consultants who ride roughshod over their client's expectations are guilty of failing to respect their client's constraints. Good project management starts before the contract has been signed: 'You need a good scoping document,' said one client. 'How a project starts is not necessarily how it finishes.' As another client put it: 'If you are very clear about your project objectives and the role you want the consultants to play, it will hugely improve your chances of success.'

Specialist experience

No client wants to waste time familiarizing a consultant with the issues faced by a particular sector. Thus, when it comes to hiring consultants, clients consistently rate the consultants' understanding of a sector or other specialist know-how far higher than factors such as an existing relationship, the geographical coverage of a firm, the size of a firm, and even price. The best consultants, they believe, bring a wealth of experience of issues they, as clients, may only encounter occasionally. According to one client: 'The days are gone when a consultant borrows the client's watch to tell him the time.'

Leadership

Specialist knowledge and practical experience provide the platform on which consultants build their credibility. But good consultants do not stop there: they use that credibility as a justification for having unambiguous, authoritative opinions. This is good news for clients, who have often found it difficult to pin consultants down to making definitive statements. Concerned to protect their liability, consultants can be too wary about making commitments, leaving clients themselves unsure what to do. Good consulting involves having the courage of your convictions; it means standing up to be counted.

Skills transfer

This is – or should be – the bottom line of consulting. Clients hire consultants because there are skills they need, but lack. They could take the option of hiring a full-time employee to plug a particular gap, but consulting firms offer clients economies of knowledge. Consulting firms not only have systems and processes to help consultants learn rapidly, but they can also spread the cost of training over several clients. While consulting fees may seem high, they are still lower than if a client were to develop the skills they want in isolation. But the economics of consulting start to fall apart if the consulting firm leaves a client no better equipped than when it arrived. Unless consultants can improve management capability, they run the risk of creating a dependency culture, in which a client returns repeatedly to the same firm for the same work. Small wonder, then, that skills transfer is one of the most important success criteria from a client perspective. Of course, importance does not necessarily translate into ease. One of the reasons why skills transfer still appears among the attributes of good consulting is that it is hard to achieve in practice. Much work still needs to be done in order to analyse how know-how can be passed from consultant

to client more effectively – it is a process that neither side fully understands at present and to which each side has been only half-heartedly
committed in the past. Consultants have tended to see it as a nice-to-
have: in an era when much consulting work is measured in terms of
output delivered, skills transfer often appears to be a distraction.
Clients, too, have paid lip-service to the idea and have been reluctant
to make the additional investment almost certainly required. This is
changing, as the cases in this book illustrate. Edengene's work with BT,
for example, depended upon BT's staff becoming as familiar with the
techniques for generating new ideas as Edengene's own consultants.
Skills transfer is an important factor in almost every project, but it
remains something much harder to achieve in practice than it appears
on paper.

PROJECTS THAT EXCEED CLIENT EXPECTATIONS

If the four attributes outlined above constitute the bedrock of good
consulting, what distinguishes the best?

Using the MCA's survey of the projects submitted for its annual
awards, it is possible to separate out the factors that apply specifically
to projects that exceeded clients' expectations, as opposed to projects
which just met those expectations.

Collaboration, communication and culture

Perhaps the single most common word across the projects that exceeded
client expectations is 'together'. 'It's amazing,' said one client, 'what
can be accomplished by a small number of people, when focused on a
challenging goal and working effectively together.' According to
another, these projects demonstrate 'the power of working together
rather than relying on just the consultant to deliver'.

But it would be easy for collaboration to become another of those
terms that become devalued by overuse and underpractice. What does
it actually involve?

Putting the right people in the right place, irrespective of who
employs them, is an important part. When clients and consultants collaborate, they each recognize that the other side has crucial skills and
try to make best use of them. 'There was absolutely no demarcation
along the lines of "I am the client, so you must do it this way"', said one
client. Open communication and honesty are also vital. 'This was an
integrated team,' commented another, 'with close relationships developing between the senior consultants and our executive directors. We

trusted each other and could discuss issues frankly.' While establishing clear roles and responsibilities at the outset may be important in good consulting, the best consulting involves both sides pushing the boundaries when necessary. 'We often asked "How would it be if ...?" or "How could we get more into this?",' recalled one executive. 'This gave both parties an opportunity to go beyond what had been initially planned.'

And the proof of the pudding is, as always, in the eating. Another client summed up the experience as follows:

> We would be hard pressed now to say which elements were generated by client or consultant. Both trust the other to deliver what they say they will.
>
> As true partners with a common goal, trust grew as we both sought the best solutions for mutual success. Issues were raised and resolved in this spirit, and [the consultants'] commitment was evidenced by the energy and single-mindedness with which they undertook all challenges.

Originality

Many of the projects described in this book are ground-breaking initiatives. It may be that the technology was untried – as with implementing the Congestion Charge in London; that the timescales were verging on the impossible – as the Apache Corporation's were when it decided to integrate an acquisition in a matter of weeks; or that the complexity of the work was unprecedented – as in Accenture's outsourcing deal with Sainsbury's Supermarkets.

Pragmatism

One of the things clients criticize consultants for most is a tendency to bring pre-defined solutions to unique problems, to be rigid in a rapidly moving environment. Thus, while planning and project control are high on the agenda when it comes to good consulting, they are superseded by pragmatism in truly excellent consulting. As one client put it, 'Planning is essential to reducing risks and increasing the chances of success, but planning can only take you so far. After that, success is dependent on a flexible and cooperative approach which enables changes in scope and timescales to be accommodated and overcome.' 'You should choose your consultants on what they can do for you, and not how much they will cost,' agrees another.

Pragmatism is not just an attitude of mind: it is also a testimony to the way in which shared risk contracts are fundamentally changing the way in which clients and consultants work together. 'The consultants rolled up their sleeves and behaved like true partners. It felt like we were in it together.'

THE BEST OF THE BEST

The three case studies in this chapter all feature overall winners of the MCA's Awards for Best Management Practice. The first two, the International Olympic Committee's work with SchlumbergerSema, now Atos Origin, and PA Consulting Group's work with Westminster City Council, are the Platinum Winners from the 2003 and 2004 awards respectively. The third, Edengene's work with BT Business, won the 2004 award for the best project by a small consulting firm.

Collaboration was important at all levels when Westminster City Council came to reorganize itself around customer needs, rather than internal functions. Long-standing internal boundaries had to be demolished, and there was a danger that, by using external consultants to help, the Council would only succeed in creating new divisions. In fact, the word that is most prominent in this case is 'help': PA did not carry out the work on the Council's behalf, but helped Council employees to develop their own solutions, ensuring commitment and building skills at the same time. The result was proof that collaborative working enables organizations to do things they could not have done by themselves, that the whole can be greater than the sum of the parts. As Peter Rogers, the Council's Chief Executive, put it: 'PA Consulting helped develop the vision and turn it into a reality. They brought the necessary skills and experience at the right times and worked with us as true partners, often meeting impossible deadlines in order to achieve a successful implementation.' But the client, too, should take some of the credit. According to PA: 'The Council is a mature buyer of consulting and understood where to give direction (and in this programme, it was from the very top), how to identify the approach it wanted for its service delivery and where to take the advice of consultants.'

There are few consulting projects where the outputs are as visible as Atos Origin's work for the International Olympic Committee. Sitting in the middle of a complex web of technology partners, the team oversaw the integration of a multitude of disparate systems and was responsible for ensuring their smooth working during the Games themselves. With the entire world watching, and records being broken by hundredths of a second, mistakes were not an option. The key here, along with tremendous amounts of energy and commitment, was getting people to work together.

Small can still be beautiful, as Edengene's work illustrates. A corporation as big as BT might reasonably expect to encounter the armies of consultants of popular folklore, but Edengene chose to put in only a small team, staffed with entrepreneurs and technology experts as well as consultants. Obtaining management buy-in for new ways of stemming customer defections would be fundamental if the initiatives were to succeed, and people might well have been cynical about solutions apparently imposed from the outside. Edengene's role therefore ranged from classic strategy consulting – questioning assumptions about market data, competitor analysis and so on – to developing the business case for the new proposition jointly with BT's own staff, advising on implementation and providing input on areas such as customer experience design and marketing. The key here was the fresh thinking the consulting firm brought to a well-trodden issue. 'Edengene's input was essential,' summarizes BT's Head of Campaign Management, Vincent Rousselet. 'In particular, their mix of rigorous analysis combined with creative thinking helped us to define and launch a major new offering in record time. This was more than consulting, it was ground-breaking team working.'

SUMMARY – KEY LESSONS FOR MANAGERS AND CONSULTANTS

- The prerequisites of good consulting are: effective project, time and cost management; specialist experience; leadership; and the transfer of skills from consultant to client.
- However, for a consulting project to exceed client expectations, it also needs to involve a combination of innovative thinking with a high degree of practical applicability.
- Beyond this is the need for genuine collaboration between clients and consultants. While many projects pay only lip-service to the idea of working in partnership, having compatible cultures, encouraging open communication and establishing common goals, in practice all play a critical role in consulting success.

CASE STUDY 2.1

CUSTOMERS DRIVING LOCAL SERVICES

Techniques of commercial customer relationship management (CRM) can transfer elegantly to the public realm, and put local citizens back in charge of the services they need.

Here is a trick question: Which is the nearest city to London? Oddly enough, the answer is Westminster. Centuries of development blur the lines between the ancient neighbours, but Westminster is a large and thriving community in its own right. The local authority Westminster City Council (WCC) provides a hugely diverse range of services, including education, environmental, housing, transport and social services, to over 200,000 residents and businesses across the area. With a budget of over half a billion pounds, WCC would qualify in revenue terms for inclusion in the FTSE 100 companies index.

What use is CRM (customer relationship management) in the context of a public sector organization like WCC? This project demonstrates how CRM can deliver tremendous benefits to customer-focused organizations in the public sector – and match the returns of such initiatives in commercial organizations.

Customer first – and foremost

WCC has a vision of putting the customer first. This means designing services to meet the needs of the citizen rather than those of the service provider. Under its customer service initiative (CSi), the council's vision has become reality, and provided a role model for the rest of the public sector. WCC has developed a radical new organizational model, in which the whole of the council is organized around a new one-stop service centre. Customer-friendly representatives now commission services and ensure that council commitments are kept.

WCC adopted five key principles of customer-focused service delivery to underpin the initiative:

- easy access to all services, including those of partner public bodies, via a single point of contact and with a choice of channels;
- empowerment by informing customers about their rights;
- guidance to the right service, first time;
- personalized relationship between customer and organization;
- delivery on service commitments.

In order to implement the 'customer first' vision, WCC teamed with PA Consulting Group to design new ways of working and to set up one of the biggest local authority outsourcing deals ever attempted. Under this outsourcing arrangement one supplier provides the entire Customer Service Centre together with many of the more straightforward council services.

At the start of the millennium, WCC had already generated considerable improvements in service provision through applying open competition for contracts. However, the annual city satisfaction surveys continued to reveal reservations on the part of customers. In the 2001–02 survey, only 38 per cent of Westminster respondents felt that their queries were dealt with appropriately and 34 per cent that they were dealt with quickly.

The council realized that simply going through another round of competition would not resolve these problems and therefore looked for a more radical solution. It had already decided to institute an experimental call centre as a step towards making services available online in accordance with e-government targets. WCC recruited PA Consulting Group to help with this project, and together the two organizations examined whether the concept of improving customer service could become a means of achieving the required step change in performance. The joint team believed it could, provided that the initiative was underpinned by the techniques and tools of e-government and genuine organizational change.

There were questions, however. For example, could CRM, developed within the private sector, adapt to the public sector with its emphasis on service rationing rather than profit maximization? Could a CRM approach cope with the complexity of WCC's diverse services? The council provides around 150 different services, many of which impact on the private lives of citizens. Given the many legacy information systems that would need to be integrated, would the cost of CRM be justified?

Perhaps the biggest single challenge was that WCC, like other local authorities, was organized around functional departments such as social services and education, rather than around the needs of the customer. To use CRM effectively would require a radical redesign of the whole organization – and there were few public sector models for such an undertaking.

Fragmented customers

CRM has suffered in the perceptions of private sector managers during the last several years. Some CRM providers and systems integrators undoubtedly oversold the benefits of CRM, so that for many potential enterprise users the technology was positioned as a silver bullet that would cure all ills. Expectations were particularly prone to over-stimulation in the areas of cross-selling and up-selling. Many CRM projects were sold into commercial organizations on the basis that they would yield opportunities to sell existing customers more goods and services.

The theory was that an enterprise's information systems contained buried indications of customer needs and propensities to purchase. These signs would be revealed by the consolidation of corporate data, its automated analysis, and its presentation to skilled operators. Linked to a proactive, sales-oriented style of customer interaction, CRM would act as a means of increasing sales to existing customer and acquiring new customers. Typically, CRM systems would guide call centre staff through the conduct of customer calls in either inbound or outbound modes. So, when a customer called in to the organization, the call centre agent would be able to retrieve a full picture of the customer's relationship with the enterprise, and view suggestions of products and services that should be proposed to the customer.

Many CRM systems have indeed brought great benefits to sales-based organizations. However, their success is almost always attributable to the combination of the technology chosen and the context within which it is deployed. The business processes surrounding CRM form the make-or-break factor for CRM success in business.

WCC is not in the business of selling products to its customers. But it has an urgent interest in gaining a complete picture of each of the citizens it serves. Having a fragmented view of its customers barred the council from optimizing its services to them. Fragmentation risked duplication of effort, or the omission of vital services. In a complex environment with tight cost controls, serving the community effectively and efficiently are mission-critical activities. For the council, CRM was to be the route towards both improved service provision and value for money.

While some customers have relatively simple relationships with the local authority, many take several services and are dealt with by many departments. Someone moving into the area might trigger a range of services, such as housing, education, social services – and even parking, if he or she needs a resident's permit.

The various professional delivery teams involved are increasingly working together to ensure that their services mesh with each other and reflect customers' individual needs. Close cooperation among departments is inspired partly by the development of professional practice, partly by economic pressures, and partly by policy at local and national levels. For example, greater attention to child protection issues is leading to increased co-working among education, health, police and social services teams. While national government policy is facilitating changes in working practice, much of the desire for closer cooperation comes from the professionals themselves. And the specialists' awareness of families' often complex needs comes from their first-hand knowledge of real customers.

The front line

WCC consciously created the right environment for its CRM initiative by building a new customer services front line operation. PA worked with WCC's leadership to develop a new service delivery model known as 'the T-shaped organization' (see Figure 2.1). This model largely resolves the difficulties of applying CRM principles within the public sector by creating an empowered front office working on behalf of the customer to commission and monitor all appropriate council services. Front line staff are even starting to make rationing decisions with the help of 'expert' IT systems.

The top stroke of the T represents integration of access to all council services via a single front office function, staffed with trained agents and supporting various channels such as telephone and e-mail.

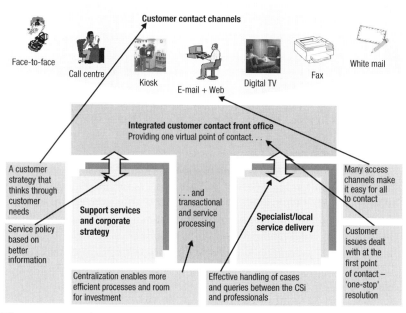

Figure 2.1 *T-shaped organization*

WCC wanted the front line to be much more than an access mechanism. Agents were also empowered to deliver services and resolve issues immediately. This empowerment is enabled in two ways. First, the downstroke of the T represents the centralization and automation of generic transactional services such as payments, and their direct integration into the Customer Service Centre. Second, specialist services such as Social Services or refuse collection are directly linked to the service centre via integrated systems.

The customer service representative now becomes a case manager, commissioning services on behalf of the customer and monitoring their delivery. As a result, the customer receives a personalized, comprehensive service through a single contact point that represents customers' interests to the rest of the organization. Performance can now also be monitored by the customer, aligning management information with CRM objectives.

The new team was formed from staff taken from different departments, who were then trained in all the other services offered by the council. This means that team members can act as generalists when taking customer calls, guiding them through the services the council can offer. The operator can work with the customer to navigate the potentially bewildering array of services available, and build a packaged set for the customer's needs. The team members' roots in the council's departments ensures that they have a personal connection with WCC's services, while the mix of departmental origins in the team ensures that specialist insight is close at hand if needed.

The CRM system is clearly acting as an aid in this context. The system serves the agent, who in turn serves the customer.

This use of IT systems runs counter to much of the more visible initiatives launched by public sector bodies in recent years. The movement towards e-government has generally been presented as one of greater customer enablement through self-service. Access to services has sometimes seemed to be merely an issue of providing user interfaces to systems, and a prompt to debates over the existence of a 'digital divide' in our communities.

PA's Rob Brown believes that while customer self-service represents the first wave of e-government, direct access to systems will never be the complete answer for all customers of public sector organizations. 'A mediated service empowers the customer more,' he explains. 'It's having someone on their side.'

Customers clearly feel the new approach works. One WCC customer left this typical message on 15 September 2003: 'Just like to leave a message about a lady called Sharon at the Planning

Application Centre who was very, very helpful, very speedy and efficient in dealing with my enquiry ...'.

Reorganizing the organization

Redesigning the organization around WCC's CRM vision was not a trivial exercise. The initiative represented an entirely new way of doing business in the public sector. 'It was a monumental challenge to change the organization, and it's a great credit to the politicians and officers that they were willing to take it on,' says Brown.

The key to reconfiguring the council's customer service operation lay in analysing generic business processes. The team studied the real business of customer interaction with WCC by following real customers as they dealt with the council. Working collaboratively with council staff, the team built faithful scenarios of customers' experiences of engaging with the council and its services. Using an extensive series of workshops throughout the organization, involving a cross-section of staff from each area, the team specified 13 core processes common to all the council's services. Each workshop was driven by the desire to 'walk in the shoes of the customer'. The team produced detailed descriptions for each process, together with definitions of required response times, hours of access and so on. The process model was developed to include an interface between the service centre and the remaining council functions of specialist and local delivery, ensuring a seamless and secure end-to-end process.

Validating and customizing processes for each department allowed the council to streamline some processes and gain savings in time and money. At the same time, realistic standards were applied in each business area. For example, while practice in some services might demand a customer should receive a decision within three working days, this might be an unreasonable demand in Social Services, where third party agency activities might be involved in progressing a customer issue.

Through to implementation

Implementing the new plan required procurement of a customer service centre, entailing a substantial investment in infrastructure and training, alongside the migration of staff. WCC decided that the best way to achieve this was to outsource the programme to an experienced private sector partner, who would provide both the horizontal stroke of the T (the front office) and the downstroke (the processing of common back-office transactions).

PA helped WCC to choose the right supplier and establish the right contract. During one of the largest outsourcing exercises seen within local government, PA supported WCC in developing the business case and service specification, managing the procurement process and negotiating the best possible deal. PA then worked with WCC and its chosen supplier, Vertex, to get the partnership off to a successful start.

Separating the business requirement from the technical implementation enabled WCC to retain ownership of the business vision while recruiting the most effective implementers. Bringing in implementation experts also continues the theme of risk management implied in the very engagement of PA. By using outside experts, the council could focus on its core business. Re-engineering service delivery and aligning back-end services took priority rather than software installation and staff training.

Elements of success

The successful delivery of the CSi involved challenges in three main areas: definition, ownership and innovation. In the area of definition, the initiative required WCC to analyse its business in radically new ways. For example, before it could set performance standards for services, it had to assess current customer contact volumes and response times. This objective information was rarely available, and the lack of comprehensive data clouded perceptions of the council's areas of weakness and strength. PA helped WCC to assemble as much information as possible, then applied sophisticated dynamic modelling techniques to define standards for Vertex to meet in the customer service centre.

Ownership of the change in business signalled by the initiative was another key challenge. The CSi implied radical changes to council staff's day-to-day working practices, together with a major restructuring of responsibilities. Not only did these changes require the formal agreement of departmental managers and councillors, they also needed the practical commitment of staff at all levels. To secure this sense of personal and organizational ownership, WCC's chief executive personally assumed leadership of the programme. Rob Brown says: 'When Westminster do something they do it well. The chief executive drove this programme personally and visibly. Every department had to buy into it, and he chaired the steering group.' The team also took care to ensure that all staff felt involved in the creation of the new service specification and in the procurement of the outsourcing deal.

Lastly, the CSi project represents significant innovation in public sector procurement. WCC was bound by public sector procurement rules dictating a level playing field for procurement and emphasizing price competition. However, the rationale for the outsourcing was to exploit best practice in private sector customer service. These perspectives had to be finely judged to ensure propriety in the process while achieving an optimal outcome.

Measuring the results

WCC's new Customer Service Centre opened in November 2002 after 18 months of intense work. Some 66 city council services from parking to libraries were seamlessly transferred to the contractor in the first phase of implementation. Many of the planned tangible benefits could be measured soon after the launch.

Customer service has indeed been transformed by the initiative. Some 94 per cent of all calls made to the council are being answered through the Customer Service Centre within defined performance standards. Call handling times exceed the contract standard – 75 per cent of calls are being answered within 20 seconds.

An increasing number of multiple enquiries are now being answered and fulfilled within a single contact, as planned in the T-shaped model. More services are now accessible out of office hours than ever before, helping to extend the council's accessibility to customers and maximizing the use of its resources. On the departmental side, professional services are being freed from the burden of routine enquiries. Professionals therefore have more time to concentrate their efforts where they are needed most. At the same time customer satisfaction is measurably increasing, since the increased capacity means more calls are being answered and more queries resolved.

Financial savings are also beginning to flow from the project. The financial benefits of the programme are estimated at over £80 million over 15 years. The council is on track to meet its targets for reducing the cost of each customer contact. In addition, the quality of management information available to WCC is now significantly improved. The council now has a much better grasp on transaction volumes, call handling times and demand. This improved information is directly aiding future service planning.

CASE STUDY 2.2

REINVENTING A CORE OFFER

Although blue-sky thinking is most often associated with would-be entrepreneurs or elite corporate strategists, BT and Edengene took the path of creative innovation to reinvent a core offering within one of the telecom industry's largest and best-established customer segments: small- to medium-sized enterprises.

BT Business provides fixed line telephone services to more than 1 million small- and medium-sized enterprises (SMEs) in the UK. In December 2001 deregulation opened the doors to competitors, each with their own aggressive pricing strategy. The new entrants gained market share rapidly. BT's own offerings were perceived in the market as complicated and offering poor value. The company was losing valuable customers at an increasing rate.

With further deregulation including wholesale line rental on the horizon and more competition moving in, customer churn was accelerating and at one point even projected to rise to 1 per cent per month. Facing this potential revenue haemorrhage, the management at BT Business knew they had to reinvent their core SME offering.

The appetite for creative change was building within BT Business, and had been strengthened by the arrival of Strategy and Marketing Director Tim Evans from the residential side of the organization. BT's consumer business had recently innovated in the residential market with its BT Together product, an offering that radically simplified calling plans for millions of customers. BT Business also needed a way of cutting through the complexity of its market and speaking compellingly to customers.

In October 2002 BT brought Edengene on board to come up with a way to reverse the damaging trends in the business, stem the flow of customer defections and shore up BT's market share – without provoking a price war. The challenge was both to retain existing customers and recapture lost ones, turning a dwindling revenue source into a growing one. Close cooperation within a combined BT/Edengene team would ensure fast progress and management buy-in, and prevent the business proposal being diluted or diverted on its way to market. Edengene's Tim Thorne says the brief was simple and compelling: 'They said, whatever you do, don't come up with a price-cutting proposition. Now go in that room and use your magic to come up with a solution. This isn't unusual with our customers: they know our ideas will be deliverable, not fluffy.'

Removing the constraints to creativity

The collection of techniques used in the project cover the entire cycle of idea generation, evaluation and implementation. Edengene has around 50 approaches to generating ideas, but the main tool used in this project is called 'breaking assumptions'. This technique involves bringing the team's preconceptions to the surface and challenging them. In this case, the assumptions under attack were those to do with pricing. By articulating people's unspoken assumptions about pricing, the team can begin to validate the solutions and test their boundaries. Inevitably, some assumptions may be widely held but found, on examination, to be out of date, or irrelevant to the problem at hand.

Using explicit techniques to remove constraints is more effective than offering hopeful advice to 'think outside the box'. Such generic notions have to be related to the actual situation of the enterprise in question before they can add any value. Releasing people from their assumptions is also the most direct way to the kind of genuine, and repeatable, innovation that Edengene is used to producing.

Many of the assumptions operating silently within organizations relate to customer expectations or behaviours. The team therefore collected a mass of market research data that had been generated for unrelated marketing purposes, and consolidated it. Adding competitor intelligence to the newly aggregated market research data created a new basis for analysing customer behaviours and preferences without the need for commissioning new research on a broad scale. Although the base data had not been collected with this end in mind, it provided a rich source of insights at low cost. The after-project value of customer data is often neglected once the projects for which it was collected have been completed. Targeted review of existing material can often create new points of departure for the business in return for marginal effort. Aggregating and reviewing in this way can help to form the 'fresh eye' that management so often needs to renew its vision.

The team also believed that reusing existing research material as fuel would avoid the danger of commissioning confirmatory or vague research. Framing market research questions without planting proposed solutions is very difficult, and conventional techniques rarely produce true innovation – they test existing propositions rather than solicit novelty. Moreover, there simply was not time to design a credible research campaign that would yield the directions and insights the team needed.

One of BT's greatest assets is its customer knowledge, including decades of dialling data, giving an unsurpassed picture of the market's habits. By studying this data and researching customer needs, the team identified the five drivers behind business telephony buying decisions: simplicity, service, recognition, price and cost management.

A striking outcome of the data analysis was the realization that business customers did not see pricing as an isolated issue. While the analysis suggested that BT Business needed to change the dynamics of its pricing, it also indicated that the company was seen as lagging behind its competitors on service. An example of perceived poor customer service was 'the BT shunt'. This was the name given to the commonly reported experience of being passed from one customer services representative to another. Customers could rapidly intuit that the business did not know which pricing plans they were on, undermining their faith in the business's competence to resolve their current problems and reducing their confidence in the business's overall ability to deliver. During the long delays generated by the 'shunt', customers had ample opportunity to ask themselves why they should stay with the provider. With the shunt experience eroding their loyalty, customers were increasingly questioning whether they should stay with BT – a company that seemed to take them for granted and offer no recognition of long-term relationships.

At the same time, the team looked at the competition. Without exception, they majored on price. Paradoxically, this welter of price offerings created a shared weakness for the smaller operators. Faced with an expanding universe of pricing options, many SME customers experienced the same thing: confusion. It became clear that simplicity and predictable cost management could be even more important than raw price: 72 per cent of customers identified unpredictable and rising costs as a business fear.

The gap in the market began to appear and take shape. The opportunity for BT Business was all about certainty. The team's research suggested that BT did not have to be the cheapest provider in order to lead the market. Instead, BT had to be competitive but, more importantly, offer the market the certainty it currently lacked. The team found that 58 per cent of SME customers did not even know what package they were using. Research also showed that better customer service and reward for loyalty would help support any new offer.

The team developed a three-part foundation for the new proposition they would deliver into BT Business's market: price, service and loyalty. These three pillars translated directly into the ultimate marketing message of the new product.

Plotting the positions of BT Business's competitors against the three pillars showed quickly that few competitors took loyalty into account when designing products for this market. One reason for this was that most of the competitors were relatively young compared to BT, which in many cases had relationships stretching back over many years and into the period when it held a monopoly over telephone services. Most of BT Business's competitors were focused on price, with a few of the leaders beginning to extend their offer into service.

The team was therefore able to choose the competitive space in which BT Business would play, and dictate the contours of that space ahead of their competitors. The team quickly agreed that service and loyalty were key areas where the company could distinguish itself and set new standards in the industry.

The price pillar

The pricing part of the equation was less easy to deal with. The brief had ruled out aggressive price-cutting. Instead, the team would have to reinvent business telephony pricing. Pricing plans in the telecoms industry are notoriously complex, and they have evolved to cover a myriad of combinations of charging bands, call durations and call times.

The team decided that the fastest way to cut through the complexity and create a pricing structure that would appeal to customers was to work through a series of targeted focus groups. Each focus group was given a set of five or six potential pricing plans as seed material, usually in the evening. During the following day the team would collect reactions to the set of plans, and generate new ones on the fly. Every type of potential plan was considered during the process, including exotic plans from very different markets such as the United States. 'It's a quick process,' says Thorne, 'not a slavish one. We do very rapid analysis in an entrepreneurial and intuitive style. We'll form a hypothesis and then follow it through.'

The team counted 27 ways to price a telephone call and tested each one in focus groups. The findings were both conclusive and surprising: capped call prices were the most attractive to customers. This was a reversal of received wisdom. The most a call could cost mattered more than the least it could cost.

The rapid, iterative nature of the business development process used in this project, and its transparency to management and customers alike, contrasts sharply with traditional practice. Edengene stresses the value of its 'venturing' approach in such situations. The company is used to thinking and behaving in an entrepreneurial mode rather than a bureaucratic one. Even the nimblest of enterprises have a natural tendency to support their own ideas, and become wedded to them even during the process of challenging them and retiring them. They may overelaborate their ideas, and seek to invest in the development of a small number of seed ideas rather than generate a large number from which the fittest may emerge. But when time constraints are tough, there simply is not enough time to follow traditional practice. Edengene excels in discarding ideas almost as much as it excels in creating them. Serial entrepreneurs like to say that failure is okay, as long as you fail quickly. Transferring this attitude to the established corporate environment entails the ability to change direction quickly, without fudging the change or apologizing for it. Thorne says: 'We're not afraid to argue passionately for a concept one day, and then tear it up with equal conviction the next week in front of the client.'

Creativity is famously composed of 99 per cent perspiration to 1 per cent inspiration. Edengene uses idea generation techniques from a wide variety of sources, and constantly adds to them. Edengene teams typically complete a high-level inventory of a proposed business and its capabilities in less than three hours. But part of the idea development process is solidly rational. As a candidate proposition is built it is tested against a set of unambiguous business criteria. These include fundamentals such as feasibility and profitability. However, BT and Edengene believe every successful proposition needs an emotional component as well as a rational structure. In the words of Tim Thorne: 'When you want to sell a product with a big uptake and you want to sell it fast, rational attributes aren't enough; you need an emotional connection.'

The core of the new offering's emotional component is the concept of certainty. The team found that the business climate into which BT Business was selling was characterized by feelings of uncertainty that were not being addressed by suppliers of business services. This sense of uncertainty was not being quantified or actively managed in terms of known risks by BT Business's customers, but it was exercising a strong influence over their attitudes. The team found that telecoms costs account for only 2 per cent of the average SME's annual spend. An unexpected overrun on telecoms costs is therefore unlikely to cause a major blow to such a company. However, no business likes shocks. The possibility of a spike in one area of the business costs can easily be joined by fear of similar uncontrolled costs in other areas.

Emotionally, a lack of certainty about the telecoms bill can transfer to completely unrelated cost items. In these circumstances, a poor experience with its telecoms provider can rapidly cause a business customer to blame the provider for problems or inefficiencies elsewhere in the enterprise, further eroding attachment to the brand.

The new offering being developed by BT Business and Edengene therefore needed a 'certainty wrap'. At the heart of the offering is a 10p cap on all local and national calls up to one hour long, at any time. The choice of 10p is boldly emotional: it has a direct, almost tactile meaning for customers. This price can be represented visually in marketing materials as a coin, and customers can readily imagine the coin in their hands. Customers also recognize the 'small change' value of 10p. The amount is not without value: people do not throw their 10p coins away. But 10p does not buy very much in the way of tangible goods. Attaching this price point to a service with an inbuilt fear of cost overruns is a smart way of capping both the factual costs of using BT and connecting with people's real-world experience of value. The 10p certainty wrap made the new pricing plan easy to grasp mentally, and almost tangible. BT Business's new offering would stand out against the complex, over-rationalized pricing plans of its rivals.

Certainty over not just pricing, but also excellent service and recognition for commitment also needed to be part of the offer. The team decided there should be a single contact number to deal with all customer issues, clear billing statements and regular account reviews. The plan would also include a 5 per cent discount at the end of the contract so that customers would feel rewarded for their loyalty. The new product now scored highly against all three pillars of the team's business blueprint: it included a capped charge (price dimension), a single contact number, clear bill and regular review (service dimension) and a reduction at the end of one year (loyalty dimension).

Delivering to the market

The entrepreneurial style of the project continued through to business planning, with the team committing to detailed financial forecasts. By the beginning of November 2002, one month after starting work, the BT/Edengene team had presented the case to BT's Investment Committee. The new product, now branded BT Business Plan, would achieve over £150 million in revenues and acquire or protect more than 120,000 customers by April 2004, just 17 months away.

Having developed the new product in concept form, the team now had to make it deliverable – within 90 days. Delivering the new proposition to the market dictated a long list of practical, urgent changes within the business. The team had to secure a single number as the new point of service contact, arrange call routing to that number and train all the call centre staff involved. At the same time, changes to the customer bill and the systems that produce it needed to be ordered.

The team's approach to meeting these demands was highly pragmatic. The key to delivering successfully was to freeze the proposition before its implementation. While the company would do everything and anything to deliver on time, it would not amend the business proposition in order to do so. Compromises would be made, and indeed encouraged; but only at the operational level. The proposition remained sacrosanct. 'We were the guardians of the proposition,' says Tim Thorne. 'The compromises are all under the surface.' The implementation plan was developed and maintained through a series of as-needed sessions, with the relevant people seeking workarounds to ensure that the proposition could be delivered on time using as much of the existing infrastructure and business processes as possible.

Thorne quotes another client's experiences with rapid introductions of innovative business concepts: 'It's funny how easy it is to deliver a good proposition.' Belief in the rightness of the offering drove BT Business's organization to mobilize the resources and the flexibility to deliver the proposition faithfully to market.

BT Business Plan was launched on 13 January 2003, just 90 days after the initial brief. Although the team had targeted 120,000 customers by April 2004, the scheme had already attracted 160,000 by January 2004, giving it the highest ever take-up of any new BT Business product and meeting its target number of customers five months early.

Vincent Rousselet, head of Campaign Management at BT Group and the sponsor of the project, says: 'Many people remarked to me that they'd never seen something happen so quickly within BT. And of all the projects I've worked on within the Group, it's the one that's remained most on track in terms of targets.'

The new offer has also provided a platform to deal with competition in other telephony markets. BT Business Plan has been enhanced to include capped international calls of 10p for an hour's call to the United States and 20p to Europe.

Importantly, the project has fundamentally repositioned BT in the SME market. A Deloitte & Touche study of UK business telephony rated BT Business Plan as 12 per cent better value than the average of competitors' best prices and calculated that UK business would be £144 million better off using BT Business Plan.

This project proves that it is possible to reinvent the core offering of even the largest organization, and revolutionize its markets into the bargain. It also demonstrates how an entrepreneurial eye from outside the organization can identify opportunities that otherwise elude management. Edengene's business strategy is to approach organizations they believe are failing to maximize their core assets and show them how they can grow their revenues by working imaginatively with what they have, rather than looking to diversify or imitate the approaches of their competitors.

This approach is a refreshing update on the maxim that successful organizations should 'stick to the knitting', or keep on doing what they are best at doing. Advising organizations to cleave to their core competencies is in any case a message that fails to chime with another popular piece of contemporary wisdom, which is that 'yesterday's solutions can't fix tomorrow's problems'. Edengene's approach to business uses creative techniques to cast an organization's existing assets in new lights, and thereby release new value from them. Try as they might, managers within an established business can find it hard to gain this kind of perspective without external help. Their vision is necessarily tainted by their knowledge of how difficult it is to create change within the organization, especially in the areas closest to the heart of its operations. Appraising the business's core assets and finding new ways to exploit them can feel like breaking a taboo, or courting disaster. The aid of a nimble and unencumbered partner such as Edengene can make it much easier for organizations to appreciate and release the hidden wealth in their existing capabilities.

CASE STUDY 2.3

HOW TO BUILD A NEW DIGITAL CITY EVERY TWO YEARS

Supplying and coordinating the information technology required for the Olympic Games presents an interesting challenge to programme managers. There is no fixed site to house operations, the partners change rapidly and the security requirements are among the toughest in the world.

In 1999 the International Olympic Committee (IOC) signed the world's largest ever sports IT contract with Sema Group for the Olympic Games in Salt Lake City in 2002, Athens in 2004, Torino in 2006 and Beijing in 2008. In 2001, Sema Group was acquired by Schlumberger and then in January 2004 by Atos Origin, which is now responsible for delivering the IT of the Athens 2004, Torino 2006 and Beijing 2008 Olympic Games.

As a moveable feast that adapts to the local circumstances of each host but must maintain its quality standards regardless of venue, the Olympic Games puts unusual stresses on technology providers. Each Games brings together a mass of specialist technology firms who must cooperate for the duration of the event. Bob Cottam of Atos Origin explains: 'The specialist companies travel the world, following the sports. So for example the downhill experts cover all the downhill events wherever they are. Then the telecoms partners vary depending on where the Games are being held. So we, along with a handful of other worldwide Olympic sponsors like Swatch, Xerox and Kodak, have to maintain the continuity.'

For the Salt Lake City Games, a consortium of 13 partners led by SchlumbergerSema, now Atos Origin, delivered all the necessary technology. Cottam says: 'SchlumbergerSema's role was to support the IOC, work closely with the Salt Lake City Organizing Committee, and then manage the consortium to deliver.'

Building a digital city

The technical infrastructure needed to run each Olympic Games is complex and extensive. As well as the many thousands of results and related statistics that are flashed up in real time on TV screens around the world, there is an enormous logistical operation behind the scenes. These unseen activities include the accreditation of tens of thousands of people, plus all security, accommodation, transport and medical services. The Salt Lake City Olympic Winter Games included around 40 competition and non-competition venues across 250 square miles of mountainous terrain at sub-zero temperatures.

The 'digital city' put together for the 2002 Olympic Games served 90,000 users. These users included 2,399 athletes from 77 countries, plus thousands of officials and media staff.

For the 17 days of events and ceremonies, a huge and complex array of networks, hardware and software had to be designed, integrated and delivered without a hitch. As Cottam says: 'At the Olympic Games, failure just isn't an option. You're working to an immovable deadline, with no second chances. And what's more, you're doing it in front of the world.'

The technology needed for the Salt Lake City 2002 Olympic Winter Games required vast resources. 32,000 miles of optical fibre cable were used, yielding a data transmission capacity of 388 trillion bytes per second. More than 4,500 workstations were installed, as well as 370 servers, 1,000 kiosks and more than 3,000 fax machines, copiers and printers.

Data from sophisticated timing devices is captured at each event and uploaded into a central database, from where it is aggregated and streamed to broadcasters locally and media agencies around the world. Data is also supplied to commentators ahead of the public, as Cottam explains: 'Skier number 10 gets to the finish line and he's now the top player. All the data has to be pulled together and provided for the broadcaster's screen in three tenths of a second – before it's on the scoreboard. He has the data before the crowd roars.'

However, the team realized early on that the project was less about creating a technology showcase and more about getting a large and diverse set of specialist companies to work as a cohesive team. Totalling 1,350 professionals and volunteers from 21 countries, the consortium represented extraordinary cultural diversity and different ways of working. The company used its experience of multi-disciplined environments to implement a proactive management framework. Jean Chevallier of Atos Origin says: 'This was about people integration as much as technical integration. We had a very short time to get our new team up and running and to achieve what a lot of corporations take years to put in place. This environment is unique to the Games. We integrate the team through procedures, a common understanding and communications lines. After the 17 days of the Games themselves, the team disbands and moves on.'

The IT team developed standards and procedures across the consortium, particularly for managing changes to systems. Specialist suppliers who might be used to making system changes at other events had to recognize that their actions had implications for other members of the consortium. For example, a company specializing in timing an event could not change the use of a particular data item without its approval in the change management system, otherwise incorrect data could be disseminated from the central databases to the world's media. The team also invested in communications channels and coaching, educating partners about the implications of working in an integrated environment.

Every system developed for the Olympic Games has to be flexible so that it can be adapted to meet unforeseen needs and amended if necessary for new requirements at the following Games. The systems have to be flexible enough to deal with the business rules suddenly changing.

Managing the programme

With time and budget constraints tightly set, and approximately 10,000 separate activities scheduled, the team decided that conventional programme management techniques were not going to be efficient. The team agreed an integrated management structure with the IOC and Salt Lake City Organizing Committee for the Olympic Games, which meant that individual team directors from different partner organizations were responsible for integrated activities. The team also introduced strategic milestones and a change control process, and empowered individual teams to manage their work within this tightly controlled framework. Cottam says: 'People in corporations take good management practice for granted, but we have to bring that in. These are companies who normally only work alone at an event. At the Olympic Games they become part of a huge family. We have to bring the sense of inclusiveness. We expected all team directors to drive their own project planning. Because we had built up such close partnerships with best-of-breed suppliers, we could do this with a high degree of trust.'

While the programme had an official lead time of three years, there were just five weeks before the Opening Ceremony in which to install complex networks and hardware. Some venues had come into live operation two to three months before the opening date, but others were only available 10 days prior to the start of the Olympic Games. The team therefore set up a test lab with 23 separate cells dedicated to mimicking venues or events. The team performed various scenario tests and then a series of stress tests, in which communications links were removed and the systems were checked to ensure that they routed successfully around the gaps. As Cottam says: 'We had to get it right. You can't ask the ski jumper in Salt Lake City, or the runners in Athens to go back to the beginning because we missed the start.'

All the system components chosen for the Olympic Games were proven solutions in their own rights, so that the overall risk of the project was contained. The team used industry standard solutions but did not tie the project's architecture to any one supplier. Several applications were developed internally by SchlumbergerSema, now Atos Origin, including integrated systems to feed real-time data simultaneously with video. The team also created a suite of Games management systems to run the logistics and back-office functions of the Games, and an intranet known as Info2002 that enabled the Olympic Family members to stay in touch. Rhona Martin, Captain of the British Olympic Team, says: 'All our travel and accommodation was dealt with very efficiently. We got stats printed daily and delivered to our pigeonholes – not just our own country's but other countries' too. In terms of the amount of information we were given, I haven't experienced anything else of that scale and detail.'

The media teams were well served as well. Cottam gives this example: 'At Salt Lake City there was a young, unknown Swiss competitor who won two medals in ski jumping. Press people could go to one of the 800 information terminals, click on "ski jumping" or the Swiss team, find him and print off his details and from that they could write their stories.'

Securing the Olympic Games

Security was a priority from the start of the project in 1999. The Olympic Games has had its share of security challenges during its history and it remains a prime target for terrorists and pranksters. The events of September 11 raised the security rating for the Salt Lake City Olympic Games. Bob Cottam says: 'With the whole of America in mourning it was difficult to see which way things were going to go.'

FBI and US Secret Service agents specializing in cyberterrorism worked closely with the team, keeping them fully updated prior to and during the Games. The consortium's IT strategy addressed external systems security by ensuring that the entire system was sealed. The team also managed internal security threats by using a 'trusted list' of personnel double-vetted by the Secret Service. Mitt Romney, head of the Organizing Committee, reassured the public about safety before the Games opened: 'If the Olympic Games were attacked, every nation in the world would react with horror and dismay. We have the time and the personnel to check every person who comes into the venue. It will be slow and it will be thorough.'

In the event, the security measures did not create unacceptable delays. Britain's Olympic champion, who led the now famous curlers to their victory, Rhona Martin, says: 'The organization at Salt Lake City was unbelievable. I thought there would be a lot of queuing for accreditation but it all happened very efficiently and our bags and van were checked quickly. Our time at the village couldn't have gone more smoothly.'

Athens and beyond

Following the Salt Lake City Winter Games, 75 per cent of the SchlumbergerSema team, which reached a total of around 200 during the Games, went to Athens and 25 per cent moved straight to Turin where they started to share learning in preparations for the 2006 Olympic Winter Games. Some of the partners of the Olympic Games involved in Salt Lake City worked on the Athens 2004 Olympic Games and will continue for Torino and beyond while other partners are local. At least 10 members of the technical team for the Beijing 2008 Olympic Games will also be in Athens to learn how to take the Games' support forward.

During the Athens 2004 Olympic Games, the technology operations centre was staffed 24 hours a day by 280 highly trained IT professionals from Atos Origin and other consortium members. They managed a team of more than 3,000 volunteers stationed throughout 60 competition and non-competition venues. The Games management system now includes nine applications including the accreditation system used to register media, athletes, staff, contractors and volunteers. The identification badges issued by the system double as entry visas into the hosting country, so the accreditation system collaborates with national databases such as those of immigration bureaux.

The 'one-team approach' used by Atos Origin has helped to deliver savings and the IOC is committed to reusing technology solutions wherever possible. A key objective is to build expertise and share best practice between Games. In turn, this objective contributes to the overall goal of containing risk. Dr Jacques Rogge, President of the IOC, says:

> The information technology operations of any Olympic Games play a vital role in the overall success of the Games. At the 2002 Salt Lake City Olympic Winter Games, this success was largely due to the commitment from SchlumbergerSema (now Atos Origin) as the lead systems integrator. All of this was achieved with significant cost and

operational savings over previous Games. The company achieved all of this without in any way increasing the risk of the technology operations; on the contrary they reduced it.

While many companies might regard the Olympic Games as simply a well-marketed event from which they can gain prestige by association, Atos Origin approaches its partnership with the IOC as the pursuit of risk reduction. The team is able to scale its IT support to the required level of each Games and work effectively with small and large suppliers alike. Atos Origin is sensitive to the unique security threats attached to the world's most prominent collaborative sporting event. The glamour of the Olympic Games; the triumphs, heartbreaks and controversies each Games produces and the technical excellence of the Games' production ultimately depend on goodwill and spirited collaboration. Atos Origin uses its involvement with the Olympic Games to prove its capabilities, but it also acts in the spirit of the Games, refusing to use the partnership merely as a spotlight for technologies. For Bob Cottam, the results of the Atos Origin work are tangible: 'We watched the athletes getting their medals, knowing that it just wouldn't have been possible if the technology hadn't performed on the day.'

3

Change management

What stops organizations doing what they want?

Everyone is aware of the often yawning chasm between strategy on paper and implementation in practice. There is no easy or single solution to the complex issues involved in gaining employee commitment to a new idea or to changing long-standing behaviour and values. Indeed, some would say that such things cannot be changed, that new people with different attitudes have to be brought in. Others would argue that the problem is primarily one of scale. While you cannot tell an organization en masse to change, individuals can be coached to do things differently and become role models for their colleagues. But the impact of even the most evangelical managers rarely goes beyond their immediate teams, its broader acceptance blunted by cynicism.

The three case studies in this chapter demonstrate that it is possible, not only to change people's behaviour, but to change it on a substantial scale.

CHANGE AND SCALE

The Living Service Programme developed at Tesco, an international retailer, was designed to improve the motivation and morale of the company's 220,000 employees. The UK's Department of Work and Pensions had to change the way its staff worked before it could start on an even harder task – encouraging people in receipt of state benefits to move away from the traditional means of collecting their allowances (in cash from local Post Offices) to cheaper, more secure payments directly into bank accounts. Transport for London and London's Metropolitan Police had to overcome long-standing cultural barriers to joint ways of working in order to make London's buses safer.

In all these cases, there were substantial obstacles that had to be overcome:

- Divisions and boundaries. A decade after Michael Hammer and James Champney, the gurus of business process re-engineering, exhorted companies to break down the barriers that divided their organizations, many of those barriers remain intact today. Tesco discovered that the strong leadership established by its head office made its store staff feel marginalized and demotivated. Rather than sending out orders from the centre, it initiated a network of local 'firelighters' whose role was to encourage other store-based staff to take the initiative. But to these 'traditional' barriers, we can now add external ones, ones that prevent organizations working together. The Metropolitan Police's Transport Operational Command Unit was the first project in Europe where police and civilian authorities collaborated, on such a large scale, in this way.
- Complexity: As organizations become more interdependent – internally and externally – the number of potential stakeholders proliferates. A feature common to all three of these cases is the effort required to reconcile different agenda and win over a wide variety of interested parties. With 13 million customers to convert from paper to electronic payment, the Department of Work and Pensions had to liaise with the companies that manage transaction processes across the UK's financial infrastructure, as well as the points of service delivery – the Post Office and retail banks. On top of this were politicians, trade unions, other government departments – and, of course, the customers themselves.
- Low expectations. One of the axioms of modern management thinking is that the pace of change is increasing. Employees, we reason, resist change because so much is changing. The experience of Tesco suggests that we are wrong to make this assumption. Here, one of the reasons for the programme's success was its difference: it did not feel like 'yet another head-office initiative', but a new departure. The approach at Transport for London and the Department of Work and Pensions reinforces this: neither of these projects was small in ambition. The Transport Operational Command Unit project was an unprecedented move to bring two public authorities together in order to solve a problem that cut across conventional transport/policing boundaries. The Payments Modernization Programme at the Department of Work and Pensions represented an overhaul of a system that had been in place since World War II. The scale of change helped galvanize those involved as it was evidence of senior executives' and politicians'

commitment to solving a problem, rather than patching it over in the hope it would disappear.

'Even at scale,' concludes a spokesperson for Tesco, 'it is possible to unlock the immense potential in individuals that will facilitate a cultural change.'

With all this in mind, change management consulting sounds like a contradiction in terms. If an organization has to change, how can external input help? Surely this is the equivalent of ordering someone to be empowered? Indeed, change management consultants often find themselves caught between a rock and a hard place. They have to facilitate rather than impose, and the moment they tell someone to do something, they have failed. However, because the most effective facilitation is often very low key – helping people find solutions rather than giving them easy answers – it runs the risk of becoming invisible. Because clients are encouraged to think the new ideas or techniques they acquire from the consultants are their own (thus avoiding the not-invented-here syndrome), there is a danger that they look back on the consulting process and question its value. What did the consultants actually do? Surely they, the client, have had these ideas all along? Indeed, the familiar complaint – that consultants borrow clients' watches in order to tell them the time – may have its origins here. You have to ask why the clients did not know to look at their watch in the first place.

PUBLIC AND PRIVATE FACES OF CHANGE MANAGEMENT CONSULTING

A closer look at the projects described here suggests that change management consulting is not one, but two things. Where they were working directly with employees, the consulting firms had to adopt an innovative approach:

▪ They had to adopt a fresh approach to old problems. A major factor in changing the individual behaviour of store-based staff at Tesco was Trilogy's use of Brad Brown's 'Choosing your Attitude': a programme that encourages people to take control of their lives and work and that was totally new to Tesco at the time. 'This has been fantastic,' commented one employee who went on the programme. 'Most important to me is that the skill of choosing my attitude has turned me from a grumpy, stressed-out guy into a

dad who has rediscovered his spark.' It is the fact of using something new – as much as the actual technique – that is important
here. A genuinely new approach can often break though the mental paralysis of which we are all guilty from time to time.

■ A different experience was offered. Trilogy's work at Tesco is also
an illustration of how important it is to think through how those
affected will feel during the consulting process. This is not usually
a factor consultants – or clients – give much thought to. The last 10
years have seen a massive shift away from the more facilitative
types of consulting ('process consulting' as it used to be known), in
favour of delivering quantifiable results within clearly defined
timescales. But Trilogy's approach shows that the means is just as
important – indeed, may be an integral part of – the end. If the local
staff on whom the success of the project depended felt they were
being told what to do, it would have defeated the object. Both
the 'Choosing Your Attitude' programme and the network of
'firelighters' were designed, not so much to command, but to
inspire – a word that perhaps does not come up enough in consulting circles.

■ New insights were gained. An important factor, in PA's work, both
with the Department of Work and Pensions, and with Transport for
London, was to be able to bring new data into emotionally charged
debates. By using dynamic simulation models to forecast how different groups of customers would respond to the proposed
changes, PA was able to help the Department assess the likely level
of take-up and the resources it would require to deal with it. With
Transport for London, the firm used a systems dynamics model to
help those involved understand the impact that traffic flow and
crime or the fear of crime had on the London bus network. PA also
worked with niche consultancies from elsewhere, notably from
initiatives to tackle urban crime in New York.

However, innovation is only one side – the public side – of change
management consulting. Behind the scenes, these projects have to be
marshalled with just as much discipline and attention to detail as large-
scale IT work. Without the backbone of such discipline, the projects
themselves might easily have been grounded by the amount of work
and the number of people and organizations involved.

In this, the private face of change management consulting, the case
studies highlight three factors critical to success:

■ Starting small. A corollary of managing the process of change so
that it is not imposed on employees is that overt programme

management techniques may be counter-productive, alienating those they are supposed to engage. It is therefore not surprising that successful change management consulting starts small: this is critical, as the cynics in an organization can see that a new idea works in practice. Trilogy trialled the Living Service Programme in pilot stores and encouraged the converts from this stage to become advocates in the next. The Transport Operational Command Unit was similarly piloted before agreement was reached for it to be rolled out.

- Speed and the perception of speed. Change management projects are notoriously difficult to keep going as they combine complexity with largely intangible benefits. Unexpected issues inevitably arise and distract those whose involvement is essential. Even where they are not distracted, progress can appear slow. One of the most important roles of the consultants involved in all three projects was to keep things moving, bringing different stakeholders together to hammer out a consensus, orchestrating activity and ensuring that there are 'quick wins'.

- Understanding that no one size fits all. Another significant cause of failure among change management projects is that they are obviously imposed from above, those responsible assume that every business unit is the same and that the process for change can therefore be uniform across all those groups affected. Fundamental to the public communications strategy developed by PA with the Department of Work and Pensions was that it took into account the likely difference in reaction between, for example, pensioners and single parents. Similarly, one of the reasons why Trilogy's work with Tesco has had such a powerful effect was that the issues facing each store were assessed individually by the people working there. In the words of one store manager, the Living Service Programme has 'encouraged [employees] to grab hold of a store and see it as theirs'.

SUMMARY – KEY LESSONS FOR MANAGERS AND CONSULTANTS

- Bringing down the barriers within and between organizations may reduce one set of obstacles to change, but it creates another – multiple stakeholders. Successful change management involves confronting and reconciling, not bypassing, the different – sometimes conflicting – aims of those involved.

■ Radical change can be easier than incremental change because it demonstrates the willingness of senior managers to resolve – rather than pay lip-service to – serious issues.

■ Effective change management consulting follows Teddy Roosevelt's advice of 'speak softly and carry a big stick'. In terms of its public interaction with employees, it needs to adopt innovative, even unexpected approaches. Behind the scenes, consultants have an important role to play in maintaining momentum and credibility.

CASE STUDY 3.1

LIVING THE BRAND – FOR REAL

The UK's biggest retailer is making strides in customer service by working at the personal level. This is a story about individual attitudes rather than information systems, and how organizations change when change becomes catching.

Tesco is the UK's most successful retailer. Its half-year profits announced in September 2003 were £628 million, and profits were expected to reach £1.65 billion for the year. The company has grown from being an efficient grocery operation to a one-stop supplier of everything from DVDs to children's clothes, and from dental floss to computers. While we might associate supermarkets with baked beans, during December 2003 Tesco sold eight pairs of jeans every minute. To give some measure of its impact on daily life, £1 in every £8 spent in Britain goes to Tesco.

The company is often used by the media to symbolize the growing homogenization of the national scene, and the concentration of power in the hands of a small number of powerful retail behemoths. The reality for customers, staff and leadership alike is very different. Tesco is, like any other customer-facing organization, powerfully aware of its role in the community and the value it represents for families. The company knows that its continued success does not just rely on excellent supply chain systems, judicious store siting and keen prices. Tesco is also a collection of 220,000 human beings, interacting minute by minute with customers, representing the store's values and functioning as its effective market presence. The company is highly aware that its brand is very much more than its name. For Tesco, the concept of 'living the brand' is manifest in the attitudes and behaviours of each member of its vast staff. Customer loyalty is not primarily a function of schemes such as Tesco's Clubcard, though such mechanisms undoubtedly help. Loyalty is, at root, driven by personal relationships.

Tesco's firm intention to remain as market leader drives the company's belief in customer service. Customer service can be a real differentiator for general retailers, and a powerful multiplier of sales. Tesco's recognition of customer service as a key determinant of continued success coincided with two concurrent research projects commissioned by the company. The results of the first project showed that customers were not experiencing consistently warm and friendly service from Tesco. The second project's results indicated that internal levels of staff morale were suffering in reaction to increasingly ambitious cost and efficiency targets in stores. As the company pursued ever-finer improvements to its processes, so its staff took the strain – with an inevitable knock-on effect on perceived levels of service.

Tesco engaged a team from Trilogy, a three-member consortium of specialist consulting companies (WhatIf, InterAction and Bridge), to help transform the quality of its customer service and raise it to the market-leading standard shared by Tesco's business processes and commercial offerings. Trilogy brought a clear, crisp and compelling belief to bear on Tesco's situation. The team maintained that in order to develop the emotional loyalty of customers through a rich experience of personal service, Tesco must create an environment that made staff feel motivated and valued. There would be no short cut to a customer service nirvana. Great service would have to be built store by store, person by person. Trilogy developed the Living Service Programme with Tesco in order to build an environment in which personal service would flourish naturally, touching the lives of every Tesco employee, and reaching beyond to the needs of its millions of customers.

Reaching the heart

The board tasked a joint Tesco/Trilogy team with delivering a service-led culture to the retail business. Central to the change would be the concept that attitude differentiates good service from great service. The team would build the skills to demonstrate this concept in action, and develop a process to deliver excellent personal service for customers while simultaneously improving staff morale in stores.

The project was also clear in its aim that the change process would not be done to Tesco people, but by, with and for Tesco people. Staff members would be trained to deliver the process for themselves, and to make it their own personal property. The project was tasked with building a critical mass of people who would act as role models of great service right on the floor of every store.

The team developed the Living Service Programme, a 26-week process to be undertaken by 660 stores. The programme's unique proposition is that a culture of service excellence for customers can only be built if the staff feel served by the organization. A revitalized, customer-centric culture cannot be grafted on to an organization, nor can it be magicked from thin air. Such a culture needs strong, flexible and consistent support from the organization. As emotional loyalty is inculcated within staff, it infects customers. 'Living Service' really does live and breathe, and touch the people who share in it.

The Living Service Programme has seven core components:

- A dedicated Tesco coach, trained to be an internal change agent, is attached to the programme.
- The programme includes in-store diagnosis of staff and customer needs.
- Leadership development workshops are run to build a service culture for staff and customers.
- The programme builds a Local Service Vision based on three unique Service Expressions.
- Shop floor 'firelighters' are developed to embody great personal service.
- Whole-store Energizer events enlist all employees.
- Learning teams are created to sustain the momentum after the 26-week roll-out programme.

A philosophy of service

Trilogy used a blend of four complementary methods to design and deliver the programme. These are brand alignment, interactive intelligence™, viral change and systemic consulting.

Brand alignment is an approach to building market leadership by fostering companies with strong personalities. The approach derives from the work of Kunde (1999). Kunde believes that great companies are created by aligning the internal brand, or the experience of the employee, with the external brand, or the promise made to the customer. The brand alignment approach stresses the need for authenticity. In conversation with Tom Peters, Kunde explains:

> The word religion derives from the Latin religare – to bind something together in a common expression. Corporate Religion is that which expresses the soul of a company and supports the building of a strong market position. In order to make a Corporate Religion come alive you have to describe your internal organization as well as your external market. These internal values create an internal movement which delivers the whole heart and soul of the company. (Source: www.tompeters.com/cool_friends)

Trilogy partner InterAction was the source of the interactive intelligence™ principles used in the project. Chairman, K Bradford Brown's techniques for 'Choosing your attitude' were a core platform for the behavioural change delivered at Tesco, and a major means of empowering Tesco's people. Much of the technique's impact lies in simplicity and transferability, enabling individuals to change themselves and sustain change over time. This principle underlies the core message of the programme: 'Everyone gains from giving great service.'

Viral techniques for spreading messages have gained a lot of attention in the marketing arena, particularly following the success of groundswell, word-of-mouth campaign for films such as 'The Blair Witch Project'. Viral marketing encourages consumers to propagate messages through their personal networks, gaining quality attention not readily accessible to the originator of the message contents. Trilogy adapted the viral approach to the propagation of the new style of working. Early adopters had real power to shape the change process, and to make sure that the project's themes were framed in the most effective, usable terms. Generating momentum among 220,000 people requires a systematic approach, and the viral change technique acts as a powerful forward force.

Lastly, the team used a systemic consulting technique to embed the new approach in the organization through the processes of recruitment, performance management and communication. Bonding the new approach with the organization's ongoing renewal processes ensures that this is no once-only exercise, having an affect on one generation but failing to affect the company's DNA.

Each technique used in the project addresses the joining of personal actions with corporate objectives in a different way. The combination of techniques lent the project unique power and durability.

Elements of delivery

Tesco built a highly successful organization based on a strong head office team providing clear guidance and direction to the store network. This hub-and-spoke design works well as a way of coordinating supply and monitoring performance, but it does not support the empowerment of individuals needed to create excellent, personal customer service. The company needed an approach to leadership that encouraged greater staff ownership and discretion. Trilogy therefore developed a series of three-day workshops for all the retail business leaders. The shift in leadership practice across Tesco has been felt profoundly. One store manager says: 'Staff feel that their managers are there for them. This has encouraged general assistants to grab hold of the store and see it as theirs. The Director now expects the GAs to set the tone as much as the management team.'

The 26-week roll-out process is owned by a cross-section of staff at every level, the critical mass being among general assistants. The in-store diagnosis tailors the approach to the issues that are particular to that store.

Part of the project's philosophy is that people must lead themselves. From Tesco's existing Corporate Values 'No one tries harder for customers' and 'Treat people how you want to be treated', three core Service Expressions emerged from the team's work with staff and customers, which are used to support individual application of customer service principles. These three expressions were:

■ Know your stuff.
■ Show you care.
■ Share a smile.

The Service Expressions are easy to understand and remember. Couched in everyday language and free of any hint of spin, they help to foster warm, personal service as a natural part of daily activity.

Living service and lighting fires

Two new roles were created to guarantee total ownership of the programme and the achievement of sustainable culture change. A full-time role – Living Service coach – was created to deliver the programme to the stores and 80 Living Service coaches were recruited from all areas of Tesco's business. According to one Living Service coach: 'To our staff, this looks like a totally Tesco-driven process. Trilogy has built deep internal capacity for us coaches, and provides invaluable support in the background.'

The coaches are trained to embody the values and behaviours of the programme so that each store has known individuals responsible for acting as low-key but consistent role models. For example, coaches are trained in advanced attitude and listening skills so that they can genuinely empathize with customers and reflect back their attitudes and needs. Being able to 'be in someone else's world' helps staff to interact with customers even in situations where they might traditionally feel helpless. So, for example, staff members are not empowered to change the price of products but they can choose whether or not to help someone who is looking quizzically at a range of products. Coaches learn to apply personal insight into customers' needs, and because they do so every day in the real store environment, their behaviour infects others around them.

One of the project's challenges was the obvious one: scepticism. Change campaigns that attempt to address hearts and minds immediately attract suspicion. People may also feel vulnerable to the importation of techniques that may appear to criticize their values or styles of interaction. Trilogy therefore made great effort to involve key decision-makers, and actively sought out sceptics. 'You can't just preach to the converted,' says Trilogy's Jane Sassienie. 'Inside every cynic is a frustrated dreamer. There's something there that they wanted, and didn't get. We can help them to make it happen, rather than waiting for life to bring it to them.'

The programme was designed to improve commitment bottom-up as well top-down in the organization. Healthy and successful organizations have always valued the people in their front line. In many ways, the Living Service Programme is Tesco's recognition, through committed investment of time and money, of that fundamental business truth. Tesco's general assistants, who operate the stores' checkouts and fill their shelves, were the key audience for the project's messages, and they supplied the key agents of change.

The project therefore introduced a second novel role dubbed 'firelighter'. Firelighters are change agents given skills to change themselves and the people around them. In each store, 5 per cent of the staff were trained as firelighters, creating a population of 20,000 committed, locally based champions of change. The firelighters were responsible for enlisting shop floor colleagues to the Living Service principles. They also performed as role models for personal service, putting the principles into practice in their daily work. As one store director says: 'The firelighters are the single biggest reason that the programme is having such an impact. The programme has switched on for the people that really matter, the customer assistants.'

Registering the impact

Tesco's commitment to the programme is evidenced by its investment over several years. The board was impressed by the results of this investment and were prepared to increase investment halfway through the roll-out of the project in order to create more firelighters.

The Tesco/Trilogy team has been careful to measure the outcomes produced by the Living Service Programme. The full national roll-out was planned to be completed in the Autumn of 2004. Key Performance Indicators tracked for the first 30 trial stores gave clear initial indicators of the project's beneficial impact. These early results set a trend for the national picture.

On the staff side, stores that had been through the programme outperformed others by an average of 20 per cent in all the key categories of an internal staff survey. These categories include morale, feeling listened to, helpful management, being first for customers, and enjoying work and celebrating success. Absence figures were down in the same stores, and staff retention was improved.

Among the project's significant intangible benefits is the widely noted enhancement in the quality of dialogue and communication within stores. Staff report that the 'them and us' culture is practically a thing of the past, with deep effects on the work climate and employee attitudes to the company. There is now a more challenging culture both within stores and between stores and the centre. Staff now have greater involvement in the shaping of decisions, and know that their ideas and opinions are valued.

A further knock-on effect, and evidence of the deep-rooted nature of the change that has occurred, is a greater willingness to embrace other change initiatives. The happy experience of the Living Service Programme has helped to recalibrate people's attitude to new initiatives. The development of the business inevitably means that staff will be involved in many subsequent changes, both at the macro and micro levels.

Perhaps most remarkably, Tesco is proud and excited to note that the programme has had a profound impact on individuals' quality of life outside the workplace. One Living Service coach says: 'This has been fantastic at work, but most important to me is that the skill of choosing my attitude has turned me from a grumpy, stressed-out guy into a dad who has rediscovered his spark.'

Customers are noticing a big difference in the atmosphere at Tesco stores, and in the attitude shown by staff. For their part, staff are enjoying work much more. One firelighter sums up the effect such a change programme can have on an individual and his career: 'To be honest, before this I was considering leaving Tesco. The ability to choose my attitude has changed my whole life. I now enjoy my job and get on with my colleagues more. Now I'm thinking about going for a section manager position. It's the best thing that's happened to me.'

The Living Service Programme is the result of a unique combination of approaches that is unlikely to occur within an organization. Driving cultural change from a personal basis is a novel technique, and not one that many companies would necessarily embrace. In this case, the mixture of elements created for Tesco added up to a holistic programme that the organization could put its faith in and roll out across the business. If it is doubtful whether such a package would be created from scratch within a large, established organization, it is even harder to imagine such a home-grown change programme gaining acceptance among its target population. Initiatives with truly innovative attributes may be treated with suspicion if they emanate from the organization's leadership: their apparent oddity can be interpreted as a failure to understand the day-to-day reality of the business, and as confirmation of the leadership's irrelevance. Equally, where innovative initiatives arise in the periphery of an organization, gaining endorsement from the leadership is often hard to achieve. One of the key enemies of change is the perception that change is being imposed by one group upon another. When the ideas, rationale and modelling of the change programme originate in an external agency, as in this project, it is often easier for the organization to swing its weight behind the programme.

Tesco took Trilogy's concepts and made them an integral part of the company's living fabric. By importing an approach, and taking complete ownership of its expression within the organization, Tesco managed to redirect the evolution of its culture in a way that keyed into its employees' beliefs and motivations while focusing faithfully on the needs of its customers. This was a project in which the personal became the practical: a case of cultural change carried out at the human scale, person by person, and action by action.

Finally, the composition of the Trilogy partnership indicates one direction in which management consultancy is developing. By turning three competitive agencies into a creative partnership (WhatIf, InterAction and Bridge), the consulting group was able to cover different aspects of the process of change while also offering specialist skills in each area: they were masters of all their trades, rather than none. But perhaps most satisfying of all for those involved is that Trilogy's team worked so closely and effectively with its client. As Sassienie says: 'Trilogy was actually four partners, because of Tesco ...' But what's in a name?

CASE STUDY 3.2

DELIVERING SAFER BUSES

Reducing crime and fear of crime on London's surface transport and improving the flow of its buses has helped drive a 13 per cent increase in users over two years. Modelling complex systems made it possible.

One of the key objectives of London's strategic transport authority, Transport for London (TfL), has been to deliver a safer and more reliable bus network for London. The bus network in London is one of the largest and most comprehensive urban transport systems in the world. Every weekday over 7,000 scheduled buses carry around 5.5 million passengers on over 700 different routes, a total of more than 1.5 billion passengers a year. London's buses are now carrying the highest number of passengers since 1968, and experiencing the fastest rate of growth in passengers since World War II.

Given the complex physical and commercial structure of the city's underground and overground rail systems, and the expense and technical difficulty of creating entirely new transport systems in a congested area, the bus system offers London's administration its best route for improving communications in the short to medium term. Buses exploit the existing roads system, so do not need direct investment in route infrastructure. Buses can be permanently or temporarily re-routed much more easily than train services. They are the preferred means of transport for short journeys, and they are the most accessible form of transport – both in terms of price and physical access – available to Londoners. Lastly, the principal technologies underpinning the bus industry are mature and stable while innovation delivers ever more efficient vehicles.

TfL is continually improving the bus system. The double-decker Routemaster bus, launched in 1954, may be a design icon and a symbol of London recognized the world over, but the poor accessibility, durability and manoeuvrability of this workhorse and its successors is no longer enough to keep up with growing demand. The new, two-segment 'bendy bus' is 18 metres long and can carry up to 140 people, at least 60 more than a double-decker bus. Bendy buses are also cashless and equipped with CCTV. Journeys are more reliable and quicker as passengers must have a ticket before boarding and can enter or exit the bus from all three doors.

However, perceptions of buses as dangerous places to be dissuade passengers from using buses as often as they might. Delays to buses are also very apparent to passengers, whether they are stuck on a non-moving bus or waiting at a stop. Poor perceptions of the safety and reliability of buses drive down their effective value to the Londoners whom they serve.

When Ken Livingstone was elected Mayor of London, two of his key election promises were to reduce congestion and to improve the public transport system. TfL was formed in 2000 to take responsibility for London's transport system and the delivery of the Mayor's transport strategy.

Traffic congestion in London costs local, national and international businesses billions of pounds every year. With the city's population projected to increase by over three quarters of a million residents over the next 10 years, the problem would have become intractable without intervention. A major element of the Mayor's strategy was the congestion charging scheme, implemented in February 2003. On its own, the congestion charge acts as an influencer on traffic flow. But without accompanying public transport measures it would have a negative effect on London's business performance as workers were priced out of the city. To make the congestion charging scheme effective, the strategy had to improve alternative methods of transport. Encouraging people to switch away from cars and towards public transport, in particular buses, was therefore a key part of the Mayor's transport strategy. While the congestion charge would act as the 'stick', removal of the barriers to greater bus usage would act as a 'carrot'.

Removing the barriers to bus usage

Consultation with Londoners confirmed that fear of crime and violence was a key barrier to increased bus usage. The crime statistics showed that there were over 9,000 incidents on buses in 2002, typically involving illegal weapons, drug dealing and aggression towards staff and fellow passengers. In order to change attitudes to bus travel TfL needed to address this criminal activity. TfL was also concerned about the number of illegal taxi touts, which reflected a failure to enforce the law relating to taxis and private hire vehicles.

The Metropolitan Police Service (MPS) is responsible for dealing with the majority of criminal activity across London. However, the MPS has limited resources. Higher profile issues of antiterrorism, street and gun crimes inevitably take priority over transport policing. Transport crime can easily be seen as merely a 'quality of life' issue.

However, the 'zero tolerance' theory of policing suggests that tackling apparently low-level crimes has a profound impact on more serious offences. Based on his experience of reducing transport crime in New York, and the policy's knock-on effect on the safety of the city as a whole, TfL Commissioner Bob Kiley agreed with MPS Commissioner Sir John Stevens and the Mayor to fund a pilot project. A unit would be created with the objective of reducing crime on London's bus network, improving bus flow and reducing taxi touting.

A further disincentive to bus travel, confirmed by research, was the length and unpredictability of bus journey times, caused in part by obstructions on bus routes. TfL was in the process of increasing the network of dedicated bus priority lanes. However, the high number of vehicles illegally using the special bus lanes was limiting their effectiveness.

The MPS Transport Operational Command Unit (TOCU)

TfL already had initiatives under way to deliver the transport strategy. However, the desired rate of increase in bus usage was not yet being achieved. A joint TfL/PA team was formed to create and deliver a detailed strategy that would:

- reduce crime and fear of crime on buses, and also in the street environment surrounding them, including waiting areas and bus lanes;
- reduce the number of illegal private hire vehicles;
- improve bus flow demonstrably.

The assignment had two phases. During phase 1, the team was to identify and validate a set of initiatives for achieving both of these objectives. At the same time, the team would establish the MPS Transport Operational Command Unit (TOCU) to deliver the pilot initiative between TfL and the MPS. The TOCU involved police officers, traffic wardens and police community support officers in the partnership with TfL staff. The TOCU would be responsible for policing agreed bus corridors on the London bus network, and enforcing the law on taxis and private hire vehicles.

Once the approach had validated the success of the TOCU pilot, phase 2 would deploy the new transport policing strategy, including the establishment of a new Transport Policing and Enforcement Directorate (TPED) within TfL. This directorate would have overall responsibility for all transport policing and enforcement activities provided by TfL and the MPS.

The TOCU had to be implemented prior to the introduction of the congestion charging scheme, due to be launched in February 2003.

The TPED management also had to be established by mid-2003 without any loss of momentum.

The team's work had three main components:

■ Strategic analysis of alternative approaches to achieving the business objectives, in order to formulate a viable change programme. This analysis was achieved using systems dynamics modelling.

■ Building a robust change programme, while taking account of the complexity of effective change in a city the size of London. This change programme was critically dependent on senior management commitment from both TfL and MPS.

■ Delivering timely, tangible results, which could only be achieved by working hand-in-hand with TfL to address issues as they arose. The team focused on providing a clear governance structure, rapid issue resolution and results-oriented management to ensure deliverables were achieved in full and on time.

Modelling for synergies

Systems Dynamics Modelling has its roots in work done in the 1960s by Professor Jay W Forrester at MIT. Forrester applied his knowledge of electrical engineering systems to other kinds of system, including 'soft' ones such as organizations. Systems dynamics has since been developed into a mature methodology that clearly and comprehensively maps cause, effect and linkages to explain complex environments.

The systems dynamics approach incorporates the concept of the feedback loop. While earlier approaches to complex systems tried to define them as static entities, systems dynamics recognizes that systems can only be understood in terms of their behaviour over time, and especially the ways in which the system's current state can influence future states. Incorporating feedback into models creates the non-linear, or unpredictable, behaviour that we associate with complex systems such as the weather.

Simulations of the system under examination provide the basic mechanism of systems dynamics modelling. A simulation can be defined, loaded with a set of initial conditions and then tested in a range of different scenarios. The systems dynamics approach lets researchers 'play with' complex systems in safety, manipulating factors that would be expensive to adjust in the real world, and measuring the impact of each configuration in a very short time. Lessons from the modelling can then be compared, refined and translated into real-world interventions. The technique has been applied in thousands of organizations around the world, and even to the US economy.

PA's Nick Chaffey describes the modelling process like this:

> We combined our experience and insights from London and elsewhere with that of TfL's managers and their suppliers in order to build a robust understanding of the factors that drive performance and then incorporated these into a model. Then we put the starting conditions in the model and say 'go'. Then we can compare different effects and see the correlation with what actually happened. We can also drill down to detail, to understand different parts of the model.

In the context of TfL's project, systems dynamics modelling allowed the team to explore the factors influencing crime and the fear of crime, as well as the factors contributing to bus flow. The team could then examine linkages between related factors: patterns that only emerge fully and repeatedly through system simulation.

In this way the team could begin to assess the potential levers that might alter behaviour within the system, and see how these levers would affect crime issues and bus flow. As measures were introduced and tested within the model, the team constructed an optimal portfolio of initiatives that would increase bus usage and improve bus flow, within existing operational and funding constraints.

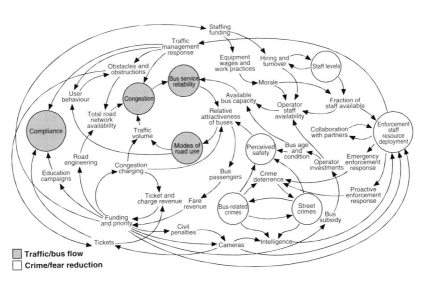

Figure 3.1 *Systems dynamics model of London's bus network*

The portfolio analysis revealed that one specific set of measures would deliver the greatest benefit to both crime and traffic flow objectives. This portfolio focused resources on increasing police presence and coordinating the activities of the many TfL operating units involved. This set of measures performed much better in simulations than packages made up of initiatives such as extra parking attendants or further investment in bus-lane enforcement cameras.

Portfolio analysis allows genuine synergies to emerge. 'Synergy' is a much abused word, often used to yoke together initiatives that may appear complementary, but whose interrelationship does not generate true benefits above and beyond the sum of the parts. Systems dynamics modelling can show that collections of seemingly beneficial measures actually undermine each other in practice. Alternatively, the method can highlight factors that have no obvious structural relationships with each other. Modelling allows such cocktail effects to express themselves in the timeline of the simulations, revealing real-world synergies that can radically change the outcomes associated with a fixed spend.

Above all, systems dynamics modelling can be used to assess the practical implications of different initiatives: the team could be confident that their recommendations would work on the streets of London.

Real-world challenges

Away from the tractable world of its models and simulations, the team had to deal with a range of pressing organizational, political and commercial challenges.

The team had to manage decisions and deliver results across the two largest agencies funded by the Mayor, each with its own culture. The TfL/PA team therefore agreed clear joint objectives with senior stakeholders across both agencies. Linked to specific performance measures, these objectives became the basis for monitoring the output of working groups set up by the team. The project also required joint working between civilian and police operations, on a scale unprecedented in Europe. Peter Hendy, TfL's Managing Director of Surface Transport, believes that successful collaboration among the different groups was a key component of the project's ultimate delivery:

> PA's contribution to the Transport Enforcement initiative has been pivotal in shaping and delivering this key programme for Transport for London and the Mayor. The PA consultants have become part of our joint team with the Metropolitan Police Service and through working

together have enhanced our capability to deliver a safer and better London Bus Network.

PA worked with US consultants to draw upon their relevant experience in New York in tackling urban crime. Several elements were used from models that had been built for other transport and crime projects, ensuring that the work for London was seeded with relevant data. The consulting team members therefore acted as an entry point for new information as well as a source of skills.

The joint team also had to move fast, given the immovable date for the planned introduction of congestion charging. The team established a timetable and clear governance structure, and was vigilant in identifying operational hitches and getting them resolved without delay. Management was encouraged to focus firmly on the project's milestones and deliverables. The great media attention levelled at the congestion charge scheme also meant that this project was under intense scrutiny.

Finally, the funding of MPS staff by TfL was an unprecedented relationship, requiring a new species of contract, tailored to the particular needs and scale of the project. TfL worked with leading UK police lawyers to create the contract while PA colleagues provided a vital bridge between the operational content and legal considerations.

Early measurable results

The performance of the TOCU was measured in July 2003, less than a year after its launch. At this time more than 45,000 fixed penalty notices had been issued to drivers of vehicles illegally parked on bus routes. In addition more than 1,800 illegally parked vehicles had been removed from bus routes. More than 1,700 arrests had been made, for crimes including serious offences such as assault, possession of offensive weapons, drugs, sexual assaults and rape. Arrests had also been made for possession of false driving documents and vandalism on buses including arson. Meanwhile, a crackdown on illegal minicab operators had resulted in 240 arrests. Sir John Stevens, Commissioner of the Metropolitan Police Service, said: 'Given that the TOCU is only a year old, remarkable achievements have been made. The unit has grown to over 500 dedicated members of staff in a short period of time and thanks to the continued partnership between TfL and ourselves will continue to grow and build on the impressive results we have had so far.'

The strategy had also contributed to a positive impact on bus usage and bus flow, with a measured 13 per cent aggregate growth in the number of people travelling by bus in London in the previous two years. Bus reliability had increased and levels of lost mileage due to traffic issues had been reduced on those bus routes covered by the TOCU.

The high profile of the initiative, as well as visible policing and enforcement activities on buses and in the street environment, has also reduced fear of crime. Feedback from customers has reflected growing confidence in public transport.

The establishment of the TPED has for the first time brought together all of the key agencies with an interest in safety and security on London's roads. This integration has greatly improved coordination and information sharing, resulting in more effective intelligence-driven operations, which have proved pivotal to identifying and targeting incidents in London.

In October 2003 the Mayor announced an extra £25 million for the initiative, intended to take the number of staff at TOCU to more than 900. The new money funded more officers for the dedicated cab enforcement unit tackling taxi touting. There were also new teams of Traffic Police Community Support Officers, to help clear critical congestion points as well as being a visible deterrent to criminals. These officers have the power to direct traffic and issue parking tickets. The TOCU's operations were extended to cover night buses and enhanced area task force teams were put in place to respond to issues anywhere on the bus network.

By December 2003 the Mayor was reporting the continued success of the cab enforcement section of the TOCU, which had now made 650 arrests.

The Mayor has said: 'This [TOCU] is another vital weapon in our armoury to tackle crime and congestion in London and I'm delighted by the results. The unit is responding quickly to crimes as they happen and shows that by tackling apparently petty criminals you frequently uncover much more serious offenders.'

TfL's success in this project demonstrates how subjective perceptions can fuel objective changes to a complex system. While the crime figures recorded for the bus system are all too real, their effect on passengers' behaviour is hard to judge. TfL could not respond simply with persuasion. The organization also had to adopt visible measures that would reassure passengers that TfL had safety and reliability at the forefront of their concerns. The TfL/PA team used scientific analytical measures to highlight workable solutions in collection of evidence, and steered clear of making unsupported, but possibly popular, gestures. Just as the zero tolerance approach to petty crime has had a ripple effect on the general quality of life in New York, so TfL's bus measures have helped to make life in the British capital less stressful for everyone. Bob Kiley is convinced that the TOCU is making a major contribution to London life: 'I'm delighted that the excellent partnership we have developed with the Metropolitan Police Service has brought results to be proud of. The unit's focus on safety, reduction of congestion to complement congestion charging and bus priority will help make London's transport system work.'

The package of measures brought to bear by the TOCU derive ultimately from the simulation work done by the TfL/PA team. Loading, configuring, running and interpreting complex, multi-variable models is not a job for the novice. The modelling of dynamic systems is clearly a specialist area, and one in which a global consulting firm can add significant value. Broadly based consultancies can foster specialist skill sets that support a range of practices while smaller organizations must concentrate solely on line-of-business services. Client organizations such as TfL, while containing the engineering and systems expertise needed to appreciate the output and contribution of an advanced technique such as systems dynamics, cannot justifiably maintain full-time modelling experts on their staff. Even if client organizations could engage full-time modellers, those experts would not have exposure to other projects and the data supplied by them. PA was able to mine its experience with other complex systems around the world, including transport projects in major cities.

This project is a prime example of the confluence of technique and experience the best consulting firms can apply to their clients' problems and opportunities. In this case, the simulation activity is matched by pragmatic general management skills, creating a service that combines the fact-based 'what to do' part of the project with an action-oriented 'how to do it' element that ensures successful delivery. The result was a rapid and assured transition from credible whatif modelling to a managed solution deployed and visible in the midst of the city's daily life. Most important of all, PA's approach ensured that the project was led by outcomes, rather than driven by random beliefs.

CASE STUDY 3.3

ELECTRONIC PAYMENTS FOR 13 MILLION CITIZENS

Large-scale public sector projects usually make the mainstream agenda when they fail to deliver. Winners are out there too, but part of their success lies in communicating with the people who count rather than feeding the news agenda. This project is bringing 13 million people into the world of modern banking, while helping to safeguard the UK's network of local post offices.

The current era of business change is notable for the sheer scale of the impact being felt by large, established institutions. As key private and public sector organizations have matured during the latter part of the 20th century, they have frequently reached inflection points where small improvements to current practice are not enough to keep them in business. Industries and governments have fallen around the world as organizations grapple with structural pressures. Others manage to flex with the pressures, and to respond with renewed vigour and vision.

This case study focuses on not one but two large concerns under pressure to effect fundamental changes: the organization delivering social security payments to more than 23 million UK citizens, and the 16,900 branch network of post offices serving local communities throughout the country. The Department for Work and Pensions (DWP) worked with PA to bring social security payment methods into the 21st century, in order to save the public a projected £0.5 billion per annum. In the process the project helped to effect change in the Post Office, revitalizing its consumer offering and protecting the livelihood of many thousands of local post office staff.

The paper trail

Prior to the modernization initiative, over half of benefits and pensions were paid using paper-based transactions at post offices. Recognizing that the process was both expensive and open to abuse, the government set a target to increase the proportion of benefits paid electronically into bank accounts from 40 per cent to a minimum of 85 per cent over a two-year period. The remaining population of 'unbanked' customers would be provided with an alternative that did not rely on the existing order book process.

The business efficiency of the payments process was not the government's only concern in setting this target. The target also addressed the government's interest in increasing the levels of financial and social inclusion within the UK. The initiative would help to improve citizens' access to services and opportunities for advancement.

The initiative was implemented through two programmes. The first of these was the Payment Modernization Programme (PMP). This programme created the strategy for converting 13 million customers' payments to electronic methods, managed the communications necessary to persuade these customers to embrace the change, and implemented the conversion process itself.

The second programme was the universal banking programme. As a result of this programme, nationwide access to basic banking services has been provided at post offices so that customers can, if they choose, continue to collect their benefits there. This new facility required the cooperation not only of the DWP and the Post Office, but also of the Inland Revenue, Northern Ireland Social Security Agency and the high street banks.

PA's support for both programmes helped to ensure that they stayed on target, with the customer conversion process starting in the autumn of 2002 and universal banking becoming available in April 2003. Andrew Heley, who led PA's work with the DWP, comments: 'This is a great achievement for the Department – one we have facilitated through some innovative management and technical approaches, plus a good deal of multi-disciplinary teamwork.'

Switch to electronic payments

The DWP and Northern Ireland Social Security Agency (NISSA) are responsible for the payment of social security benefits and pensions in the UK. Until recently, around 13 million customers received these payments via order books and Girocheques, cashable at the post office. The remaining 10 million customers were paid electronically via their bank accounts. Analysis of the existing system revealed that the paper-based payments cost over 50 times as much as their electronic equivalents. Electronic payments can be processed for just 1p each.

Clearly, if all customers could be paid electronically, enormous savings would follow – savings that could be spent on other public service priorities. The move would also eliminate counterfeiting and other abuses associated with paper-based transactions.

Desirable as it was to transact all payments electronically, the DWP also has to cater for those unable or unwilling to use conventional banking facilities. The Prime Minister had publicly assured customers that they would continue to be able to access benefits via the post office. The primary solution was to be 'universal banking', a scheme allowing everyone to open a basic account, either with a bank or with the post office itself, into which benefits can be paid electronically. The money can then be withdrawn at a post office counter using a card and personal identification number (PIN).

The aim may appear simple, but succeeding with a change of this nature is far from assured. In the first place, the planned conversion was the largest of its kind in the world to date. Having 13 million customers convert from paper to electronic payment would affect hundreds of thousands of staff in government departments, post offices and banks. Transaction volumes would increase dramatically in all these organizations, causing a massive rise in the number of transactions passing through the UK's financial infrastructure, principally BACS (which makes electronic payments between banks) and LINK (the national cash machine network).

To make matters even more challenging, the timescale for conversion was tight. Conversion could not start until April 2003, when universal banking was to be launched. Between that date and the government's 2005 deadline was a two-year window in which the conversion task had to be completed.

High volumes and tight timescales are easier to manage when the project team commands all the resources and stakeholders involved in the change. In this case, however, there was a complex web of relationships to be understood, negotiated and aligned. Universal banking activities had to harmonize with other government initiatives, including the Inland Revenue's new Tax Credits programme that also offered universal banking options among its payment methods. Then there was a large number of stakeholder groups, each with its own interests and information needs. These included the public, politicians, trade unions, financial institutions and government departments. The change process and its success (or otherwise) would be highly visible, not least to voters.

Finally, the novelty of the proposed change meant that uptake rates were uncertain. Government cannot compel customers to convert. Nor would the government offer financial incentives for customers to give up their order books. Media coverage and the activities of pressure groups have unpredictable effects on the public's response to change. Essentially, the change would have to be managed in an environment the project team could neither control nor predict. The team would have to influence rather than instruct.

Making conversion a reality

The DWP formed a multi-disciplinary team with PA to develop its conversion strategy and support business processes for the Payment Modernization Programme. PA gathered specialists in programme delivery, strategy, IT, modelling and contact centre design. Colleagues from PA worked closely with DWP staff at all levels, and remained on hand throughout the programme to advise departmental senior management on everything from overall feasibility to detailed security issues. PA's overall role was to manage the entire process of the conversion. Heley says: 'We had to understand the dependencies among all the tasks and maintain an end-to-end picture, so that things didn't fall down cracks.'

An early task was to design a strategy for informing customers about conversion, recognizing the differing needs of groups such as pensioners and child benefit recipients. The team produced a dynamic simulation model to evaluate alternative approaches, varying the frequency and timing of invitation and reminder letters, telephone calls and other marketing activities. This model allowed the team to compare the impact of the various scenarios not only on conversion timing, but also on the DWP's ability to deliver 'business as usual' and the demands on its resources.

The simulations fed directly into the conversion strategy. Within a 12-month period, the team specified a customer conversion centre and arranged for its operation to be outsourced to a third party. This supplier, managed by DWP with close operational support from PA, now handles most communications relating to conversion.

Meanwhile the DWP developed the Direct Payment 'Giving it to you straight' campaign in order to communicate the changes underway. The campaign gave clear, straightforward information to make sure that people understood the changes and how they would be affected. The strapline 'Giving it to you straight' signalled the campaign's commitment to clear communication, while referring to the direct payment of benefits and pensions.

The campaign explained the account options, so that people could choose one suitable for themselves. It also highlighted the fact that people would have more options for when and where they collected their money; for example cash machines and supermarkets operating a cashback facility could now be used to collect payments. The campaign was set to run for two years, using press, radio and TV advertising, and posters and leaflets to support direct mailings to customers.

The pattern of simulation, specification and implementation used for the communications strategy was reflected in the team's approach to stakeholder relationships. The team worked with stakeholders to create an integrated Critical Milestone Plan giving shared visibility of key tasks and dependencies. This plan balanced the programme's requirements against the DWP's other commitments – a capability that was particularly valuable when it came to allocation of scarce IT resources.

The team also developed a management information capability to provide an integrated picture of progress. This was achieved in the face of the fragmented nature of the DWP's legacy IT environment, which included 17 separate benefit systems with limited ability to communicate with each other. The management information yielded was high-level enough to support ministerial reporting, yet detailed enough to drive programme decision-making.

Banking for all

The Post Office is one of the UK's largest and best-known businesses. In 2003, the Post Office estimated that it served around 29 million people making some 42 million visits to its branches each week. The Post Office also calculated that 27 pence in every £1 circulating in the UK passes through a Post Office branch. Its pivotal role in the lives of countless people is summed up in its slogan: 'For the little things that make the big things happen™.'

The objective of the Universal Banking Programme was to make banking services available to everyone at post offices, so that any benefit claimant can receive payments electronically. The leading UK banks developed basic accounts that can be accessed electronically at the post office. The Post Office itself developed its own card account, accessible only at its branches. The Post Office card account can only be used to receive benefits, state pensions and tax credit payments. No other payments, such as wages, can be paid into it. This account suits customers who want a simple account without overdraft facilities or charges. No credit checks are carried out for customers opening the account. The simplicity of the account makes it suitable for any customer, including the homeless. Customers can take cash out, free of charge, at any post office, using a plastic card and PIN.

The introduction of the card account was not just a key part of the universal banking programme, but a major element in the modernization of the Post Office network. Post Office branches were already under threat from lost business. Thriving branches were adding newsagent and grocery services to their offerings in an attempt to stay profitable. The government's contract with the Post Office to pay benefits via order books was already due to cease in 2005. Without that guaranteed income, and the customer traffic the payments service brought, the future existence of many Post Office branches was in doubt.

The card account was introduced to meet the needs of universal banking, but it has also had other benefits for the Post Office. Being part of the electronic banking network means that it can offer cash withdrawal facilities to bank customers, increasing each branch's utility to the community it serves. Research suggests that many customers prefer using post offices to banks, so the introduction of banking facilities to post office outlets may have a multiplier effect on customer visits and spend.

Joined-up government in action

Implementing universal banking brought together a large number of stakeholders. As well as the main government departments and the Post Office, the programme also impacted the Inland Revenue, Treasury, Department of Trade and Industry and the UK banks. Several private sector suppliers were also involved. At the outset, the PA team helped to establish a decision-making and programme management structure to ensure that all these participants could work together effectively. A monitoring framework was created to gather information continually from all players, together with a reporting structure to keep stakeholders, including government ministers, informed of progress on both programmes.

The team's role, as in the conversion programme, was to understand the relationships among all these players, ensure continuity of activity and make sure that everyone involved knew their role in the unfolding project. Heley says: 'It's been a huge task for everyone involved. PA's support has been the part that glued it all together. We could act as the catalyst, do the end-to-end assurance role. People see things from their own perspective; the hardest thing is looking at [the project] across the piece.'

The team also had to deal with inevitable conflicts of interest, and ensure that they were resolved in ways that met the best interests of the customer. For example, in stark terms, the government would benefit more if customers opted for direct payments rather than Post Office card accounts, since the former have cheaper transaction costs. However, the Post Office's interests would be better served by a greater uptake in card accounts. Communicating the options as clearly as possible to the target population therefore became even more important. In this way the customers would drive the eventual profile of payment delivery, not marginal interests among the service providers.

While most stakeholders' objectives were interdependent, there were occasional clashes in the priority and timing of different organizations' activities. In order to pre-empt such clashes, the team devised governance structures that gave all parties early warning of issues that would require action. The team also put considerable effort into encouraging collaboration across organizational boundaries.

The programme team also implemented cross-programme risk management and critical contingency planning mechanisms, focusing on areas introducing new business processes, or where transaction volumes were set to increase substantially. In this way resources and management attention could be directed to potential failure points before problems occurred.

The scale of the undertaking and its tight timescales demanded regular assessment of progress towards the launch, and early warning of any risks threatening it. The reporting framework provided ministers and other decision-makers with clear, consistent and focused information on both progress and risks. The information delivered was always related to programme objectives, and made appropriate to the current stage reached in the programme. By managing the horizon in this way, the team ensured that issues were dealt with in a timely way but also within the context of the greater plan.

Top-level governance of the work was the responsibility of a Cabinet committee. Unusually for such committees, officials were invited to meetings and key implementation scenarios were often pursued in detail. Hands-on involvement from ministers made an important contribution to the success of the programmes. Heley says:

> Although [conversion] was a policy issue, it has very far-reaching consequences for millions of voters. It was clear to ministers what the effect on voters would be, so they were interested in details. For example, this letter is going to an 80-year-old person who can't read. It'll be read by her relatives, so what do you want it to sound like?

Delivering true benefits

The ultimate measure of any change initiative is the promptness and fullness of its delivery. Both these programmes were delivered on time and on budget. The Customer Conversion Centre went live on schedule, with war pensioners and child benefit claimants the first to be invited to convert. By March 2004, over 10 million invitation letters had been issued, and over 65 per cent had received a positive response. This response rate was in line with the aggressive targets that had been set.

In April 2003, the Post Office and banks switched on universal banking. By March 2004, millions of transactions had been conducted over the Post Office banking infrastructure and more than a million customers had opened a Post Office card account.

Mechanisms were also firmly in place to allow tracking of conversion, and to manage the delivery of the Payment Modernization Programme's projected savings. The quality of these mechanisms gave ministers the confidence to launch the programme on time, and facilitated its successful completion. By March 2004 more than 5 million of the targeted 13 million customers had already converted, with every indication that overall conversion goals would be met in full.

In classic management consulting style, the joint DWP/PA team acted as a catalyst for business change. PA deployed an appropriate mix of internal expertise at each stage of the programmes, but also tapped into DWP's know-how. The collaboration between colleagues in government departments and consultants has been genuine and sustained. Skills transfer was assured throughout the programmes by handing over programme elements to operations staff as soon as they were established.

PA has shown the great value of an independent consulting presence in the management of a complex, time-constrained initiative. The PA team members were able to manage all the streams of activity without being themselves on the critical path. They could maintain a '30,000-foot view' and turn their attention objectively to any detailed area that needed addressing to keep it on track. This would have been less easy to achieve if the firm had had an interest in, say, the development of the systems components involved in the solution. A clean separation of concerns put PA clearly in the driving seat, and also allowed the firm to act as an effective link between the government and its agencies. With its focus on delivery, the PA presence was the pacemaker of the process, making sure that every activity contributed to the achievement of the overall goal. Public recognition for the firm's achievement has, however, to be measured by the overwhelming silence of the media. Heley jokes: 'It hasn't been in the news because it's worked!'

Meanwhile, the DWP's achievement is being acclaimed as a prime example of best practice in joined-up government. The modernization initiative combines a major delivery effort with cross-departmental and industry working. Other public sector programmes continue to benefit from the lessons learned.

Payment modernization and universal banking have been highly successful programmes. Neither programme has had much exposure in the media. We have become used to stories about large project failures in the government sector, and can even find it hard to comprehend the achievements of those unsung projects that deliver their planned benefits on time and to budget, despite the foreseen difficulties and unforeseen challenges with which they have to deal. Experience at the DWP, and by extension at the Post Office, show that sound programme management techniques can effect change to timescale even where large populations and systems are involved.

Above all, these two programmes demonstrate the primacy of communications in making change happen. Communicating in the right styles and at the right times for the right audiences has been crucial to the enduring success of both programmes. Allowing different stakeholders to appreciate each others' perspectives, and maintaining support for a diversity of goals, has saved the state operational resources, reduced fraud, safeguarded local post offices, expanded payment options for customers, and brought a new population into the modern electronic banking era.

The last word goes to 83-year-old pensioner Edith Richardson, describing her experiences of the pilot in the *Sun* newspaper of 26 March 2003: 'I haven't had any problems getting used to the new system .... I know some of my friends are worried about the changes but it is quite simple .... I can take all [of my pension] out or take out £10 at a time if I want.'

There is no better description of the convenience and security modern banking offers to people of all ages and needs.

4

Human resources

The HR function of popular mythology is staffed by short-sighted bureaucrats bogged down in inventing ever more labyrinthine rules: more Stasi than strategy. As in any myth, there is an element of truth in this. While publicly upholding the view that 'people are our greatest asset', it is a rare organization that puts its HR function on equal footing with operations, sales or marketing. Like IT managers, HR managers typically find themselves falling between two stools. These two groups are guardians of an organization's most important assets – its people or technology – but they are also under constant pressure to minimize the costs of that asset. HR managers are responsible for overseeing compliance to an increasingly heavy burden of regulation, but they are also expected to be flexible and responsive. While they are in the forefront when it comes to reshaping organizations through mergers, acquisitions, outsourcing and offshoring, budget cuts often force them on to the defensive when it comes to developing and motivating individuals.

Squaring these circles is not easy but it is critical to success, as the case studies in this chapter demonstrate. The Apache Corporation characterizes itself as having a sense of urgency: 'We get things done.' That attribute was tested to the limit when the oil company acquired BP's interest in the Forties oilfield in the North Sea. Cultural differences between the two oil companies, as well as a host of regulatory issues, could have lengthened the integration process and threatened Apache's aim of increasing efficiency. Instead, the whole process was completed in just six weeks.

Evotec OAI is a newly formed drug discovery company, formed from the merger of two other companies. Losing staff almost as fast as it was recruiting them, the company needed to look beyond conventional thinking on retention. At the UK's Ministry of Defence (MoD), scale was the biggest potential stumbling block – how to set up a service capable of preparing around 14,000 service men and women annually for new careers in civilian life.

While vastly different in focus, these projects show just how hard HR managers are working to change people's perceptions of their role.

Making short, sharp interventions

All of the projects in these case studies illustrate the importance of good project management disciplines. Without clear planning and a real sense of energy and momentum, the cultural differences between the BP and Apache organizations might have delayed the integration of the Forties operation and eroded the expected benefits – a common failure when it comes to mergers and acquisitions more generally. Similarly, the MoD's resettlement programme was just the kind of initiative to get bogged down in red tape, but was up and running within a very short space of time. Moreover, it was not enough for the department to offer counselling: the service men and women needed a network of offices and resources, backed up by slick administration, if they were to be able to compete effectively in the job market. As Apache's and the MoD's experience demonstrates, HR work is shifting from the continuous maintenance of an organization's 'steady state' to project-based work. Getting things done – to use Apache's words – and getting them done fast is one of the most important ways in which the HR function has been reinventing itself.

Thinking on your feet

Momentum has to be balanced with flexibility, and none of the projects in this chapter were designed to a pre-determined formula. Clearly, there are always constraints, but the ability to accommodate change at short notice was a theme emerging from all the entries for the HR award. As one client put it: 'The need for increased flexibility to manage projects of this size and scale was fundamental to success.' Indeed, it is harder to think of a process more grounded in rules and regulations than that of transferring a group of people from one organization to another. Yet Apache sought to cut through potential bureaucracy by ensuring that its staff were briefed. It also used a dedicated Internet site to keep people fully informed and to give them the information to make decisions for themselves as much as possible.

Going to the people, not expecting them to come to you

The stereotypical HR manager is stuck behind the desk of an organizational backwater: nothing could be further from the case here. The only way Evotec could understand the roots of its high turnover of staff was to go and talk to those staff. Apache's HR team took its messages out to North Sea oil rigs. The MoD's Career Transition Partnership could not expect busy service people to come to it, but established a network of offices at nine regional centres, supplemented by local support in places as far apart as Germany and Nepal.

Helping people to help themselves

Empowerment is a much misused word, reminiscent of Dilbert cartoons in which some petty bureaucrat 'orders' a humble worker to take charge of his life. Moreover, cynics might attribute the idea of self-service HR to tighter budgets: companies are, in effect, asking their employees to do some of the work which HR administrators did for them in the past. Yet each of these projects shares the belief that the best way to help employees is to give them the information, resources and expert support – to help themselves. The projects are indicative of a significant shift away from the paternalistic approach to HR in favour of a more facilitative model.

Avoiding fuzzy thinking

HR is often regarded as one of the woollier areas of management, yet all these cases indicate that information – hard facts – plays an increasingly important role. Misconceptions and assumptions were clouding Evotec's understanding of why employee turnover was so high: although the workshops and questionnaire yielded some uncomfortable – but incontestable – messages. 'A certain amount of heart-searching went on,' says the company's HR director. 'But you couldn't ignore data like this.'

ADVISING VERSUS DOING

It is also clear from these three cases that consultants are playing an increasingly important role in the day-to-day running of the HR function. Consulting here is not a nice-to-have, an optional extra: instead, consultants are performing fundamental and necessary work.

The key here is specialist knowledge. As one of the more mature consulting markets, bound by regulatory barbed wire, consultants have to be experts in very specific fields. The MoD selected Right Management Consultants to work on the Career Transition Partnership because of the company's record in career management and counselling. At Evotec, HR Director Martyn Melvin made a similar choice:

'By working with Penna Consulting, we were able to tap into real experience that made the project work extremely smoothly.' 'We were immediately impressed by the professionalism and knowledge the group possessed,' says Jeff Bender, the Vice President of HR at Apache. 'It was readily apparent that they had "been there and done that", and could answer any questions we put to them.'

From the MCA's Awards Survey, HR clients appear significantly more likely to choose a consulting firm based on expertise in their particular sector. They are also much less concerned about having an existing relationship with the individual consultants or firm involved, and are less likely to pick a firm based on the recommendation of someone else.

The nature of specialist knowledge in the field of HR means that it is important that the consultants who possess it can work side by side with their clients as far as possible. HR consulting cannot be in a 'black box' but requires client involvement every step of the way, and it is therefore not surprising that all of these projects involved joint client–consultant teams. Of course, it is one thing to put people from different organizations together in the same office, and quite another to get them to work together in practice. On top of the conventional barriers, Right Management Consultants found the culture of military life very different to that to which it was accustomed, but was still able to work with MoD personnel to resettle 30 per cent more people than originally planned, largely due to the openness of both sides. Similarly, Jeff Bender at Apache believes that frequent and effective communication between his team and that from Mercer was critical.

These views are borne out by the other projects submitted for the HR Best Management Practice Award. 'I felt I mattered to the consultants as much as they did to us,' commented one client. 'Communications were good throughout and they always delivered each part of the project on time. As the project progressed we became more used to their ability to contribute and consequently got more out of the project as a result. The relationship was friendly, professional and demanding.' According to another: 'We have been increasingly willing and able to challenge decisions and actions on both sides of the relationship, thus improving the quality of the final process.'

Underpinning this, however, is a delicate balance between advising and doing. While relying on Penna's input, Evotec wanted to ensure that the participants in the focus groups and all those subsequently affected by the changes the company made, saw the project as driven by Evotec itself, not imposed upon it from outside. 'We respected Penna's input, but it was still very much a company-led initiative,' said Evotec's Martin Melvin. 'This made it a powerful combination for carrying out effective change at a critical time for the business.' 'We worked hard to develop close working relationships,' agreed Penna's project manager. Rather than put in a big team of consultants, Penna chose to involve only a small number of experts. 'From our experience, we've found that working in a collaborative relationship with a client always produces better results. It's essential that the client's resources are used where they make a difference for their people. In this example, a collaborative approach with carefully budgeted actions led to a tremendous and rapid improvement in results for the HR team.'

Other consultants make the same point. 'The solution must be owned by the client and they are responsible for it. As a consultant, you need to be able to advise and challenge where appropriate on the basis of your previous experience. There is a fine line between trying various ideas and what you would do in a client's very specific situation. You also need to be able to back off at times and let things take their course – if you sell a long-term benefit you must be ready to measure it in the long term and not get sucked in to short-term meddling. Combining a light touch with a high impact is possible.' Not surprisingly, HR clients are much more likely to be concerned about finding a cultural match between themselves and the consultants they use, than other types of client.

The need for consultants to support their clients, but not dictate to them, is a mirror image of the challenge HR managers face with their internal clients. A consulting firm's input may involve advice, help with implementation or most commonly, a mixture of the two. But whatever the consulting firm's exact role, the project has to be owned and fronted by in-house staff if it is not to encounter resistance. The same is true for the HR function: success may involve supporting employees and carrying out administration on their behalf, but it depends on winning the commitment of those employees in the first place.

SUMMARY – KEY LESSONS FOR MANAGERS AND CONSULTANTS

- HR managers are habitually in a difficult position, caught between the conflicting needs of organizations to cut costs while retaining employees' energy and commitment. Caught between two stools, they often fall down the gap.
- Overcoming this institutional handicap depends on five factors:

- dividing more HR work up into short-term projects with definite end-dates;
- being flexible;
- working with employees wherever they are based, instead of expecting employees to come to them;
- adopting a facilitative approach, providing employees with the information and tools they require to take their own decisions, rather than taking those decisions for them;
- replacing gut instinct with hard data when it comes to pinpointing and resolving employee issues.

■ HR consultants are an accepted part of the HR function, providing specialist expertise on HR techniques and regulatory compliance. However, while know-how may be an important factor when it comes to selecting an HR consulting firm, success during the course of the project is dependent on a firm's ability to get things done, the extent to which it can work in joint client-consulting teams and achieving the right balance between doing things on the client's behalf and allowing the client to remain in control of the work.

CASE STUDY 4.1

PROTECTING THE BENEFITS OF STAFF IN TRANSITION

Moving 250 far-flung oil industry staff from one employer to another without spilling a drop of oil or losing a single employee benefit is hard enough. Making the change in six weeks demands creativity too. Excellent communications and fast-track processes for legal compliance helped to safeguard the future of the UK's oldest and largest North Sea oilfield, as well as the futures of all its workers.

Founded in 1954, Apache Corporation is based in Houston, Texas and employs more than 2,350 people around the world. The company is known for its ability to acquire oil production assets from other producers and improve their efficiency, profitability and life expectancy. Apache is also active in oil exploration and the opening up of new fields. The company produces some 430,000 boe (barrels of oil equivalent) per day and has a market capitalization of more than US $13 billion.

Apache completed the US $630 million acquisition of the Forties oilfield from BP in April 2003. The Forties field is the largest oil discovery ever made in the British sector of the North Sea, and on its transfer from BP immediately became Apache's largest asset worldwide.

The Forties field was discovered in 1970 and began production in 1975. After 28 years of continuous production, delivering around 2.5 billion barrels of oil (around 15 per cent of the UK's total historic offshore production), Forties still ranks in the top 10 fields for liquid hydrocarbon production and reserves. The field has estimated reserves of 147.6 million barrels of oil equivalent and anticipated 2003 net production of 45,000 barrels of oil per day. (A barrel is about 35 imperial gallons or 42 US gallons.)

The North Sea is an extremely harsh environment in which to locate a complex industrial process. For Apache, coming to the North Sea presented technical problems very different from those the company was used to solving in the more benign waters of the Gulf of Mexico. Technologies and operating procedures have been specifically developed for the North Sea oil industry over more than a quarter of a century. But the technical context was not the only challenge for the new market entrant. Apache also had to absorb, comply with and master the complex employment landscape within which its new asset was set.

An opportunity with added responsibilities

Apache acquired the Forties field at a time when the major players in the North Sea oil industry were looking to redistribute their assets. From the point of view of an incomer, the North Sea has a mature and sophisticated infrastructure, including a highly skilled workforce. Apache saw clear opportunities for cost reduction, and ways that the company's expertise could be exploited to wring further enduring value from Forties without compromising on the safety or compensation of the people involved.

Forties is also surrounded by known fallow fields, indicating potential expansion opportunities for Apache. Assessing the profile of known, probable and possible oil reserves within the field allowed the company to make the immediate deal, while the wider context enabled Apache to plan Forties as a base for long-term expansion in the North Sea.

Forties immediately became Apache's single most valuable field, and attracted the management and investment attention that accompanies such status. The change of commercial ownership would mark the arrival of a new generation of energy management, focused on revitalizing a key European industry.

The asset Apache bought from BP included a total of 350 people continuously offshore and an infrastructure that was up to 28 years old. The age of the equipment created reliability and maintenance issues, which Apache experts could immediately measure in business terms. The team estimated the company could add 7,000 bopd (barrels of oil per day) to the field's production simply by improving the reliability of rig equipment. Apache estimated that work scheduled for rig maintenance was blocking a further 8,000 bopd.

While the Apache team could rapidly turn its attention to production improvements using the expertise developed by the company throughout its global operations, the company knew that employment issues would present novel challenges. Following a rapid competitive tendering process, Mercer was engaged to provide actuarial, administration, investment and legal services together with advice on communications, employment law, healthcare, HR operations, employee performance and reward. The Forties deal had been announced in January; Mercer were engaged in February; more than 250 staff were to be transferred to Apache by the start of April. Speed and accuracy would be paramount in making the transition work, especially given the complex nature of the staff's existing employment rights, which had to be protected.

Creativity was important too. Apache needed to replicate the big-company benefits its new staff were entitled to, but without an existing profile in the market.

The Apache/Mercer team set these objectives for the project:

- Ensure a smooth and trouble-free transfer of staff by the beginning of April.
- Agree a three-month Transition Service Agreement with BP to allow time to establish payroll and benefit continuation arrangements.
- Develop a compensation and benefits arrangement for the newly created company that would meet the new business obligations and objectives.
- Communicate with staff throughout to maintain morale and productivity.

Protecting benefits

The UK's Transfer of Undertakings (Protection of Employment) legislation, universally dubbed TUPE, provides a legally binding guarantee that employees' contractual terms and conditions remain intact when they move to a new employer during a change in ownership. TUPE is based on the European Community Acquired Rights Directive and requires new employers to respect employment terms including salary, hours, overtime allowances, redundancy packages, holiday entitlements and union recognition. TUPE applies for mergers and acquisitions, and also for outsourcing deals that involve the movement of staff between employers. The regulations do not just apply during the period of transition and a following honeymoon, but for the full duration of employment. Employees can sue employers for unfair dismissal if TUPE is not complied with at any time.

However, TUPE does not cover non-contractual elements such as pensions and benefits. Apache agreed with BP that staff moving to Apache would receive pay and benefits 'broadly comparable' to those at their previous employer. In particular, Apache undertook to continue to provide a defined benefit pension plan for current employees. However, despite this commitment to provide similar compensation and benefits, the company needed to contain or reduce employment costs per unit of production to be more efficient. In order to respond to the six-week timeline for implementation, the team's solution needed to be as clear as possible and involve minimal bureaucracy.

Shared vision, shared visibility

One of the early tasks on the project was to share understanding of the relevant UK laws and precedents around TUPE, Data Protection and employment law issues as well as the general human resource climate in the UK. These areas were all new to Apache's management, but the team absorbed them rapidly and looked for creative solutions that would match the company's strong commitment to getting things done quickly. A steering committee communicated regularly between the United States and the UK using conference calls.

The shape of the project and its management style were dictated by the strict time frame. The team focused on the 'end game' defined by the project's objectives, and worked backwards from the deadline to define the necessary tasks. Mercer's Peter Wallum calls this kind of project 'do-by-close': the project is defined by tasks that must be completed by the closing date.

A dedicated Apache Web site was set up to support collaborative work across the continents and around the clock. All project papers were filed and available to the client and consultants working on the assignment, giving shared visibility of the authoritative status of every factor in the project. The team also maintained an ongoing log of tasks, issues and risks associated with the project. Budgets were agreed for the streams of work and were monitored on a weekly basis.

Mercer drew together experts in retirement benefits, healthcare, share schemes, employment law and employee communications to ensure that all areas of the project were covered. The firm's collective experience in mergers and acquisitions was also tapped by the team using Mercer's knowledge management systems. Mercer's actuary for Apache, Nigel Roth, says:

> We have 13,500 consultants worldwide, and an M&A network within the business, so we've got someone ready to respond and deliver in every geography. We nominated individuals from different parts of the business with the right range of skills to meet Apache's needs. We worked well together as a team and had highly complementary strengths.

Each of the different work streams presented its own set of challenges. On the benefits side, it was agreed that Apache would establish a new Defined Benefit (DB) pension plan offering broadly comparable benefits to the scheme previously provided by BP. Employees of the Forties field were to be given access to this new Apache DB pension plan, and the ability to transfer past benefit rights if they requested. Mercer recommended changes to the way contributions were made to the scheme in order to produce savings on Apache's National Insurance bill, but at no detriment to staff. A new Defined Contribution (DC) pension scheme was also set up for new employees and any existing Forties employees who opted to transfer into it.

The new pension programme had to be approved by the Inland Revenue and in place by July 2003. By that time, employees needed to be informed about the pensions options available to them. It was important to communicate the scheme's details and the available options face-to-face to ensure all employees understood their rights. Presentations were given in a number of workplaces, including the oil rigs themselves. Mercer used financial advisers from its sister company, Marsh, who, uniquely in the industry, had the required flying licences. Tim Wagstaff of Marsh explains: 'This means we are licensed to visit rigs. Anyone doing so needs to have practised for possible emergencies – by escaping underwater from a helicopter and so on.'

The team also produced personalized benefit statements (along with other communication literature) to help employees make informed decisions. Wallum says: 'You can't do this sort of thing with a video. We had real people walking around and talking to people. We provided the background materials and provided the Marsh people to do the advising, on the rigs and at home. We used every technique we could to contact people.'

Keeping the show on the road

A critical aspect of the project was helping to maintain employee motivation and productivity during this period of major change. Throughout the assignment the team's communications specialists adopted the 'Apache style' when preparing for briefing groups and supporting question and answer sessions. The Apache style is plain-speaking and direct, reflecting the need for speed and accuracy in its sphere of business in its avoidance of ambiguity or vagueness.

The distributed nature of the workforce presented particular problems for the communications exercise. Staff were mostly at rigs or on shore leave: there was no question of gathering everyone in a hotel for a half-day's session or drawing up a schedule of one-to-one meetings. The team visited individuals and used a range of channels to communicate, including e-mail.

The biggest hurdle to installing the new pension arrangements was the transfer of Apache staff records from BP. The team found and appointed a payroll bureau to handle the complexity of pay arrangements in the North Sea oil industry. Additional complications included replicating BP-specific calculations, and especially dealing with situations where employees had been members of several successive schemes as a result of previous corporate acquisitions within the BP group.

Apache also needed to replicate the previous DB pension arrangements as far as possible. These involved complex investment strategies that would be costly to model. Mercer used a consulting solution covering risk assessment, objective setting and investment strategy through an approach called Mercer 360. This approach enables smaller pension schemes to implement an appropriate investment strategy at an affordable cost. The team was also able to use this structure to design the new DC arrangement.

The team also had to ensure that the new pension arrangements were formally approved by the Inland Revenue before the launch date in July. The legal team shifted the approval process on to a fast track by submitting a simplified draft of the arrangement ahead of the final version. This allowed the team to prepare a final submission that it knew would gain rapid approval.

The team then had to train the new pension fund trustees. The appointed trustees were mostly from the United States and had little experience of UK pensions and benefits. The training programme was designed for fast consumption, and tailored to the exact requirements of Apache's new schemes for the Forties business.

Benefits packages

The Apache/Mercer team created risk benefit arrangements for employees working in the North Sea that mirrored, as far as possible, those offered by their previous employer. These benefits included private medical insurance, disability cover and life assurance. Some of the benefits in the new ranges had previously only been available to big benefit purchasers – companies with larger populations of staff. The Apache/Mercer team managed to negotiate discounts similar to those made available to larger companies, ensuring that staff didn't miss out on big-company benefits with the change in ownership.

Under their previous arrangements, employees in the Forties business had benefited from a Save As You Earn (SAYE) share option plan and a Share Incentive Plan (SIP), where the company matched the purchase of shares by individuals. The transition team replicated the SIP in all its features, and added extra beneficial features that could be introduced in a US share scheme but could not be applied to UK shares. A tax-qualified discretionary share option plan was implemented by Apache to replace the SAYE scheme. Early Inland Revenue approval was sought and obtained for both of these plans, meaning that the re-engineered share benefit packages were fully implemented on time.

Wrapping up the new pensions and benefits arrangements called for the creation of a new staff handbook and contracts of employment for every member of staff. The Forties business had previously had two staff handbooks, and like many such products they were not always easy to navigate or update. The team replaced these handbooks with a single, simplified handbook that covered all the relevant details, met the legal requirements of TUPE and fitted with Apache's approach to staff management. The team also worked with Apache's solicitors to develop new contracts of employment for staff in time for the transition date.

A smooth transition

Mergers and acquisitions are famously unpredictable in their achievement of the business goals designed for them. Sometimes macro-level faults cause such deals to come unstuck. In these cases, one or more external factors in the companies' environment turn out to have been incorrectly analysed, or to have changed in their relevance or impact by the time the deal is completed. Other mergers and acquisitions are derailed not by inappropriate or unsustainable visions, but by failures of execution. In particular, deals can often fail because key staff members melt away during the transition. How people are treated during the process of change, and the care applied to their future security and opportunities, are significant determinants in the retention of staff and hence the overall success of mergers and acquisitions.

Jeff Bender, Vice President of HR, Apache Corporation says: 'We've experienced negligible turnover since we've taken over the field operations from BP. Our production has already improved significantly, with more expected over the ensuing months. A significant cultural change process is in place and we've already seen the results of this throughout the organisation.'

The team's commitment to regular and consistent communication with all the affected staff made the change process a transparent and inclusive one. The level of senior management attention given to pensions and benefits issues gave a strong message that the new owners were committed to the personal obligations they had undertaken in acquiring the Forties business. Apache was in fact able to sustain productivity throughout the period of the transition project. The company had managed to replicate an inherited pay and benefits regime without the significant costs normally borne by a new, 'outsider' company entering an unfamiliar market.

Despite having no existing management infrastructure in the UK, Apache was able to show staff how quickly the company could get up to speed and take firm control of the issues it was facing. The deal was completed on time, a successful Transition Services Agreement was made and implemented, stakeholders were communicated with throughout and new services such as payroll and pensions administration were created and launched without major hitches.

Mercer's contribution to the successful transition took its lead from the entrepreneurial way the consultancy was awarded the contract. Peter Wallum explains how his firm became involved with Apache:

> I read about the deal in the *Financial Times* at the weekend, and I knew they'd need help. So I talked to some people in our Houston office and they found out the Apache management was coming to see three potential consultancy providers the next week. We were allowed to do a quick presentation on the Tuesday morning, with the understanding they'd want a fully costed proposal by Thursday night. We were about to send it out when all the power went off in the city – a total blackout. I rang Jeff Bender on my mobile phone and he said that if we could get it to him in the morning, he'd read it. I sent him a hard copy on Friday morning by courier along with – rather cheekily – an engagement letter to sign. Which he did, on Monday. And we started on Tuesday. It really helped us that Nigel Roth went to Houston to visit Apache's top management the following Friday to outline many of the benefits, issues and challenges already identified and to present effective solutions.

Wallum did not doubt that his team were exactly right for Apache's needs, a conviction which drove his actions. But this style of thinking also matched Apache's own approach to business remarkably well. Both organizations could be said in this case to be operating out of opportunism. 'Opportunism' is commonly used in a pejorative sense, but it is a term that is due for rehabilitation in business. Apache's success lies in seeing opportunities where others see problems, and acting upon those insights. Similarly, Mercer's success in helping mergers and acquisitions lies in their ability to recognize situations in which they can make a crucial difference for their clients, and communicating their value directly with the prospective client. Summing up his team's activities in winning the engagement and delivering its goals, Wallum says simply, 'We really wanted to do it.'

This project also demonstrates that the 'soft' values of employee rights can receive the same attention as the harder issues of commercial takeovers without being lost in a flurry of technical tasks – providing the right kind of specialist attention is committed to the transition. The North Sea is a dangerous environment, and the personal risks taken by those who work there are to some extent balanced by the long-term security represented by their benefits packages. Protecting employee rights in this industry therefore has a moral weight that is hard to ignore, but which should not go unaddressed in other business sectors. A sense of urgency is demonstrably not incompatible with attention to employee needs, aspirations and sensitivities.

CASE STUDY 4.2

DIAGNOSING AND TREATING WORKFORCE AILMENTS

How the commitment of a group of highly valuable knowledge workers was revitalized through a simple process of exploration and change.

Evotec OAI is a drug discovery company, performing technical research and development services for pharmaceutical and biotechnology companies. The business is knowledge-intensive: the company's highly qualified scientists create novel compounds and design new drugs in the very earliest stages of the pharmaceutical development process.

Evotec OAI was formed in December 2000 by the merger of Germany's Evotec and the UK's Oxford Asymmetry International. The merged company's ability to offer integrated services across the entire drug discovery process makes it a partner of choice for many of the world's major pharmaceutical and biotechnology companies. Evotec OAI's applied expertise in chemistry, biology and compound screening enable it to accelerate its clients' product development processes. Using Evotec OAI also allows client companies to manage risk by outsourcing this complex and knowledge-intensive process. The result is a reduction in both the time and cost of bringing new drugs to market.

Throughout the industry, relevant scientific knowledge and skills are at a premium. As previous generations of 'blockbuster' drugs lose their patent protection, pharmaceuticals companies must replace them with new products. At the same time disease profiles continue to evolve, leading to searches for new treatments and new markets. Competition and consolidation within the pharmaceuticals industry is intense, and companies such as Evotec OAI who are at the leading edge of the innovation process must work hard to keep their people. The greatest problem with businesses based on human capital is that human capital's habit of leaving the building every evening – and sometimes not returning. But the same competitive pressures mean that few companies can solve their retention problems simply by throwing money at the problem.

Staff turnover among Evotec OAI's knowledge workers had reached 25 per cent, an expensive and potentially business-threatening level. The high level of churn was not only draining the company of valuable expertise, but challenging the continuity of its projects. Replacing staff is a costly and time-consuming process, and even the best-qualified and motivated new staff cannot reach their full productivity potential on day one. Evotec OAI urgently needed to know why staff were leaving, and what the company could do to turn the tide. Evotec OAI asked Penna to help management understand the company's staff retention issues, reduce recruitment costs and build a more engaged organization: one whose people are committed to the company for the long term, and who feel that their needs are well met by the company.

People as vectors of knowledge

As an organization that depends on intellectual capital and research for its competitive advantage, Evotec OAI is wholly reliant on the knowledge of its people and their ability to apply that knowledge. The competition for scientists who have the mix of talents needed to succeed in this field is intense. The best people combine high intellectual abilities with deep knowledge, attention to detail, and the ability to work with others. While the mainstream media often depicts this area of activity as a somewhat mechanical business of manipulating data on screens, taking its keynote from advances in imaging and the development of the human genome project, the reality of drug discovery work combines data processing, individual insight and collaborative teamwork. Knowledge cannot exist in a vacuum, and only has value when people can use it to solve real problems. The delivery channel for knowledge, in other words, will always be people: human beings with all their quirks, passions and needs.

In the years immediately following the merger of the two predecessor companies, the business grew strongly. The company was growing by 30 per cent every year. However, the staff turnover rate of 25 per cent meant that the company was continually short of people. With a workforce of specialized scientists, 40 per cent of whom have PhDs, finding people of the right calibre is a challenge. Such people are not easy to attract and are expensive to replace.

HR Director Martyn Melvin had tried a number of traditional methods of finding out why staff turnover had increased and remained stubbornly high. For example, he improved the exit interview process in order to learn more about the motivations of those leaving the company and to retrieve as many leavers as possible. Melvin felt that these kinds of actions addressed symptoms rather than underlying problems. His work with Penna was aimed at moving away from firefighting towards an employment environment better designed to satisfy and motivate the company's people.

The Evotec OAI/Penna team's first task was to design and deliver a set of employee diagnostics that would reveal the reasons why staff were not completely engaged with the company. The research would also help the team understand the factors that had most impact on engagement levels, so that the company could begin to influence how strongly staff identified with the company. The team would then develop a strategy to increase employee engagement and thereby strengthen retention. Finally the team would implement its strategy and measure the results.

Asking the right questions

The team worked with a tight budget and decided on a simple and collaborative approach to the project. Focused, light-touch and personalized projects work well in human resources situations, where any suggestion of unnecessary spending – especially on external consultants – can be read as compounding whatever criticisms staff may already have of management's priorities.

The team first ran a series of focus groups to identify the organization's key issues. The first focus group involved members of the senior team, so that they could understand and commit to the process, and further sessions were run throughout the business. Themes that emerged from the focus groups included the lack of clear career paths, inconsistent management style, the pressured work environment and the high local cost of living.

The themes from these focus groups then helped shape the design of a questionnaire for all employees. The questionnaire was implemented as a form on a Web page, so that it could be efficiently delivered to and completed by every member of staff. The process was confidential as well as easy to use, with completion of the questionnaire taking no more than 15 minutes. The online questionnaire was hosted externally by Penna's partner PeopleMetrics, so no systems had to be installed at Evotec OAI.

Penna's Alasdair McKenzie says: 'We used the focus groups to understand the working experience at Evotec OAI, and then used that understanding to design the questionnaire. It's better than using an off-the-shelf questionnaire because it's unique to the organization while drawing on best practice from elsewhere.'

The response rate for the questionnaire was 88 per cent, which compares extremely well to the average 40 per cent response rate expected for surveys of this kind. The team tested the validity of the questionnaire results using statistical analysis methods. McKenzie stresses the importance of validating the questions before developing a strategy based on the answers: 'Knowing that we'd asked the right questions gave us confidence in the actions we were going to take based on the results.'

Some of the questions required a specific answer and a value judgement. These questions asked respondents to agree or disagree with a statement using scores ranging from 5 ('strongly agree') to 1 ('strongly disagree'). But the questionnaire also included open questions. The team was particularly keen to identify and explore the factors that led to increased job satisfaction, people's desire to stay with the company, and the levels of employee advocacy. Would they, for example, recommend Evotec OAI as a place to work to friends? As well as being a good indicator of employee engagement, such attitudes can actively help with recruitment. Therefore qualitative data on questions such as 'What do you like about working here?' were captured and provided helpful and constructive feedback. The questionnaire also included a blank space for staff to add their own observations about life at Evotec OAI.

Analysis of the questionnaire returns revealed the real issues within the organization, and indicated which factors were affecting individuals' engagement. With this knowledge gained, the team could now identify the 'levers' the company could use to improve employee attitudes in general and staff loyalty in particular.

The research took less than two months to complete, including data capture and analysis. The results showed that a small number of key areas held a disproportionate sway over employees' sense of engagement. This discovery allowed the company to direct its attention and resources to those areas, rather than constructing an unfocused programme of change.

There were three key areas of concern affecting Evotec OAI's fragile retention situation. The team called the first issue 'role fulfilment'. This meant the extent to which employees could stretch within their defined roles and thereby feel the achievement of working to their full potential. Melvin and McKenzie make the point that knowledge workers enter their professions largely for the rewards of intellectual achievement, and that when opportunities to fulfil themselves professionally go stale, they can rapidly lose their attachment to the company. McKenzie believes this is a two-way street: 'Knowledge workers have high expectations, but when you engage them correctly their productivity is enormous.'

The second area of concern that emerged from the research was the somewhat directionless nature of the company's career development processes. The existing appraisal process focused on assessing

Overall Model

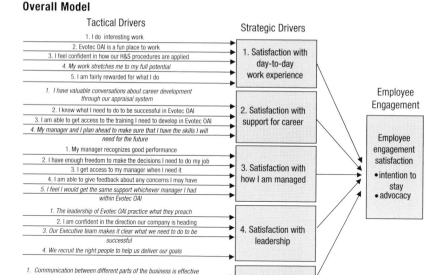

Figure 4.1 *Summary of the team's findings*

past performance, and setting appropriate rewards. This regular opportunity to review the individual's progress and aspirations needed to become more forward-looking, and focus on where the employee wanted to go rather than where he or she had been. Melvin says: 'We weren't asking those questions, we were just making appraisal judgements. Now we also ask about career aspirations, and what [people] are doing to develop their own career.'

The final area affecting employee engagement was the visibility, or perceived lack of it, among the company's leadership. Employees felt that they did not have enough contact with senior management and were not confident that direction was being set for the company as a whole. Any perception that an organization lacks attention to the rudder quickly combines with other frustrations to fuel a sense of detachment in employees. This is one area where no news is definitely not good news.

Presenting the evidence the team had collected to the company's leadership was a challenge in itself. 'A certain amount of heart-searching and budgeting went on,' says Melvin. 'But you can't ignore data like this. You may think you know what your people are thinking but these figures make it real. You can track the responses on a graph: this is what they are telling you. It's not simply about making people happy. It's about making the business perform better.'

Small changes for large effects

The data gleaned from the research pointed to a number of areas where Evotec OAI's management could make beneficial changes. According to Martyn Melvin, the business needed to effect a number of small changes that would target key concerns: 'It hasn't been one big change, but a lot of small changes. We've taken action on a broad range of issues, all of which were brought to us by the employees.'

The company wanted to demonstrate clearly that it had listened to its people's opinions and taken appropriate actions, even where there was no complete solution within the company's control. This was particularly true in the case of the cost of living in the local area. Melvin says: 'We couldn't do anything about the local cost of living, though we recognized it as an issue. But what we could do was help with the make-up of the benefits package. We can make employees feel more valued, and treat them as adults with choices.'

Benefits packages were redesigned to provide a choice from the benefits that employees said they valued most. So, for example, employees can now choose to swap earned extra holiday entitlement for pay if they wish. The ability to craft their own compensation packages gives people a degree of control over their lifestyle choices which they can otherwise feel are frustrated by general economic conditions. 'More money' is rarely the answer to any problem, though it is unsurprisingly the first answer most of us produce to most challenges that we face in business and in private life. By tackling this expectation with employees, and finding a workable solution, Evotec OAI's management could show the link between the business's commercial parameters and the compensation of its people. The company does not have the option of raising its prices to customers in order to increase wages; nor can it easily relocate to a cheaper location (and expect its employees to follow). Management and employees need to appreciate each other's perspectives, and design reward systems that address both commercial realities and individual aspirations. Often, as at Evotec OAI, the key to satisfying both parties lies not in raised costs but additional flexibility and personal choice.

The company also set about revitalizing its training, development and career support activities. The intellectual and professional development of staff is close to the hearts of Evotec OAI's scientists. For many professional staff, the opportunity to explore new areas of research or go deeper into their existing specialisms has no price. For such people, their own development cannot be replaced by other incentives such as money or improved working conditions. Without a sense of forward intellectual development, many such professionals feel that they are going backwards. The urge to stay at the leading edge of developments in the sciences sustains researchers throughout their careers, and Evotec OAI realized it needed to support that motivation much more explicitly. The company now also looks for opportunities to broaden the experience of its people as well as advance them in their existing specialisms.

The company also decided to strengthen the bonds among its people, so that they would identify more strongly with each other and forge a greater sense of common purpose. Supporting relationships among staff is also a means of extending the company's training effort and spreading knowledge throughout the organization. Actions taken included the extension of the induction period to a whole year. Weaker departments were partnered with better performing ones for guidance and benchmarking. The company did not neglect the informal networks that do so much to power the creativity and motivation of companies, especially companies dedicated to innovation. A new restaurant was built so that staff could enjoy meals with each other on site, and strengthen their personal networks in a relaxed setting.

In order to improve the visibility of management, the existing quarterly directors' communication exercise was redesigned to include more 'face time'. The changes resulting from the project were in fact communicated at a quarterly meeting, so that staff could see that the senior leadership were completely supportive of the project's recommendations. On the broader issue of management visibility as the business develops, Melvin and McKenzie acknowledge that management skills do not always arise naturally or predictably in scientific research environments. According to Melvin: 'Exposure to responsibility for anything other than their own work doesn't tend to happen until their mid to late 20s'. The company now actively looks to source managers from among those staff who show an aptitude for juggling several activities at once. They may not be the best scientists in their groups, but they have the ability to take an overview and pursue several strands of activity at once. There is an explicit recognition within the company that it needs a mix of skills to succeed, and a renewed commitment to supporting excellence across all the disciplines required for commercial performance. Those whose fulfilment derives from technical development are encouraged to pursue their goals, while those whose finest talents lie in other directions are supported. By selecting and developing managers from within its own ranks, Evotec OAI will help to ensure the credibility and accountability of its leadership as the company goes forward.

Other 'small changes' were introduced to support the company's internal communications and bolster a sense of belonging to a unified and directed organization. A company magazine was started, and the intranet began to be used for more cross-site activities between the UK and German offices, particularly for arranging job swaps.

From project to toolset

This project began as a means of discovering why Evotec OAI's retention rate was poor and creating a set of actions to correct the situation. The result, however, has been a much deeper impact on the business. The project has given the company a means of exploring issues as they arise in the future, and intervening in order to change course. Melvin gives the sense of an organization newly empowered with additional skills to drive the business forward: 'It's never finished! We're currently looking at doing another phase of research. We're always trying to move in the right direction, and always looking for the next set of coordinates. Now that we know the levers we need to pay attention to them, so that we have a satisfied and productive workforce.'

Evotec OAI also now has a hard measure of its current level of employee engagement and can track this measure regularly as the firm progresses. The organization now regards this kind of self-examination as a regular attribute of its business methods, and a behaviour that feeds directly into the improvement of the working environment, career prospects and company harmony.

The staff turnover rate halved following the implementation of the project's recommended actions. The company now does far less recruiting, leading to a significant reduction in HR costs. The reduction in churn also means that the company retains more knowledge for a longer time, giving it a competitive advantage over firms with higher staff turnover rates. Productivity and morale have also increased. Martyn Melvin estimates that the company saved several hundreds of thousands of pounds in the period following the changes. The UK project was subsequently repeated at the German office with similar results.

Professional environments are notoriously difficult to staff and motivate. Monetary incentives often have little real priority among knowledge workers, though they may focus on money issues as an acceptable proxy for other concerns. The relationship between the work they do and its external commercial value is not always clear to researchers, and arguably their freedom from immediate commercial pressures is a factor in their ability to experiment and explore. But the absence of this lever, which tends to apply by default in most businesses, creates unique problems. A knowledge-intensive company such as Evotec OAI cannot assume that its people share a set of obvious drivers that can be appealed to or manipulated. As has been said of many professional environments, managing scientific researchers is 'like herding cats'.

This project demonstrates that returning to first principles by asking people what they feel is wrong with their environment can reveal the actual drivers that pertain within a particular company. Discussing the results frankly and relating them to commercial realities can then allow creative solutions to come forward. It is striking that all the 'little changes' actioned by Evotec OAI share the trait of addressing the employees as 'big people'. Flexible benefits packages give the message that individuals are recognized as adults with choices, but so does flexibility over the professional development paths they take. Scientists are used to structure in their work: structure is at the heart of the scientific method. The commercial world delivers little in the way of reliable, persistent structure and companies cannot pretend that this is not so. By supporting their people's own sense of personal responsibility, direction and development, companies like Evotec OAI show that this apparent conundrum can be, if not solved, managed with excellence.

Penna has shown with this project how a low-budget consulting exercise can produce deep and lasting benefits for an organization. Many employees are cynical about HR projects, expecting them either to be sinister exercises in covert criticism or blatant propaganda campaigns. The human scale of Penna's work at Evotec OAI and the team's faithful concentration on the opinions and aspirations of the employees created workable solutions that benefited everyone in the company.

It is doubtful whether the kind of information gathering and analysis performed at Evotec OAI would have been successful if it had been conceived and undertaken solely by the management team. There is often a sense, especially within organizations that have recently undergone major changes, that management ought to understand how everyone is feeling without having to ask. The direction and endorsement of an external partner can help management break the ice that quickly forms around employee dissatisfaction, and give everyone involved the necessary permission to share his or her views.

CASE STUDY 4.3

STANDING DOWN, MOVING FORWARD

Helping members of the armed services make the transition to the wider world of work required a sensitively tailored package of information and counselling services.

The issue of what to do with those who are no longer needed to fight for their country has been around as long as warfare itself. The treatment of those laying down their weapons and returning to more peaceful activities has varied over the centuries from total indifference to support from the very top. An early initiative that combines a certain randomness with high-level support is commemorated in a common pub name throughout England. After the Battle of Warburg in 1760, John Manners, the Commander-in-Chief of the British Army, generously set up each of his disabled non-commissioned officers with a public house. The new landlords called their establishments The Marquis of Granby in honour of their patron, who died in 1770 leaving massive debts. For many years, Manners's gesture remained the highpoint of military resettlement services.

Resettling military people in 'civvy street' took on a more official aspect during World War I. The scale of the national call-up meant that the many hundreds of thousands of men returning from the hostilities could not be naturally absorbed into the civilian community. As the number of people in uniform changed during the 20th century and the range of service roles multiplied, resettlement became an ever more complex issue. At the same time public perceptions of the community's duties to its service people changed. The development of the modern welfare state after World War II and the convergence of education and employment policy-making towards the end of the century both helped to create a climate in which the transition from service to civilian life became an opportunity for support.

Today, more than 24,000 personnel leave the UK Armed Forces annually and make the transition to civilian life, of whom around 17,000 are eligible for some form of resettlement assistance. These leavers are of widely different ages and have a diverse range of qualifications and aspirations. They are also dispersed throughout Britain and overseas. Each person approaching his or her date of leaving has different personal circumstances and ambitions, but adjusting from the military environment to the civilian world is an issue common to all. This change in life stage is certainly a challenge, but also a chance to take stock and focus on the opportunities and possibilities that lie ahead. Leaving the services need not be seen as the end of the line, but as a point of change within a larger career.

In October 1998 resettlement services for the UK Armed Forces were taken over by the Career Transition Partnership (CTP), a partnering arrangement between the MoD's Directorate of Resettlement and Right Management Consultants. The initial five-year contract was subsequently renewed for an additional two years to September 2005. CTP has merged the best of commercial HR consulting with a military context, creating a unique bridge between two very different worlds. The new organization is clearly working to set leavers on the right path. A leading air engineering mechanic from the Royal Navy says: 'All the people were extremely helpful. They pointed me in the right direction and supported me every step of the way.'

Creating the partnership

Three objectives were defined in the initial contract for CTP. The first objective of the new organization was to set up a resettlement service for all ranks and all services, with the capacity to handle an estimated 17,000 eligible service leavers every year. The service would have to be in place by October 1998; the contract was agreed in July, giving the team a very short time in which to design and staff the organization.

The second objective targeted CTP's impact on the population of service leavers. The aim was to increase the take-up of resettlement services from the existing 40 per cent of service leavers to 50 per cent, or up to 8,500 individuals per year. The third objective was to place 75 per cent of service leavers within jobs within six months of their leaving date.

The team proposed delivering flexible, personalized career change and job-finding support through 120 civilian staff based at nine specialized centres. These Regional Resettlement Centres (RRCs) were already in place at military bases across the UK. The Directorate of Resettlement, representing the MoD half of the partnership, was to form resettlement policy for all three services.

Initial access to resettlement was also to be managed separately by each service through their respective education departments. Unit resettlement staff would provide information and administrative services to leavers, while Service Resettlement Advisors provided more comprehensive briefing and advice. Those eligible for resettlement help would then be directed to the nearest CTP Resettlement Centre to start their programme.

The package available to eligible service leavers through the RRCs begins with individual career counselling. Each person is assigned a career consultant as his or her key point of contact for advice, guidance and support throughout resettlement and for up to two years after discharge from the services. Leavers can then attend a Career Transition Workshop (CTW). This is an interactive three-day workshop, during which service leavers are helped by a training consultant to identify, evaluate and market the skills, attributes and experience they have gained in the services. Leavers explore how they can break their experience and expertise down into meaningful elements that may be repackaged into compelling offers for employers. One RAF Junior Technician advises other leavers: 'Whatever else you intend doing for your resettlement make sure you do a Career Transition Workshop.'

The RRCs offer other workshops and seminars on topics such as self-employment, CV writing, interview techniques and personal networking. There are also financial advice briefings given by reputable financial organizations and housing briefings delivered by the Joint Service Housing Advice Organization.

Further practical assistance includes trial attachments with civilian employers that enable service leavers to spend time with a potential employer while being paid by the MoD. These attachments give service leavers work experience while enabling employers to assess their ability and fit without obligation or cost. Leavers also enjoy administrative support and research facilities including careers libraries, PCs with Internet access, telephones and career guidance software packages.

The RCCs share access to a Resettlement Training Centre based at Aldershot where leavers can join a broad range of training courses. Current courses include computer maintenance, roadside vehicle repairs, security systems and aerial installation, facilities management, project management and IT skills. There is even a workshop on becoming a management consultant. Courses are regularly adjusted to meet the needs of employers and many lead to the award of civilian qualifications.

Finally, the CTP works with a sub-contractor called the Regular Forces Employment Association (RFEA) to place leavers in jobs. More than 25,000 vacancies are generated annually by the RFEA through 29 branches across the UK. Candidates are matched with vacancies using a central database networked to the RCCs.

This story, from an air engineering officer in the Royal Navy is typical of many:

I was very quickly introduced to the CTP by the Royal Navy resettlement office in Portsmouth. This proved to be the turning point in making my departure from the Royal Navy a successful one. Eight months since leaving the Royal Navy my business partner and I have established an organizational development and management training company, with a growing list of clients from small- to medium- sized enterprises to large blue chip organizations. I am convinced that many of the mistakes that I could have made I did not, due to the advice and guidance of the CTP.

Changing emphasis

The CTP service was the first example of a military resettlement service being provided by a partnership of private and public organizations anywhere in the world. The biggest challenge facing CTP at the outset was the need quickly to integrate a civilian organization into a military environment. The key issues were communications, confidentiality and culture.

For example, since the RRCs are based within MoD facilities they initially lacked the communications technology that is standard in the private sector. CTP quickly installed a wide area network (WAN) and enhanced telephone systems to enable better communication. In addition, specific steps were taken to understand the culture and traditions of the services. The delivery teams designed for CTP integrated individuals from both civilian and military backgrounds. Right's Tim Cairns had himself served in the armed forces, so was well placed to appreciate the differences between team members:

> There was a natural caution borne of not quite knowing how other people work. It's a fear of the unknown. People have perceptions that quite often are wrong. They get their perceptions from the media, which is not quite the truth, because they are selective or exaggerated. In my experience, what helped was that the civilian side tried very hard to understand how the military operates. Many of our staff are ex-military and over time civilians with no military background have learned a lot about the military ethos – the impressive aspects as well as the frustrating ones.

In order to meet the key objective of increasing the number of individuals taking up resettlement services, the CTP team decided to track and keep in touch with individuals as they were assigned to different areas within their service. This is a significant departure from previous practice, which ensures continuity of planning in the run-up to leaving.

To provide international support an RRC was opened in Germany and local support provided to ex-Ghurkhas in Nepal. Additionally, workshops and career consultancy have been delivered at military establishments (such as RAF Lossiemouth in Scotland and RNAS Culdrose in Cornwall) where service leavers find it difficult to travel to other venues. Online support has also been continually improved and updated.

The issue of confidentiality arises from the high proportion of personal information divulged in the CTP process. For example, some leavers have medical histories that should not be divulged to potential employers, though employers may need to know about any implications for the individual's ability to perform or keep a particular job. Since leavers' files contain a mixture of private and public information, access to records has to be through an authorized individual.

From the cultural point of view, life in the armed services is highly structured. While collaborative and creative techniques have begun to cross over into the armed forces from general management practice, it is fair to say that the trade in approaches has historically been in the other direction. The 20th century's big corporations were initially modelled after military organizations, with specialization, hierarchical structures and a reliance on orders. Today's business organizations target innovation, quality and flexibility as well as efficiency, creating a need for more motivational management, empowerment and openness. These approaches are irrelevant and indeed dangerous in the battlefield, so service personnel are valued for their ability to perform as ordered, use their initiative when appropriate, and persevere in the face of adversity. The ethic of loyalty to the team is also highly prized in the military environment. These qualities have a high value in the civilian world, but must be exercised in a less structured environment.

Workers in the business world need to accept rapid and radical changes to their goals, and must be able to tolerate high levels of ambiguity. CTP is often the first place in which service people experience these aspects of the outside world. According to one army leaver: '[CTP] made me realize I've got to start thinking for myself'. Meanwhile a flavour of the traditional military attitude comes over in this excerpt from the Royal Marines' robust advice on how to work with a CTP consultant: 'His experience is in commerce and industry and therein lies his strength – use it. He is well paid for his services so make sure he is working for you. Know his name, telephone and fax number and his e-mail address.'

Right's Cairns says: '[Attendees] don't know what to expect from the workshops but they come out positive about it. It's facilitative rather than chalk and talk, which is different to what they're used to. They are very adaptable people, though sometimes institutionalized – but they're aware of that.'

Performance of the new unit

Nine RRCs were opened within the target time of three months. The centres were able to help current leavers, plus a backlog of leavers who had postponed registering with the existing resettlement services in anticipation of the launch of CTP. A tenth centre was subsequently opened in Germany to support service leavers based there. CTP consultants also delivered face-to-face advice to people on active duty in Gibraltar, Cyprus, Brunei, Nepal, Kosovo and many other overseas locations.

Over the initial five-year contract period, CTP provided personal career transition services to over 50,000 people of all ranks leaving the UK armed forces. This throughput equates to more than 70 per cent of those leaving, and 15,000 more people than set out in the project's initial objectives. More than 3,000 Career Transition Workshops were delivered in the UK and Germany, and more than 30,000 job vacancies were generated every year by the RFEA.

As a result of the advice they received from CTP, service leavers are now better prepared than ever to face the civilian world. Recent surveys of leavers assessed by the MoD indicate that between 93 per cent and 96 per cent of service leavers gained employment within six months of leaving the military, over 20 per cent more than targeted in the initial objectives.

CTP staff act impartially, aiming to give the right guidance to each individual. Sometimes the result is a recommendation that an individual remain in the services. Leavers can be advised that they will ultimately be better placed for a civilian career by staying in the armed forces and gaining more experience and qualifications. For example, during 2002–03, 30 per cent of the 900 people who re-engaged with the services during the resettlement process did so directly as a result of CTP advice and information. Retaining these people represents a win-win situation: the individuals have their career prospects enhanced, while the MoD saves hundreds of thousands of pounds in recruitment and training costs.

The CTP philosophy is empowerment, so that individuals treat the resettlement process as a preparation for life, not just a means of getting a first job. CTP enables service leavers to invest in their future through a proactive approach to their own career development, to make their own decisions and to act on them. For many leavers, personal ownership of this kind is a new experience and one that provides a steady foundation for their onward progress. The advice leavers receive is impartial and the interest of the individual is paramount at all times. This attitude has helped individuals to find the most suitable long-term career, rather than just a short-term job that may not last and lead to later unemployment and lack of direction.

Tim Cairns himself went through the transition process before CTP existed. Of his own experience, he says:

> There was a lot of help available, but you had to seek it out for yourself. And there was a lack of ongoing support – no centre and no assigned career consultant. CTP gives leavers a named person, assigned to them in a one-to-one meeting at the end of their Career Transition Workshop, and that relationship persists for up to two years after they have left.

The work of the CTP has also improved the reputation of the armed forces as an employer, both to future recruits and to civilian employers. Those who have been well supported during their transition to civilian life are more likely to recommend the services to friends and relatives. Employers are also more likely to gain benefits faster from employing service leavers who have had the benefit of CTP. For example, Ray McMahon, Service Support Manager for railway company GNER Scotland says:

> We have been delighted with the calibre of staff that have joined GNER from the armed forces. The transition of staff joining GNER has been remarkably smooth. We are a customer service industry led business and the staff we have recruited have all shown that their training in the forces has been invaluable when dealing with people and providing customer service. Our relationship with the CTP is going from strength to strength and we are pleased to provide employment opportunities for those leaving the forces and entering back into the civilian world.

Right's contribution to the resettlement service centres around its ability to tailor HR consulting for the military environment. The company took best practice from commercial outplacement and career guidance services and adapted it to the special circumstances of those leaving the armed forces. It was able to respect and preserve the best qualities of the CTP's clients while introducing them to the realities of the wider world of work.

5

Operational performance

At any point in the economic cycle – bull years and bear years – the vast majority of businesses are performing neither very well nor very badly. Their markets are not growing; their cost bases are relatively stable; there are no major threats or opportunities on the horizon. The reasons for stalling may be many and varied; some may be familiar, others less obvious. They are united only by the fact that they are hard to solve.

Improving business performance is the traditional backbone of consulting, stretching back before World War II. Today, when people calling themselves 'consultants' abound in almost every walk of life, it remains the standard by which the consulting industry differentiates itself from other forms of temporary labour – body-shopping, contracting, even interim management. When the MCA revisited its definition of 'management consulting' in 2002, it concluded that it is: 'The creation of value for organizations, through the application of knowledge, techniques, and assets to improve performance. This is achieved through the rendering of objective advice and/or the implementation of business solutions.'

This differed from the MCA's previous definition in two important respects. First, it allowed for the fact that much consulting today takes the form of implementing business solutions and is not confined to providing objective advice. Second, it stressed that the work of genuine consultants is directed at improving performance, not simply maintaining the status quo.

This emphasis has been particularly relevant since the millennium, as the consulting industry has faced a client base that is simultaneously desperate to make improvements during a period of economic stagnation and cynical about consultants' ability to make a genuine difference. Mike Bird, a partner at Kepner-Tregoe (one of the consulting firms featured in this chapter) says:

Many consultants have been selling quasi-academic solutions, but clients are turning round and saying 'What does all this add up to?' The real game is the how: how to equip clients to run their businesses better; how to configure those businesses more effectively. The consultants who'll make money will be those doing this hard-nosed work. For all the talk of recession, this is a good market for consulting firms that can demonstrate tangible, practical, non-IT business solutions which clients can see and use to get results.

THE FIVE PILLARS OF OPERATIONAL CONSULTING

The case studies in this chapter highlight five fundamental ways in which consulting firms help organizations to improve their performance.

Seeing the wood for the trees

One of the key ways in which consultants can help improve performance is by pinpointing the underlying cause of a problem. Every one of us finds it hard to step back from our daily lives: even the smallest organization can become bogged down dealing with the here-and-now. We apply the same thinking to the same problems, but expect different results. For someone to come from the outside, as a consultant does, and see a situation clearly and disinterestedly can be enormously helpful. This is just what Kepner-Tregoe was able to do at Sun Microsystems when they realized the key to improving complex customer problems was the quality of information transferred from one shift of support engineers to another as they worked around the clock – and around the world. Ashridge Consulting challenged long-standing assumptions at the Norwich Community Hospital by suggesting that improving patient throughput was more than just a matter of more money, but depended on improving the efficiency with which patients were discharged. BT Retail was not short of information about consumer behaviour and market trends, but that did not mean it could see how to buck a stagnating fixed line telephone market. It needed to stand back and, with the help of Edengene, brainstorm a welter of possible options for generating new business before it appreciated that solving the micropayment issue was critical.

Still seeing the trees

Of course, problems viewed in isolation can be highly misleading. Cut out as much of the white noise as possible that typically surrounds a business problem, and you can be left with something that can look deceptively black and white. Good consultants therefore marry their identification of a problem with an understanding of all the constraints that make the problem difficult for that client to resolve independently. For the UK Government Communications Headquarters (GCHQ), the challenge was not so much reconfiguring existing systems and processes, but doing this without interrupting the highly sensitive work involved. At Sun Microsystems, Kepner-Tregoe realized that training would not be enough to change the behaviour of Sun Microsystems' engineers; the consultants had to insert clear points in the problem-handling process which would trigger additional tasks.

Know-how – and knowing how to implement it

Although apocryphal, it is still a pertinent story. A critical machine in a large factory breaks down, holding up production worth tens of thousands of dollars a day. When the in-house experts cannot fix the problem, the factory manager calls in an external mechanic. For a few minutes, this outside mechanic walks up and down the machine, occasionally poking things with his screwdriver. Then, in a flash, he leans in to tighten a screw and the machine starts up. But the factory manager is less delighted a week later, when an invoice for US $10,000 hits his desk. He rings up to query the amount. 'That's right,' says the mechanic. 'It's a dollar for tightening the screw – and 9,999 dollars for knowing which screw to fix.'

The value that a consultant brings is not determined by the amount of time he or she spends working on a problem, but by the experience and techniques he or she can bring to bear on what appears to be an intractable problem. Perhaps more than any other area of consulting, 'operational' consulting benefits from a wealth of management tools and techniques. However, the skill of the consultant does not just lie in bringing a briefcase full of techniques to a given problem, but in knowing which are appropriate and how to apply them. Consultants are often criticized for coming up with ideas that prove impossible to implement in practice, but that is far from the case with the projects represented here. Ashridge Consulting used Eli Goldratt's Theory of Constraints to demonstrate that a system – in this case a community hospital – could only run as fast as the speed of its weakest link. Kepner-Tregoe brought clearly defined intellectual capital to its work at Sun Microsystems – a problem-solving methodology. But the firm's contribution was not confined to telling Sun Microsystems' engineers something new, but in ensuring that it was used on a consistent basis. PA Consulting Group's Systems Engineering methodology was one of the main reasons why GCHQ wanted to work with the firm, providing

it with a means of analysing the interactions between its complex processes, 5,000 staff and more than 60 independent IT systems. The Chief
Executive of BT click&buy described the consulting team from
Edengene as pragmatic as well as smart: 'Edengene's delivery was
really excellent, from the more academic analysis at the start of the
project, right through to implementation.'

Passing the baton from consultant to client

Skills transfer is something that clients consistently put high on their
agenda when it comes to hiring consultants – it is not enough to use
consultants to solve a problem, they have to show the client's people
how to solve it for themselves in the future. To quote Bird at Kepner-
Tregoe again:

> The best clients say 'show me how, and I will execute'. Consultants have
> to leverage a client's internal resources rather than their colleagues; they
> need to have people who are credible, and consulting teams that are small
> enough to be flexible. They have to multiply their impact, not by bringing
> in more consultants, but by transferring skills.

Skills transfer was one of the aims of Ashridge Consulting's work with
the Norwich Community Hospital. Here, the consultants helped the
hospital's employees to learn, based on a combination of practical
experience and analysis of how people learn in different ways. Kepner-
Tregoe focused on training Sun Microsystems' trainers in order to pass
on problem-solving techniques. At BT Retail, Edengene were involved
not just in generating and evaluating new business ideas, but in helping set up BT click&buy, working side by side with BT's staff to pass on
entrepreneurial know-how.

Providing incentives to change

Resolving operational problems often depends on getting diverse
groups of people to work together. The fifth and final facet of the best
operational consulting is to ensure, once a change has been made, that
it sticks. At the Norwich Community Hospital, anyone – from porter to
senior clinical staff – could have blocked the initiative. To get around
this potential obstacle, Ashridge involved as many people in the process as possible, giving them a stake in the solution. Kepner-Tregoe
realized that Sun Microsystems' engineers were unlikely to use its
process-solving on a consistent basis unless it gave them a positive
incentive to do so – as long as they collected the information required,
they could offload the problem on to the backline support team.

MIRACLES AND PARABLES

What's common across all five of these factors – as well as across all four of this chapter's case studies – is that clients and consultants have to work closely together. If the consultants are bringing a new approach to solving a problem, then the client brings intimate knowledge of the context for that problem, what kind of solution is being sought, whether any attempt to resolve it has already been made. Each side needs the other in what is the antithesis of the out-sourcing model – where suppliers (consulting firms, IT service providers and so on) solve problems on their clients' behalf rather than show-ing them how to solve them themselves. The organization that allows a supplier to take over the resolution of a problem learns how to manage suppliers, not how to resolve the problem. In some areas, this makes good economic sense: using a supplier's specialist knowl-edge to solve one-off problems is far more efficient than trying to build up in-house skills. However, where the problem affects an activity at the heart of your business (as dealing with complex and urgent customer issues was at Sun Microsystems) knowing how to solve the problem is vital.

Knowing how to solve critical problems is important for a more fundamental reason. One of the reasons why an organization's perfor-mance stalls is that the people within it find it hard to challenge the status quo. They do things the way they have always been done, and cease to believe that it is possible to change. Performance improvement is therefore just as much about altering this perception as it is about fix-ing a problem. By fixing a problem, people start to see that things can be different.

There is a famous story about Greg Brenneman, who joined the ailing Continental Airlines in 1986. Seeking to restore the company's image, Brenneman asked how long it would take to repaint all Continental's aircraft in the new corporate colours. Told that it would take three years, Brenneman said they would do it in six months – and they did. For the employees of Continental Airlines, it was a mir-acle – they had achieved something they did not think they could. Stories like this gain currency, illustrating important values intended as standards for the organization as a whole. They become, in effect, parables.

One sign of excellent consulting is that it knows when to stop. 'Miracles' can only be performed by employees of an organization because it is their perceptions about their own capabilities that need changing – and bringing in consultants from the outside does not do this. Consultants can help improve operational performance – they can pinpoint a problem and provide some of the know-how to fix it. But they cannot perform miracles.

SUMMARY – KEY LESSONS FOR MANAGERS AND CONSULTANTS

■ Improving operational business performance has long been, and still remains, the bedrock of consulting.
■ The best operational consulting has five characteristics:
  – being able to distinguish the precise cause of a problem from its symptoms;
  – appreciating the constraints the client is under;
  – bringing management tools and techniques that are new to the client and which help resolve the issue;
  – ensuring that the consultants' skills are passed on to clients;
  – ensuring that the changes made are sustainable.
■ However, the best operational consulting also recognizes that it requires the combined efforts of consultants and clients. This is not just because each party brings different, but equally important, skills and expertise. Clients have to learn how to solve operations problems themselves, if they are going to be able to raise their overall performance.

CASE STUDY 5.1

BLUE SKIES, BLUE BILLS AND ONLINE BREAKTHROUGHS

BT managed to build a successful new consumer business that exploits its core assets while simultaneously solving a problem previously relegated to the wildest frontiers of the Internet – online micropayments.

BT Retail provides fixed line telephone services to more than 18 million homes in the UK. Since deregulation BT has performed well, maintaining an impressive market share of 73 per cent. However, in the midst of a static or declining market, BT had to find new revenue opportunities and plug a projected revenue gap of £1.5 billion by April 2006. Through a process of creative, entrepreneurial business development, BT discovered a business opportunity that would yoke together two compelling forces, and attach them to one of BT's most powerful engines, its billing capabilities.

The first of these market forces was the growing significance of online spending in the UK. The progress of consumer e-commerce is no longer reported on front pages, perhaps because there are fewer high-profile failures to be covered. However, the figures speak for themselves. According to Interactive Media in Retail Group (IMRG), which monitors the development of the UK's online markets:

> The online shopping market was 72 per cent bigger in 2003 than in 2002 and has grown more than 16-fold during the 45 months in which the IMRG Index has collected market data. In the first month, April 2000, the e-retail market is estimated to have been worth just £80 million. Since then, an estimated £21.8 billion has been spent online by UK shoppers.

Focusing on the key Christmas shopping period, IMRG adds: 'Online sales for November and December 2003 combined were worth a cool £2.5 billion, representing some 7 per cent of all UK retail sales.' (Source: IMRG, *A cracking £2.5 billion e-Christmas*, 19 January 2004). These figures speak eloquently of the steady growth of online shopping, showing how e-commerce is becoming an established retail channel.

The second force that BT wanted to harness was the emerging market in the kind of premium online information that people would be prepared to pay for. Pundits have long predicted huge global consumer markets in pure information, whether it be written, pictorial, video or music. These markets have been slower to take off than mainstream e-commerce offers such as online grocery shopping. However, recent successes in paid-for content, especially Apple's iTunes music download service, suggest that the big time may be around the corner. BT's own market research showed that people wanted quality content on the Internet and that 46 per cent of UK Internet users were prepared to pay for it. These findings matched experiences in Germany and the United States where high demand for quality, paid-for online content was already established. BT wanted to position itself as a leading carrier of transactions for such digital goods.

Tapping these growing markets would require a new solution: micropayments. The ability to make relatively small payments via a simple electronic means had already been pursued by many Internet industry players, but with little success. For many analysts, micropayments fell into the frustrating business category doomed to be labelled as 'a good idea'.

BT has confounded the conventional wisdom with click&buy, the micropayments scheme it launched in September 2002. By February 2004, there were 110 content sites in the scheme including *Hello! Magazine*, The *Independent*, Multimap, Channel 4 and *Encyclopaedia Brittanica*.

The click&buy concept, and its transition from idea to operational business, was developed by BT with its consulting partner, Edengene, beginning in the autumn of 2001.

Producing ideas

The first phase was idea generation. A small team of six BT people and five Edengene people was formed. The BT contingent brought the essential understanding of BT's business and deep knowledge of current trends in the market. The Edengene side included entrepreneurial talent and consultancy experience plus technological and financial expertise.

The joint BT/Edengene team set to work looking for market opportunities in and around BT's core business, studying market trends to identify emerging opportunities. Long-cherished beliefs and assumptions were challenged in order to reveal areas for renewed analysis.

The team also assessed BT's key assets and how these might contribute to a new business stream. One of these assets was its trusted brand. Another was its efficient, itemized billing process, which produces regular detailed bills for more than 18 million customers.

In four weeks the team generated more than 200 ideas. Nine of the ideas went forward to be worked up into full business propositions, complete with work on sizing the respective markets and studying the competition. Of this collection of nine, four were selected for implementation, including the proposition for online micropayments. The remaining ideas were not wasted: in the intervening period, a total of 21 ideas from the original 200 have since been developed into business streams.

Edengene's Tim Thorne recalls that the idea that became click&buy emerged when two other ideas collapsed together: 'We had an idea for getting involved with micropayments along the lines of paying for vending machine items with your telephone number. The other idea was to set up a huge library of online content. Neither of these ideas made commercial sense.'

Paying for content

Following the deflation of the dotcom bubble and a widespread reduction in investment on online ventures by established businesses as well as start-ups, business developers have been struggling to find ways to make money from online services. The days when a snappily-titled Web site with a sketchy but compelling business plan could command attention and funding based on its potential future revenues have gone for good. With the hype largely removed from the sector, decision-makers focused on creating traditional business plans based on proven customer needs and revenue streams.

Until the decline in the dotcom market, online advertising had reigned as the supposed revenue engine of the Internet. However, the effectiveness and value of online advertising now attracted greater questioning. Advertisers withdrew their support for indiscriminate banner advertising. Those who remained in the online channel switched their spending to 'pay per click' advertising spots, where the advertiser paid only when users clicked through the banner to a linked page. Soon the number of companies willing to run pay-per-click campaigns also shrank as companies began to run simple commission schemes based on actual purchases. While advertising survives on the Web, particularly in the form of paid-for advertisements on the leading search engine Google, content providers have largely given up on this method of funding their activities.

With the online advertising model generally discredited, many content providers turned reluctantly to subscription strategies. Since most of the best-known content providers on the Web are associated with print titles, it was logical that the failure of advertising would send them to the other source of revenues traditional in the print world. Leading sites such as that of the *New York Times* shifted quickly to subscription services, using the strength of their brands in the print world to assert the intrinsic value of their online content. After all, if a customer would pay for the *New York Times* from a news vendor, why should they expect to get the same content free online? The costs of producing the product did not dwindle to nothing just because the paper stage had been removed.

However, consumers have the same kind of resistance to online subscriptions as they do to offline ones. Despite the overall savings usually offered by subscription packages, many consumers are put off by the high up-front costs of a subscription and the long-term relationship it implies. While businesses understandably pursue customer relationships and are investing increasingly in maintaining them, too many companies forget that many customers are not looking to make commitments. In the realm of digital content, impulse buying is a particularly strong factor. We have been trained to buy print media, music and films as impulse items, strongly influenced by word-of-mouth recommendation and point-of-sale display techniques. These behaviours translate poorly to the online subscription model. The record companies have been among the first to learn of customer resistance to relationships of this kind. Services set up to offer paid-for access to the music of one or other record label have foundered on the simple truth that music buyers do not buy record labels: they buy music. And as the consumer population continues to migrate online, users increasingly want to be able to transact in the way they do in the real world. They want the convenience of simple billing, the anonymity of cash, the spontaneity of shopping. BT's research showed that over 80 per cent of consumers preferred 'pay as you use' to annual subscriptions.

Subscriptions and pre-pay accounts, such as PayPal, work well for certain groups of customers but do not scale well to the mainstream. While regular *New York Times* readers may be happy to recognize themselves as such and enter into a subscription relationship, and loyal eBay traders are attached to PayPal as a way of transacting within the online auction community, less motivated consumers need a less committed channel to online payments. The simplest payment option for such users is the credit card, which is by far the preferred mechanism of Internet users. However, credit card transactions are not viable for small amounts. The handling fees charged by credit card companies make this mechanism unusable for amounts of under £5 or so. For the dollar-per-download model of most content providers, credit card is clearly an inoperable route. Even where the price of a piece of content makes the credit card mechanism a credible option, customers are reluctant to enter their credit card details repeatedly, and are especially suspicious of vendors they do not know well.

The concept of micropayments plays strongly to both consumer preferences for payment and the commercial realities of the credit card system. Micropayments offer a single, simple, secure system covering a range of approved content providers. Payment is made as simple as possible for the user, so that there is little practical or perceptual barrier to making the transaction. Micropayments add convenience and confidence to the e-commerce world, and grow that world to encompass a broader mass of consumers.

Hidden strengths

Various micropayment schemes had been launched for the Internet, often to loud flourishes that were not repeated at their eventual windings-up. The schemes ranged from quirky, entrepreneurial Web-based currencies like Beenz and Flooz to Compaq's heavyweight Millicent project, via bank-supported digital money schemes such as Mondex. These schemes failed for a number of reasons. In the first place, they suffered from inductive failure: a user would be asked for a special currency to pay for something, but only users who already had the special currency would be able to buy the item. Which would come first, the chicken or the egg? Few users were willing to transfer real-world money into invisible online money, especially if they could not see any vendors in their areas of interest who were prepared to take the novel currency. Where users confronted the digital money barrier from the merchant side, rather than interrupting the purchase process to sign up for the new payment mechanism, most preferred to find an alternative supplier.

The second reason that the majority of first-generation micropayment schemes failed is to be found in their supporting brands. Consumers simply do not look to technology companies like Compaq to act as a mint. Although Compaq's Millicent scheme involved the production of secure, digital tokens that could be used to store value, users were unwilling to make the mental leap between physical and logical currencies and to grant a technology company the right to create such tokens. Paper money had to be forced on to suspicious coin-users by law. It is unlikely that consumers will accept the further dematerialization of money just because its technical feasibility can be demonstrated.

Consumers have also proved to be less keen on the idea of traditional banks handling their online payments than we might have expected. Although retail banks have very detailed information on their customers and therefore try to develop business around customer relationships, customers stubbornly refuse to feel quite so warmly about their banks. Any bank's primary means of communication with a customer is the statement, which is (for most of us) a regular and depressing list of outflows and possibly debts and charges. The bank's utility to a consumer might be best represented in its ATM network, a facility consumers use largely on impulse. Thorne says: 'We asked the question: If someone launched a micropayments system, who should it be? And people said that their first choice would be a credit card company. But their second choice was their telephone bill.'

BT has two particular assets that make it a natural provider of micropayments. BT is regularly voted one of Britain's most trusted consumer brands. The BT endorsement would give content providers the ballast of security and trust they needed to attract online customers. BT's size, reach and longevity tells customers that the products and services it provides are reliable, scalable and good value.

The other key asset identified by the team was the telephone bill, known within BT as the 'blue bill'. BT is the UK's largest biller. Every quarter, millions of homes receive accurate, detailed, timely bills that show even the smallest transactions. Line by line, the blue bill itemizes every transaction on an account, right down to penny charges. Billing is the lifeblood of any telecoms company, and often an area of technical challenge: many telecoms companies run scores of separate billing platforms, with complex bridges between them. The idea that the blue bill could be a route to new revenue, especially revenue derived from online activity, was a revolutionary one. Edengene's Thorne says: 'The blue bill is a micropayments system. There are 2p and 3p transactions on there. And people believe what the bill says. They trust it.'

Creating the new business

BT gave the click&buy project the green light in January 2002. The team was asked to come up with a fully worked-out business plan. Within six weeks the team had built the business case, researching the market further, refining the proposition, developing an implementation plan and detailing a robust financial model.

The team also had to consider technology during this phase. The micropayments scheme would need a robust and secure system, otherwise it would fall prey to some of the failures that had destroyed previous micropayments initiatives and rebound adversely on the wider BT business. Building a system from scratch would have been possible, but BT wanted to launch the scheme as quickly as possible. The team did not want the project to disappear into a 'big systems' development programme – an especial danger given the scheme's relationship with the business's core billing systems. The team decided to look elsewhere for a solution, and particularly in the German market, where the micropayments concept had had most success to date.

The German consumer market differs from those of the UK and United States in having very low credit card ownership. Micropayments had flourished in this environment, capturing the majority of online transactions in Germany from the nearest rival solution: cash on delivery.

Edengene explored and rapidly rejected a technology known as 'drop dialling'. Thorne explains:

> Drop dialling is a technique that's been used in the porn industry. The user is flipped over on to a premium-rate line for a few seconds and that's how the content provider collects. We had two major factors in our minds: great convenience, and a good customer experience. We found drop dialling just wasn't reliable enough. We watched a demonstration from the leading German player – and it failed. In any case, BT wants to encourage broadband access, which is an always-on connection, so switching the line doesn't apply.

The convenience factor applied as much to potential suppliers as customers, according to Thorne: 'We needed to keep costs down for merchants to cooperate with our scheme. It's very expensive [for merchants] to implement e-wallets, for example. Their budgets for e-commerce have gone down in recent years.'

The team quickly found Germany's Firstgate Communications. The Firstgate micropayments solution had attracted some 400,000 customers in less than two years. Firstgate now has more than 1.4 million customers. The Firstgate system worked well, was scaling well, and was provably secure, standing up to a BT security audit.

Firstgate did not have the resources to bring their micropayments model to the UK but were happy to license the technology to BT in a deal brokered by Edengene.

The technology works by exploiting the simplest element of the Web: hyperlinks. A merchant can charge for any item simply by allowing users to click on a special link that takes them to a charging page. Merchants have a great deal of flexibility in how they use the system, and can amend prices whenever they want. For example, a content provider can specify that a story is available for £1 on its date of publication, but 50p thereafter. Users sign up for the click&buy service by getting a simple username and password combination the first time they use a merchant in the scheme. They can then choose their preferred method of regular settlement: direct debit, credit card, or telephone bill.

With the technology in place, the project began to accelerate towards launch. The management team was appointed, including an interim CTO, Strategy Director and Business Development Director from Edengene. Despite the organizational support of BT and its brand, the team was effectively setting up a small standalone start-up business. The team therefore designed the business as an entrepreneurial unit, and included an incentive scheme for staff.

The team also committed to making its first sales before the formal launch of the business. While the technological implementation went ahead, the team worked to find 40 initial content providers. The challenge here was to overcome scepticism in the vendor marketplace and demonstrate how micropayments could deliver more customers for online content. Case studies were built, demonstrating the potential and putting the case for moving quickly.

The trial of BT click&buy went live in July 2002 with 20 content providers, delivering its first revenues just 10 months after the initial brief to Edengene. The full public service with 40 content providers was launched in September 2002. Payment by credit card, debit card or direct debit were the initial options offered. The option to pay via the 'blue bill' – a core element of the proposition – was challenged by competitors but the industry regulator ruled in favour of BT. Click&buy became an option on BT telephone bills, first to selected customers in March 2003 and then, by the summer of 2003, to all 18 million BT domestic accounts. Currently around one third of click&buy users use the telephone bill option.

Today BT click&buy is the UK's leading micropayments service, allowing all BT home customers to pay for quality online content through the telephone bill. In July 2003, BT click&buy launched a new 'roaming' initiative, giving the online payment solution access to an additional 1.4 million click&buy account holders in Germany, Austria, Switzerland, France, Spain, Holland and the United States. Recent enhancements to the service include the launch of click&vote, which allows users to register TV poll votes online, and click&give, an easy way for users to make donations to charity. Mobile payments have been added to the scheme as well, enlarging the scope of the service still further.

Prior to the launch of click&buy, BT was not seen as a leader in the UK's online industry. In fact, it was often seen as a brake on progress, especially with its national broadband roll-out. Click&buy plays to BT's key strengths as an enabler of valued services to the mass market. The business stream fits well with its core competences of infrastructure development and trustworthy communications.

Click&buy also releases exceptional value from one of the most important business relationships in the modern world: the itemized telephone bill. With the familiar 'blue bill' now evolving to encompass every kind of digitally ordered or delivered service, BT is well placed to carry the bulk of transactions in this steadily growing channel. This project has proved that with the combination of imagination and robust business thinking, it is possible to create ventures in and adjacent to a company's core business that will both leverage existing assets and meet customer needs, now and into the future.

Edengene's Tim Thorne is adamant that click&buy makes a major contribution to BT's market positioning: 'This is what BT should be doing: acting as an enabler. This is a very strategic move for them. First, it encourages people to put content up for charging. Second, as broadband evolves, this gives them a wide platform for [charging for] different content.'

Thorne describes his firm's service as 'outsourced business development for business ventures'. In practical terms, this service delivers unusual insights that can then be converted into functioning business processes. Those on the inside of an organization can easily become estranged from the business's own assets, and even fear them. Certain practices or products can become untouchable, as a sense builds that they are too difficult, mysterious or fragile to tamper with. The 'if it ain't broke, don't fix it' attitude can further encourage people to avoid reassessing, and reapplying, their core competences. External entrepreneurs such as Edengene's consultants do not share the same taboos and have nothing to gain by subscribing to any erroneous beliefs they encounter when working with their clients. They think the unthinkable, in order to do the undoable.

Using this kind of external consultancy is also one of the few safe ways that an established organization can import an entrepreneurial spirit into its own community. It is hard to create an authentic 'start-up' experience within a large organization, although many have tried with so-called 'incubator' divisions where pet projects are given some shelter from the typical reporting requirements and team members may be offered a share in resulting profits. However, these in-house initiatives often suffer from a sense of unreality. The parent organization is always there to catch the fledgling business if it fails. No one's home is on the line. By exposing staff to consultants such as Edengene's, an organization of the massive size of BT can exploit the urgency, verve and nerve of a group of entrepreneurs without taking on any significant risk. Staff are shown a different way of thinking and working, and thereby shown that perhaps the obstacles they assume exist in their day-to-day environment may not be so permanent after all. This kind of intervention not only creates new businesses in short order, but also sparks a new sense of vision in the staff who are involved.

CASE STUDY 5.2

SMARTER METHODS TO BEAT CONSTRAINTS

A community hospital used a theory associated with the manufacturing sector to confound cherished assumptions about wringing greater value from constrained resources. Patient treatments are soaring, but neither the hospital nor its staff or its funding have been enlarged.

Managers in all types of businesses often find themselves confronted with zero-sum situations. Their experience and intuition tell them a win-win solution is the optimum exit point for any challenge to the business, be it big or small. But sometimes the constraints leave so little room for flexibility that even the most creative manager is forced reluctantly to conclude that 'something's got to give'.

Tony Hadley, Head of Community Services at the Norwich Community Hospital (NCH), faced such a dilemma in the summer of 2002. He needed to increase the number of patients that NCH could treat, in order to improve patient care and to relieve pressure on beds in the acute hospital. However, no additional budget was available and it was hard to imagine his hard-pressed team could work any harder.

Various change initiatives had already failed. Yet, working with Ashridge Consulting, NCH increased the number of patients it treated by 40 per cent within three months, with no changes to its existing resource levels. Together NCH and Ashridge worked some latter-day alchemy: they measurably made something out of nothing. The transformation in the hospital's operational performance is living proof that 'more money' is not the answer to the health service's problems. There is a smarter way.

Creating something from nothing

Achieving change in the National Health Service is a constant challenge. The government's high profile 10-year NHS Plan embraces a full agenda of change initiatives. Targets have been introduced throughout the service, driving a shift to a culture that values performance and accountability alongside clinical excellence. Throughout its history the NHS has tried to match the growing expectations of its users as medical advances have widened the range of treatments it can offer. Government, media and NHS staff have been unanimous in their belief that the service can only meet ever-growing needs by securing infinite resources.

From one perspective, they are of course right. Take any individual part of the system, and one can make a case for meeting targets through the application of further resources. Manpower and capital can solve problems in isolation. The difficulty arises for managers who have to decide where to allocate resources in order to benefit patients across the whole health system. Given the mass of competing demands, any individual allocation decision will appear to deny other areas. If there is one belief to match the idea that a bottomless well of resources will cure all the NHS's ills, it is the belief that existing methods make too many areas of healthcare into a lottery.

Ashridge's Gary Luck says: 'From our experience, current practice within the NHS is to allocate resources as evenly and as fairly as possible across the organization. Unfortunately, this practice of spreading resources fairly and evenly can prove damaging to the quality of patient care and doesn't enable the NHS to treat more patients.' Ashridge therefore took a different view. The consultants agreed a three-part primary objective with NCH. The team would use a combination of techniques to increase the number of patients going through the NCH and increase the quality of patient care without increasing resources or making staff work harder.

They also set a secondary objective of capability transfer, an objective Ashridge adds to all its health service projects. Ashridge would transfer learning and skills so that NCH could build its own internal consulting capability. The transfer process would run throughout the project, rather than being added at the end of the process as an afterthought. NCH would emerge as an organization ready and able to identify and address its own problems, long after the initial consulting intervention was completed.

Applying the theory of constraints

The theory of constraints is a model created by Eli Goldratt and successfully applied in organizations around the world. Initially used in manufacturing, this model is now being used to great benefit in other environments, including the NHS.

Goldratt's key insight was that organizations tend to be structured, measured and managed in parts, rather than as a whole. While breaking large problems down into smaller parts is a rational method for dealing with complexity, the result is often an overall reduction in performance standards and a seemingly endless list of chronic inefficiencies and conflicts.

The barriers erected within organizations are usually apparent to their people. Few staff are happy to work in 'them and us' cultures, but they feel powerless to challenge the organizational boundaries. Short-term targets focus minds on immediate actions, and leave little time for planning the future. At the same time, proposing change exposes the organization to new risks. Achieving a healthy, integrated business demands the removal of those barriers to success, but the day-to-day reality of running the business seems to preclude improving the business.

Goldratt's theory of constraints enables organizations to apply change in a way that creates long-term, systemic benefits. The process is described in terms of three questions:

1.   What to change?
2.   What to change to?
3.   How to cause the change?

In the first step – What to change? – analysis of cause and effect is used to trace the relationships between observable symptoms and underlying problems. The method looks for 'core conflicts': central unresolved dilemmas around which the organization is frozen or trapped. Core conflicts are often surrounded by palliative measures such as policies and measurement processes designed to deal with symptoms rather than the underlying problem.

The second step – What to change to? – challenges the assumptions sustaining the organization's newly revealed core conflicts. Solutions can now be developed and evaluated to replace the conflicted area. Such solutions are tested to ensure that they do not create undesirable side effects of their own.

The final step – How to cause the change? – involves building a transition plan to ensure that the designed changes take place, and take root, in the host organization.

Ashridge applied the theory of constraints using an application known as 'drum-buffer-rope' which recognizes that a system can only run as fast as the speed of the weakest link. This is 'the beat of the drum', the pacesetter of the organization's overall activity. The 'buffer' safeguards the bottleneck, ensuring the most constrained link in the system is always active to its full capacity. 'Drum-buffer-rope' has been widely applied to manufacturing processes. In these settings, material is released according to the pace set by the drum. The relationship between the 'drum' and 'buffer' is controlled by an operation known as 'rope'.

At a two-day workshop, 25 staff were introduced to the theory of constraints via these two tools. A dice game using dice and tokens representing patients was used to demonstrate the effects of uncertainty and variation on dependent events and whole-system behaviour within the hospital.

The joint team agreed that modelling system behaviour would only have a real-world impact if they could create a fertile environment for change. Soft skills would be needed to allow the organization to learn its way into new processes and behaviours. The team therefore developed a project plan to roll out changes while securing buy-in from all staff. Support of innovation and the challenging of existing working practices and boundaries would be key to effective and permanent change.

Boundary effects

The team's analysis of cause and effect showed that the overriding constraint on NCH's performance was a chronic bottleneck at the point of patient departure. Patients could not be released from the hospital at the earliest appropriate moment. Resources were essentially being tied up with inactive cases, blocking new cases from entering the start of the care chain.

A conflict that occurs at the edge of an organization can be one of the hardest to tackle and resolve. In this case, the slowdown at patient release was not entirely within the control of NCH. Other agencies had a major part to play, notably Social Services.

In order for a patient to be discharged safely, a number of events need to be synchronized. These include, for example, availability of prescriptions, transport, home improvements, support packages and accommodation for continuing care if appropriate. The complex nature of care packages provided by Social Services was the most frequent cause of delayed patient discharge.

Solving this boundary issue required the team to enlarge their understanding of the hospital system to include colleagues in Social Services. This non-traditional view of the hospital's scope rapidly emerges from a patient-centred analysis of NCH's processes, but is hidden by the structure of the organization and its partners. Following patient experiences in terms of events and outcomes rather than their sequential ownership by care agencies is a growing theme in the modernization of the NHS, and is elsewhere helping to refocus resources in general practice and public healthcare information services.

NCH/Ashridge team therefore included members from the relevant Social Services teams in the pursuit of potential solutions. Working together, the combined team managed to isolate and resolve what seemed at first to be a rigid, insurmountable obstacle. The obstacle was disguised in terms of the protection of patient confidentiality – a vital human right, and one that was inadvertently working against the best interests of the patient. The barrier was surrounded by laws and codes of practice. In other words, the team had found a classic core conflict.

Data protection laws prevent Social Services staff access to patient information until the patient has been discharged from hospital. The legal brake on information handover contributed greatly to NCH's terminal bottleneck. If colleagues in Social Services could begin planning patients' aftercare before they were discharged, there need be no inherent delay at this point in the chain of care. Ideally, social workers needed to be planning patient aftercare before the patient was admitted to the hospital.

The team found an imaginative workaround that immediately made sense and could be supported by all parties. A member of NCH staff would begin the patient's discharge plan and manage it until the point when it was legally correct to hand it over to Social Services. It is a simple solution, but one that only became visible and doable in an open and trusting environment. The team generated an elegant and lasting solution to a major problem by working with each other, with respect for the appropriate laws, and with committed concern for the patient's best interests.

Team-think revisited

The core team had to be capable of transferring skills and knowledge throughout the hospital and other associated agencies such as Social Services. This involved a programme of support and just-in-time skills training and development as the theory of constraints change programme unfolded.

The team was trained to deliver the key messages of the dice game and to facilitate workshops for stimulating new thoughts to address old problems. The majority of the workforce, from porters to medical consultants and totalling some 180 individuals, were introduced to theory of constraints thinking through a series of two-hour lunchtime

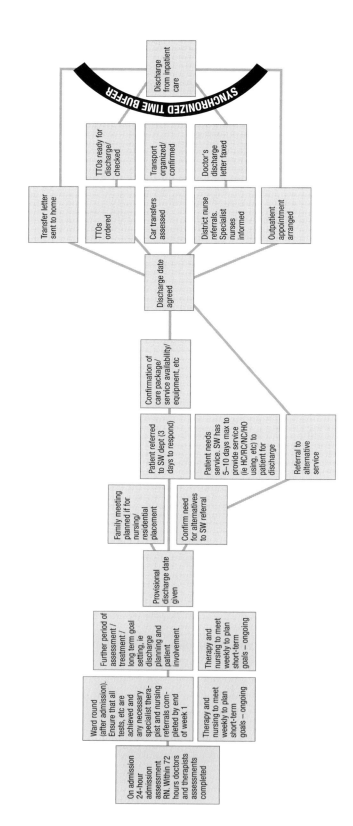

Figure 5.1 *Dependent events with time buffer*

sessions. This transfer of knowledge replicated the principles inherent in Ashridge's training of the core team, which included:

- avoiding jargon where possible;
- allowing staff the space to develop their own solutions;
- giving staff the opportunity to think about the significance for them as individuals, for their department, the hospital as a whole, and – crucially – for the patients;
- providing the opportunity to say 'No' as well as 'Yes'.

Gary Luck says that guiding the team's thinking habits and attitudes is crucial to avoiding the traps inherent in any organization susceptible to a blame culture:

> We treated [the project] as an enquiry into what we might be able to do. Each time we met we offered different thoughts and explored together whether they'd be helpful. It's an exploratory way of finding benefits. I often started workshops by reminding people they could also say 'No'. That way you can build a true consensus.

The size and disciplinary diversity of the organization could easily have blocked the change initiative. The workforce embraces a range of responsibilities and viewpoints spanning porters' to consultants'. Various departments and organizations such as community hospital, physiotherapy, occupational therapy and Social Services have their own management targets and professional issues to guard.

Potential problems in executing the changes were pre-empted by the transfer of facilitation and consulting skills to the core NCH team. Staff from cross-functional and multi-disciplinary areas were involved to co-create and implement the content and process.

Genuine new thinking was stimulated by creating an environment in which staff felt they could be open and honest about views and feelings. Meetings held in the era before the project have since been described by participants as being like rehearsals for a play. Actors spoke the lines they had laboured to learn and voiced the entrenched views of their sectional interest. Trapped in the evolved habits of their culture, they lacked a simple analytical model that might help them find ways forward in situations of uncertainty and complexity. This project helped them understand that whereas linear styles of leadership are relevant in situations of low uncertainty and high agreement, a more facilitative approach is required in situations of high uncertainty and low agreement as so often found in today's – and tomorrow's – NHS.

Better patients, better staff

The project's results were immediate and outstanding for patients, the hospital and staff alike. After 20 days' consulting input, immediate breakthroughs in performance were achieved without extra funds and without staff having to work harder. The average length of patient stay was reduced from 35 days to 20 days, enabling a 40 per cent increase in the number of patients going through the hospital. This step change was achieved within a few months from the start of the project in August 2002, with continuing month-on-month improvements. By March 2003 the average length of stay had fallen further, to 19 days.

Based on the measured increases in throughput, the team calculates that an additional 700 patients can be treated each year. Funding the treatment of 700 extra patients through traditional routes would have cost the hospital around £2 million.

Readmission rates of patients discharged from the hospital are also declining. This finding indicates there has been no reduction in the quality of patient care.

On the organizational side, the core change team has become a group of very able internal consultants. The team members' newly acquired learning and techniques have changed NCH into a learning organization, able to identify and address its own problems on an ongoing basis. Staff were given the time, leadership and support to develop their own solutions. They were also given the opportunity to think about the significance of change for themselves as individuals, for their department, for the hospital as a whole and – crucially – for the patient. This way of thinking has now become orthodox throughout the organization.

Several months after the dramatic improvement in results, staff are constantly overcoming new problems. They are also beginning to look at other areas within the Health and Social Care system with which they are linked, including general practice and care homes. They are sharing their learning, and helping to create environments for new learning in the organizations with which they share the responsibilities of care.

Problems with recruitment and retention have receded at NCH, described recently as 'the place to work' for medical staff in the area. An occupational therapist says: 'I have turned down other jobs because I don't want to move away from a theory of constraints environment.'

Confidence among the staff has also soared. A Social Services employee says: 'Before, if I had a problem I would want to blame someone and walk away from it. Now it's just an issue that I know I can tackle.'

Meanwhile Chris Price, CEO of NCH says: 'TOC has captured the imagination of staff at NCH. It has got everyone pulling in the same direction and has been a great tool for team building as well as service redesign.'

This project proves that a combination of rational, analytical tools and a supportive, open communications environment can dissolve zero-sum situations and radically alter the performance and capability of an organization. NCH and Ashridge have shown it is possible not only to make existing resources go further without loss of quality, but also to foster a culture eager to seek and implement further changes.

NCH's experience also implies that extra resources, applied blindly, can easily be consumed in buttressing broken structures and bypassing broken processes. Decision-makers owe their stakeholders the duty of questioning the band-aid solutions holding their operations together, even if – especially if – they mask the most politically sensitive and culturally loaded aspects of the business.

The theory of constraints and the adaptations made to it by Ashridge formed an entirely novel approach to management within the NHS, demonstrating how academic models can be put to practical use in the business environment via experienced consultants. It is unlikely that such a technique would be discovered at random by a manager within an organization like the NHS, or that such a lucky discovery would attract the support needed to apply it successfully to any area of the business. This is an important role for the consulting industry: good consultants act as conduits for the effective dissemination of valuable techniques that would otherwise not exact their maximum benefit.

NCH is an organization that has literally been refreshed by its use of the theory of constraints and the associated tools and techniques Ashridge introduced. As core conflicts are brought to the surface and eliminated through collaborative enquiry by motivated staff, a new health begins to spread through the organization, strengthening its ability to act and changing the lives of the customers it touches. Gary Luck says: 'While the actions we took here may be specific to this organization, the principles of what we've done are relevant to others. Real change isn't like a cog that you can move from one machine to another. Businesses are living entities that need developing from the inside.'

CASE STUDY 5.3

RELOCATING THE ORGANIZATION AND REDESIGNING
ITS MIND

*Designing and managing Europe's most complex IT relocation created
the opportunity to redesign the way GCHQ works, refitting it for the
new challenges of the 21st century.*

The genteel spa town of Cheltenham has been the discreet home
of the Government Communications Headquarters (GCHQ) since it
moved there in 1952. Long referred to vaguely as a department of the
Foreign Office, GCHQ functioned outside the public conscious-
ness until 1983 when the organization's role was formally explained
to Parliament. GCHQ reports to the Foreign Secretary and works
closely with MI5, MI6, the Ministry of Defence (MoD) and law
enforcement authorities.

GCHQ is responsible for two functions: signals intelligence and
information assurance. Signals intelligence is the lawful interception
of electronic emissions to protect the vital interests of the nation and
to support military operations. Information assurance defends government communication and information systems from eavesdroppers,
hackers and other threats, and protects the UK national critical infrastructure (such as power, water and communications systems) from
interference. Both of these functions operate around the clock, and
GCHQ is supported by one of the most advanced IT facilities in the
world. The UK's national security depends on GCHQ's operational
integrity and continuous availability.

The ending of the Cold War gave rise to a new role for the intelligence and security agencies. The 1994 Intelligence Services Act
(ISA) identified national security, economic well-being and the pre-
vention and detection of serious crime as the main threats to our
security.

The organization responded to the challenges, introducing new
ways of working, with the key areas of focus being on better team
working. However, it has been extremely difficult to achieve this
transformation in working style, because the organization occupies
more than 50 buildings spread across two sites some four miles
apart. Many of the buildings date from World War II and they are
served by a vast array of different computer systems.

In 2003 GCHQ began the process of moving its 4,500 staff from
its existing sites at Oakley and Benhall to a purpose-designed facility
in the western part of Cheltenham. The building cost £337 million,

and it forms part of the largest private finance initiative (PFI) project yet undertaken in the UK. The total cost of the PFI project is around £1.2 billion, including a 30-year service contract covering the provision of ancillary services such as security, logistics, telephony and maintenance. An additional £303 million covers the cost of technical transition, the move and the installation of the IT infrastructure to the new site.

The new building, known as the Doughnut, was completed in June 2003. Business units began moving in during September 2003 and by March 2004 some 2,200 staff had been relocated. The move was scheduled for completion in the summer of 2004. Part of one existing site will be kept operational for several years in order to ensure operational continuity.

The Albert Hall would fit comfortably inside the space at the heart of this immense building. The Doughnut contains over 5,000 miles of communications cabling, a length that would stretch from Cheltenham to Cairo and back again, and 1,850 miles of fibre optics. The fully equipped computer rooms cover an area equivalent to three football pitches.

New methods in intelligence work

A move of this size is complex enough, but GCHQ saw the New Accommodation Programme (NAP) as more than a logistical exercise. GCHQ used the move as an opportunity to enhance considerably its new ways of working to become a more joined-up and flexible organization. It needed to alter both its business behaviour and develop new systems while integrating with existing legacy systems to ensure business continuity.

A GCHQ spokesman, speaking at the start of the relocation project in September 2003, said:

> A lot of our business improvements rely on good teamwork, and the design of the Doughnut will make it a lot easier for our mathematicians, linguists, technologists and intelligence analysts to share information either face-to-face or through a common computer system. Additionally, when we face new threats, the open plan design is flexible enough to allow us to set up new teams in the space of a few hours – people will not be tied to specific desks any more.

The workforce at GCHQ is unusual. The organization employs more mathematicians than the average university mathematics faculty, and its linguists are fluent in 67 languages. A range of specialisms peculiar to intelligence work makes for a multi-disciplinary environment in which events are being tracked and interpreted from a range of viewpoints in real time. The complexity of modern threats and the globalization of terrorism are both publicly quoted reasons why modern intelligence work requires a greater degree of collaboration than it did in the relatively ordered world of the Cold War. GCHQ staff attempt to find meaningful patterns from a mass of data of different types, and there are few fixed assumptions they can apply in their work. Sharing information and ideas across disciplines is therefore a key tool in their method.

The obvious answer to the challenge of sharing information is the provision of excellent information systems. But, appropriately enough for the intelligence activity, the obvious answer is in this case misleading. According to David Stupples, formerly of PA Consulting Group and now at City University in London, human communication is the key:

> In the old buildings [staff] were physically compartmentalized in different rooms, and even in rooms within rooms. They need a more global picture today, and it helps when people can talk to each other. They need more openness within their world, to share views and ideas. Today's terrorism is in a global context, so [GCHQ staff] being part of a wider collaborative community is good for the country.

Merely swapping or copying more information between individuals would not have helped to produce that collaborative community. 'The information flowing around these people is already dense,' says Stupples. 'Passing more of it around wouldn't help.' By 'dense' information, Stupples means highly complex and apparently unstructured information that needs to be analysed into meaningful components before it can be understood, or related to other information. Different experts need to 'unpack' the information and discuss it with each other. Since all information is potentially related to everything else, it is not possible to predict who needs to see what at any given time.

The situation at GCHQ is the opposite of that which pertains in a highly structured expert environment, such as a hospital. A hospital's casualty department can screen incoming patients using 'triage', a French word meaning 'sorting'. Triage nurses determine who needs to be seen most urgently by doctors, based on a preliminary examination of each patient. Patients are then processed through the hospital via a series of diagnostic sessions and tests, each aimed at excluding certain possibilities, and eventually a course of treatment is decided upon.

GCHQ, on the other hand, is a perfect example of a highly unstructured expert environment. The typical escalation process used at a hospital would fail to identify and prioritize threats at GCHQ, because the behaviour being examined by the organization is designed precisely to thwart detection and categorization. GCHQ must be organized to 'expect the unexpected' but nevertheless determine what is important among the multiple streams of data coming in.

A moving experience

The primary objectives for the New Accommodation Programme (NAP) were to complete the move to the new headquarters within a self-imposed, aggressive schedule while maintaining continuous operations throughout, and to deliver significant business and cultural improvements. To achieve these objectives, four major issues needed to be addressed.

The first issue was the assured continuity of GCHQ's service. The programme could not stop the running of GCHQ, even for a single moment. A programme of this size and complexity would normally require downtime for systems' installation and testing, but GCHQ's importance to national security ruled out any loss of service.

The second issue was the complexity of GCHQ's computing facilities. The organization had a large number of separate systems, each one larger than the IT facilities of most corporations. The organization had also developed many connections among the systems, creating a highly interdependent 'system of systems' that was hard to understand and maintain. While the systems remained in place, they delivered excellent service. Contemplate moving them, and their fragility became apparent. At the purely technical level, GCHQ was also running what was estimated to be the largest supercomputer cluster outside the United States. This meant that professional expertise in relocating the systems was scarce.

Third, the project's milestones could not be altered. The nature of the contracts supporting GCHQ's move across town set the timeline in stone. The move had to be completed within aggressive time limits and delivered within an exacting cost and specification constraint.

The final issue compounded the impact of the first three and raised the stakes still further. Not only had the team to move these complex systems within a fixed timeline without any interruption to service, but it also had to improve the systems architecture in the process. A substantial number of legacy systems had to be fully integrated with each other, and redesigned to allow continuous improvement in the future. In the words of the project's Design Authority, this 'was a bit like rebuilding an aircraft carrier from the keel up, whilst it is at sea and flying its aircraft operationally'.

Adapting a methodology

PA Consulting Group was appointed to help GCHQ with its move because of the consulting firm's leading expertise in systems engineering. 'Systems engineering' may sound like a generic term, but it is in fact a specific professional discipline with a long history. The International Council on Systems Engineering (INCOSE) defines systems engineering as: 'an interdisciplinary approach and means to enable the realization of successful systems. It focuses on defining customer needs and required functionality early in the development cycle, documenting requirements, then proceeding with design synthesis and system validation.'

The key to systems engineering is its holistic approach. Each stage in the process is analysed in relation to the overall problem being attacked, using the seven dimensions of operations, performance, testing, manufacturing, cost and schedule, training and support, and disposal. Systems engineering has been traditionally used for building new things in a static situation, such as a nuclear submarine in a dry dock. It has also been used extensively in NASA's space programme, where mission objectives and timetables are fixed many years in advance.

There were two reasons why a traditional systems engineering approach would not work on NAP. First, GCHQ already existed, and so this was a case of a major role change for an existing operational facility, rather than building anew. Second, and equally as important, GCHQ needed to evolve continuously to align proactively to new threats. The earth and planets move in predictable cycles; but GCHQ's business is anything but predictable. PA therefore modified its systems engineering approach with GCHQ to create a methodology tailored to GCHQ's unique circumstances. The modified methodology took into account the volatile external environment in which the organization exists.

This special adaptation of the systems engineering approach made it possible for changes to be safely applied without impacting current

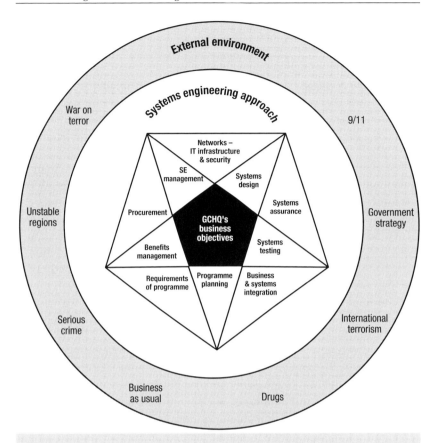

Figure 5.2 *Systems engineering approach taken at GCHQ*

operations. PA's skills and knowledge of systems engineering were combined with GCHQ's knowledge of its systems and goals to form a highly capable and integrated team, able to deal with the immense complexity involved in the delivery of a successful solution.

Working through the move

Even the most sophisticated methodologies only succeed in practice if they are applied in a well-managed, flexible environment. The PA/GCHQ team planned the style of the relocation project to ensure success, paying careful attention to risk reduction, morale and direction.

First, the team designed a step-by-step approach to the relocation in order to minimize risk. Business continuity dictated that the systems, people and data could not be moved in one single bound. Instead, the team developed an incremental plan that involved the re-engineering of the legacy systems, integrating these with new systems while addressing business issues, and finally moving the people. This means that a large proportion of the necessary technical redevelopment effort was carried out prior to the physical relocation, thereby breaking any critical dependency between systems and people.

Second, the team determined that meticulous planning, issue management and dynamic testing were all needed to make the complex relocation task achievable. For example, to assure business integrity during enhancements to existing IT applications, the team implemented 'roll-back' systems. These ensured that if a change was applied to an existing service and it did not work as planned, then the service could quickly revert to its previous stable state, without any interruption to GCHQ's operations.

The third plank of the delivery approach was to use computer simulations. The team ran a range of different simulations to analyse the pros and cons of different ways of tackling the move. The simulations included trade-off analyses to show how different sets of tasks would impact on each other, allowing the team to define an optimal series of activities. Other simulations covered performance analysis and failure mode analysis, enabling the team to design a relocation plan that would minimize the likelihood of loss of service.

The team also performed scenario testing to help decide on how the business could be supported under all foreseeable circumstances. For example, simulation was used to develop a programme schedule that could accommodate massive parallel working. This parallel working was instrumental in meeting the aggressive time schedule.

The fourth aspect to the delivery approach was 'the people element'. The team knew that moving people physically was only part of the challenge. Ensuring their commitment to the new systems environment, and their flexibility during the move, were key components of the project's overall success. The team developed a change management approach that would fully engage GCHQ staff and ensure that they exploited the changes in their IT systems. This change management strategy had three elements. The first element was operational pilots, with early versions of new systems exposed to staff so that they could begin to familiarize themselves with the coming changes. The second element was the involvement of users in systems design, testing and integration, so that staff had a sense of ownership of the systems being built. The third element was the transfer of learning from other organizations that had experienced the magnitude of large-scale change, which was achieved by liaising with other PA clients.

The final aspect of the delivery approach involved demonstrating the combined expertise of a multi-disciplinary team working in a collaborative style. The project called for strong technical leadership and insights from mission-critical industry sectors, such as air traffic control and rail transport. PA drew on the whole range of its capabilities, including IT skills, programme management, change management, modelling, systems integration and network design. To supply all these competences, PA assembled a team averaging 40 members and representing more than 600 years' experience with complex computing systems. This was the most experienced team that PA had ever fielded, and it was matched by a similarly experienced team from GCHQ. The two groups formed a joint team that exemplified, and encouraged in others, the collaborative style of working that GCHQ wanted to foster in the new headquarters.

Negotiating bumps along the road

Shipping GCHQ across Cheltenham was clearly not a simple matter of ordering a fleet of pantechnicons and a mountain of boxes. Unpicking the existing IT environment, designing a new target environment and calculating the transforming steps that would turn one into the other called on a range of intellectual skills. Designing the delivery approach called in a number of softer skills, such as issue management and system piloting. Despite these careful preparations, the team still had to deal with unexpected problems – not least the escalation of the organization's role after September 11. The relocation programme coincided with a period of major world conflict, but the systems engineering-driven scheduling approach provided the flexibility to accommodate these events, some at very short notice. The pattern of the relocation was successfully reconfigured on a number of occasions to allow changed priorities to go ahead.

GCHQ has always had to change its IT facilities and business processes as it adapts to changing world conditions. Given the global crises that occurred during this programme, changes were constantly occurring. Configuration management, or knowing the status of GCHQ's systems at all times, therefore became crucial. The specially tailored systems engineering approach meant that

NAP could accommodate these changes relatively easily, thereby maintaining the integrity of the overall facility and the viability of the programme.

Even without these unprecedented challenges, GCHQ presents a tough environment for external agents of change. The organization's IT facilities and working practices have evolved over many years and interact in highly complex ways. There is an immense body of knowledge at GCHQ, and in order for the PA people to become effective quickly they had to tackle an extremely steep learning curve. Maintaining the team's level of expertise on a long-term assignment was also a challenge. Careful 'succession planning' ensured that the PA contingent remained effective over the several years of this assignment, despite inevitable staffing changes. A training scheme quickly brought new team members up to speed.

Knowledge also flowed in the opposite direction, from consultancy to client. Prior to NAP, the government standards for projects and programme management (MSP and Prince 2) were not explicitly aligned with systems engineering. The GCHQ/PA team developed a successful alignment that has since been endorsed as the preferred method for future change programmes.

In its World War II guise as the Government Code and Cipher School (GC&CS) at Bletchley Park, GCHQ created the world's first electronic computer. Called Colossus, the machine enabled the decryption of messages sent from the German high command, playing a vital role in the allied war effort. Today, the organization is using its experience of moving colossal systems to ensure that the increasingly complex technical environment continues to yield vital intelligence in the fight against global terrorism. By marrying the strength of information-processing systems with human teamwork, GCHQ is now developing a new collaborative culture to replace earlier compartmentalized styles of working.

CASE STUDY 5.4

BRINGING RATIONALITY TO BEAR

Convincing experts that the way they solve problems can be captured and taught helped Sun Microsystems claw back more than 16,000 lost days for its customers every year.

Support: an innocuous sounding word implying a sturdy, reliable, and probably simple structure that props up an edifice. But in the business context, while 'support' may designate a quality that users or customers take for granted, from the point of view of the support provider it can be a major headache – and a cause of critical business failure.

Excellent support is crucial to the IT business, and increasingly to other kinds of business as the goods and services on offer in our markets become ever more complex. While not all customers invoke support, for those who do so it rapidly becomes the defining feature of the customer experience. Getting support right, on a predictable and repeatable basis, directly influences service renewals and repeat product purchases.

The 'always-on world'

Sun Microsystems is an established provider of hardware, software and services to the business market. By 2000, Sun's worldwide revenues of US $18 billion were being fuelled by sales to large organizations with heavy transaction volumes, such as banks and telecoms companies. These customers are 'always-on' businesses, responding to customer needs in real time and often working on a global basis. When there is a problem that affects delivery to a customer, every second counts.

Sun was solving most customers' problems quickly and effectively. Many customer problems were rapidly and accurately resolved by generalists and specialists within a country organization. However, problems that escalated from Sun support organizations in individual countries to Sun's worldwide backline support were taking too long to fix.

The engineers in the backline support are the most experienced in Sun, and they see the toughest customer problems. Sun invests continually in their training, support software and processes. With the best people available at the point of pain, what else could Sun do to fix problems faster?

Sun managers found that the handover point between country teams and the backline was a key determinant of success in resolving customer problems. A traditional view of the support function might begin to analyse this situation in terms of structure, and look for ways to change the support team organization. After all, 'support' sounds like a structural element. Sun, with the help of consultants Kepner-Tregoe, had a key insight that led them to take a different path. They realized that the transition between teams was a process embodying the transfer of information. If the team could improve the capture and presentation of critical information at this point, Sun could mobilize its existing resources to greater effect.

In simple terms, when the backline first heard of a customer problem from their colleagues in the country organizations, information was often missing or vague. Backline staff had to spend additional time gathering problem-specific details before they could progress. If Sun could improve the quality of this vital information, then they could fix their customers' problems faster.

Sun therefore launched the Sun Global Resolution ^{SM} (SGR) troubleshooting project in July 2000. The goal was dramatically to speed up resolution of customer problems by using rational troubleshooting processes. The new processes would be institutionalized within the customer support service chain: baked in to the way Sun dealt with all customer problems throughout its global operations.

Experts in action

'Rational troubleshooting' may sound like a contradiction in terms. Our mental image of troubleshooters is of lone, taciturn and expensive individuals who are called in to work some kind of magic when mere mortals have failed. If leading managers are lauded for their ability to take 'a helicopter view', troubleshooters are the daredevils dangling beneath the spinning rotors.

Consultants Kepner-Tregoe have a different take on troubleshooting. Founded in the 1950s, Kepner-Tregoe was built on the premise that people can be taught to think critically. The firm's founders had studied breakdowns in decision-making at the US Strategic Air Command while working for the Rand Corporation. They discovered that successful decision-making by Air Force officers had less to do with rank or career path than the logical process an officer used to gather, organize, and analyse information before taking action. Their work proved that applied expertise can be mapped, and taught. Shifting their studies into the civilian world, Kepner and Tregoe observed the practices of both effective and ineffective decision-makers responding to complex, repetitive challenges.

They developed their findings into the 'rational process', which became the Kepner-Tregoe method for effective organization management. The firm also pioneered the 'train-the-trainer' concept, an approach to skills transfer now widely implemented throughout the business world.

Kepner-Tregoe's cultural origins are similar to those of Sun. Both companies share a heritage of academic rigour and garage start-up pragmatism. Working together on Sun's support capability, the combined team was able to maximize the expert value of Sun's engineers to improve the customer experience radically.

Sun asked Steve White, a UK-based senior backline engineer trained to coach his colleagues in Kepner-Tregoe troubleshooting, to lead the SGR troubleshooting project. White says:

> We already knew that Kepner-Tregoe's troubleshooting processes gave us what we needed to create the SGR troubleshooting project. But a project of this scale needs genuine partnership, not simply intellectual property. Right from the start we established a baseline of trust with Kepner-Tregoe's consultants. Kepner-Tregoe's processes gave us a common way of working together that meant that when issues arose, we could sort things out quickly.

Escalation ping-pong

Like almost all technical support organizations, Sun used a management escalation process to deal with problems raised by customers. Escalation allows organizations to tag problems for priority and severity depending on the age of the problem, and the degree of customer pain it is creating. The escalation process itself notifies an increasing number of senior managers, so that more and more of the organization's resources are steadily applied to the problem in the pursuit of its resolution.

According to Kepner-Tregoe's Mike Bird: 'Most organizations have a blurred escalation process that's driven by perceptions of expertise. And the support organization is structured according to those perceptions.' In other words, organizations' structures and processes are based on how people believe problems are solved, rather than direct, objective evidence of the reality.

Sun's support approach had developed alongside its product and service set. However, the business value of its offerings had begun to change in the customers' perceptions, and not always in line with Sun's own preconceptions. Many businesses had moved online – a development partly inspired and encouraged by Sun itself – and now relied heavily on their systems for business survival. Traditional back-office functionality was now being operated directly by customers. If that functionality failed, the bottom line registered the failures immediately. Problems now attracted much greater exposure than in the past.

The existing support structure used four escalation levels. Level 1 comprised call handling. At this stage, incoming problems would be logged and routed to generalists at level 2. A generalist would be able to address common problems within defined standard response times. A typical example would be remedying a well-understood Unix problem within a 15-minute call-back period.

The support structure's level 3 was made up of product specialists. These specialists were trained in particular Sun products, such as its enterprise servers. In most cases level 3 specialists were grouped within a Sun country organization, although in some territories level 3 staff were shared at a regional basis.

The fourth level was the backline: Sun's engineering gurus. Level 4 specialists form an elite corps drawn from the teams that create Sun's hardware and software. They were used to taking support calls from all over the world, but did not interface directly with customers.

Sun was finding that in the lower levels of its escalation structure, many of the easier problems needed to be fixed faster. With Sun boxes taking enterprise-critical roles, quick fixes needed to be quicker. The company therefore brought in a knowledge base and a range of support tools. These remedies gave level 1, 2 and 3 staff faster access to the organization's knowledge, streamlining its ability to respond to the classes of simpler, well-described problems. However, the new tools did not address efficiency and effectiveness at level 4.

By running a troubleshooting pilot in two sites, the joint team discovered that the problem affecting the level 4 handover was bound up with the quality of information contained in the transition. At this point in the escalation, the problem effectively became invisible as the interfacing teams attempted to communicate without a shared language. The organization suffered from what Sun called 'escalation ping-pong' as colleagues batted undefined problems between themselves. Level 3 staff would take a problem to level 4 colleagues precisely because they did not understand the problem. But level 4 staff could not grasp the problem because their level 3 counterparts could not describe it.

One of the team's insights is that problem-solving loses visibility because it is conducted privately and silently by experts. Bird says: 'The quality of the solving is invisible because the diagnosis is going on in their heads, and their outputs are questions and suggestions.'

The sources of the experts' comments remain obscure to the person with whom they are working, leading to a lack of shared understanding and trust. In a situation lacking a tangible, shared agenda, it is easy for the belief to arise that every problem is unique.

Information in transit

Sun use the example of medical experts to explain how problem-solving actually works, and its generic features. A doctor making a diagnosis asks lots of questions, most of which will seem baffling to the patient. However, the doctor is not asking questions at random. His or her questions are designed to rule out areas of enquiry as quickly as possible. The diagnostic process is one of pruning: carefully discarding those branches of the solution tree that are not relevant to the case in hand.

Medicine also provides a good example of how clear information sets assist in handovers between levels in an escalation process. For example, at the scene of an accident a police officer will use first aid skills to make the victim safe and comfortable, and report to the paramedic a defined set of information, including the time elapsed since the accident, any obvious wounds and any observed behaviours. For their part, the ambulance team will make a next-level report to the receiving medical team at the hospital. This team's report will include data on vital signs and the results of any first-line tests they have completed during the journey. The information package delivered alongside the patient is standardized and acceptable throughout the medical profession within a country. This practice of capturing diagnostic data at each escalation level is repeated throughout the healthcare profession, notably at the interface between general practitioners and consultants. This particular professional interface is similar to the level 3–4 handover point at Sun.

The hard graft of making change in organizations comes down to influencing the day-to-day, minute-by-minute behaviour of a large number of individuals: individuals with opinions, experience and pride. Computer engineers, in particular, live with a stereotyped view of their profession that casts them as uncommunicative and arrogant. Managing such individuals, and suggesting that their working practices can be improved, requires sensitivity and openness – and the ability to see beyond limiting stereotypes. Steve White, an engineer himself, was not encumbered by prejudice. But he was aware that querying the processes of any professional risks damaging organizational relationships and delivery: 'Sun's engineers are among the best in the world. How could we persuade these engineers to change the way they work on the most complex and difficult problems? And do so without damaging the great work they are already doing? There was more to the solution than training.'

The answer came in two parts. The first part was the concept of triggers. A trigger is a defined point in the call workflow when an engineer should use the new process. So, when a country engineer has spent a short time trying to solve a problem on his or her own and then wants to escalate the call to the worldwide backline, the trigger asks for the problem data to be handed over in the precise format defined by the team. Every problem call passed to the backline now contains answers to the same questions, in the same format, regardless of the technology of the problem.

The data format combines questions that together isolate and compare the problem. Basic questions formed around 'What ...', 'Where ...', 'When ...', 'How big ...' and so on provide structural elements to the problem definition. Comparison questions help to refine further the problem boundary and distinguish it from unrelated problems with which it might have surface similarities. For example, if the answer to a 'What' question is 'Box A is broken', then a follow-on comparison question might be: 'Is Box B broken?' The method uses logical operators such as 'is not' to explore the space around the problem.

The method also uses scale to narrow down various dimensions of the problem. For example, when exploring the time attributes of a problem, the user may be asked: 'When did Box A break down this time? When has it broken down in the past? How many times has it broken down in its lifetime?' Again, these are very similar questions to those asked by a doctor seeking to establish a historical context for a current condition.

A troubleshooting environment

The new information format and the triggers associated with its use provided the vehicle for the improvement Sun needed to make. Achieving a change in actual practice required further actions. As Roy Garcia, Sun's leader of the SGR troubleshooting method in the

United States says: 'Sun engineers are smart, practical and experienced people. We needed to set up the process so that the engineers wanted to use it and so that customers saw the benefit as quickly as possible.'

Applying triggers meant extra work for country engineers – but the backline (and the customer) would see the benefit, not them. What would country engineers get in return?

The team's analysis identified two factors impacting any scheme's usability in this environment. First, when country engineers handed over poorly defined problems to the backline, it was usually the country engineers who had to go back to the customer for additional information. Second, country engineers handed problems over to the backline because they had reached the end of their known roads. They had nowhere else to go.

The team brought these factors to the surface, and used them as the fulcrum of the new process's rationale for its users. The message was formulated in terms of typical situations, and their consequences. So, the message went, if you are a country engineer wishing to escalate a problem case to the backline, then pass it to them in the SGR troubleshooting format. If it is not in this format, then the backline will request that you do so – and you will have to explain the delay to the customer. But if your request is in the SGR documentation format, the backline will take it over, immediately, cleanly, and without quibble. Do the wrong thing, and life will become harder. Do the right thing, and life will become easier – for everyone. The new information format encapsulated a contract by which the different support teams would cooperate to solve customers' problems.

Enabling experts

The project's style of solution differs from typical interventions made to improve modern business processes, in that it does not take the form of a discrete item that can be installed, or integrated. Nor is it a form of broad behavioural change. The change the team was looking for was rooted in a very tangible and specific mechanism, and the obligations that go with the mechanism. Training is therefore key to the method's success.

Sun staff took a four-day course, designed not to bludgeon them with an alien way of working, but to let them see that the proposed new way of working actually recognizes and encapsulates the way they already work. The course leaders found that people may approach such courses with wariness, but generally emerge as advocates. They realize that the best experts ask the best questions. As Bird says: 'The people who take to it best become champions. They realize: "this is what I do". They also learn that making those questions visible and sharing them across interfaces is a way of cloning the best people.'

Kepner-Tregoe insists that its training is based as much around real problem-solving as possible. Mike Bird estimates that 25–30 per cent of any training engagement involves working on real, live problems. The trainers may be completely unversed in the special subject matter of the business area – all the better for demonstrating how rational problem-solving crosses specialist boundaries, and how all problems share common generic features in the questions by which they are defined. The train-the-trainer approach ensures that the new method is rapidly embedded in the workstyle of the organization, and transmitted to as many colleagues as quickly as possible.

The Sun/Kepner-Tregoe team spent two months defining and planning the worldwide project. The project included:

- creating a bespoke course based on the troubleshooting method, named the Sun Global Resolution Troubleshooting class;
- training 70 Sun Global Resolution[SM] (SGR) leaders – high-calibre Sun engineers trained to train their fellow engineers;
- training 2,400 backline and country engineers;
- facilitating the SGR troubleshooting method on serious customer problems;
- launching new procedures for customer problem management;
- managing implementation of the SGR troubleshooting method in more than 30 countries.

Visible value

From the start of the project, newly trained engineers solved numerous outstanding customer problems. SGR troubleshooting process leaders also helped to resolve serious customer issues, with considerable success. Peter Brentnall, for example, had only just emerged from his process leader training when he was asked to help a major customer who was very unhappy with a persistent system problem. The problem was one of the most complex and demanding problems Sun had ever seen, but Brentnall guided the support team to resolution so successfully that the customer has become a willing reference for Sun's support services.

Engineers were now solving problems more effectively and cleanly. When action was needed, it was happening sooner, and more incisively. Fewer engineers were getting stuck on problems, and major incidents were being managed more smoothly.

John Ryan, Sun's director responsible for the backline in EMEA and Asia Pacific regions, also trained as an SGR programme leader to coach and facilitate his colleagues. He says:

> The amazing part of this project has been the 'fringe benefits'. The SGR troubleshooting process now forms the basis of our technical problem resolution process, but the spin-offs have been considerable. Customers are delighted when we do on-site SGR process facilitations because we show rational process and help them participate in finding root cause to their own problems. Engineers communicate better using the structures embedded in the process. There is less conflict in the system because everyone knows what is needed. Managers are using techniques such as decision analysis to make better choices. Everything considered, the SGR troubleshooting process is tremendous value for money and we are well on the way to rational thinking becoming part of our corporate DNA.

The SGR troubleshooting triggers for use were introduced on 1 December 2001, with immediate performance benefits. In June 2002, an independent group within Sun measured how the company's support performance had changed. The results were unequivocal. The project had been driven by the need to resolve Sun's toughest customer problems faster. Compared with the previous year, the SGR troubleshooting process had streamlined the process of meeting Sun's customers' needs by 16,060 days. These benefits continue to accrue for Sun and its demanding customers around the world, second by second.

Kepner-Tregoe's contribution to the upgrading of Sun's support capability lies in its expertise in the process of diagnosis. While other techniques for improving customer support focus on pulling together information sources or driving operators down prescriptive paths of enquiry, the Kepner-Tregoe approach aims to discover the questions that will in turn reveal the nub of a particular problem. The company helped Sun to think about how it thinks, and gave Sun a means of capturing and replicating those habits of thought throughout its professional support community.

6

Business strategy

Strategy has not had an easy time since the millennium. Squeezed by a combination of economic downturn and endemic scepticism about the visionary ideas of the e-business boom, most strategic planning departments – if they still exist – have retrenched. They have focused on the operational issues like how to yield bottom-line improvements in more acceptable timescales, and on the organizational changes often ignored by the high-flying strategy of convention. Now, with the global economy starting to pick up, managers are rightly asking: What role does strategy play in our organization? How can we ensure that the ideas we have on paper can be realized in practice?

The two cases in this chapter represent the full spectrum of responses to this question. At one end, we have Capgemini, assessing the strengths and weaknesses of the Duke of Edinburgh's International Award programme and developing suggestions for future direction. Hugely successful (more than 100 countries run Duke of Edinburgh award schemes), it was still important to ensure that the programme reflected the changing needs of young people. This was traditional strategy work at its best: a period of intensive data gathering by the consultants followed by client workshops aimed at brainstorming a new vision for the organization. At the other end of the scale, there is RightCoutts' work with the Harrogate Healthcare NHS Trust. Like public healthcare systems across the world, the Harrogate Trust found that it needed a more corporate style of management, something that was likely to have a profound impact on the culture of the organization as a whole. The appointment of a new chairman and chief executive, and the advent of a new executive team, provided the catalyst to improve the effectiveness with which administrators and clinicians worked together on strategic issues. This is strategy as cultural change in which data gathering cedes to appraisals of individual managers, and facilitation to mentoring.

It is significant that neither of these case studies comes from main-stream corporations. While commercial organizations batten down the strategic hatches, it is in the public and not-for-profit sectors that strategy is looking to prove itself again. Moreover, unlike most exercises to develop new strategies in the private sector, these initiatives were not taking place against a backdrop of declining performance: change, and the timing of change, was a matter of choice.

Taken together, the very different projects described here share three important lessons:

- *Strategy cannot be developed by one part of an organization, or by one group of stakeholders, in isolation.* At the Harrogate Trust, service delivery would not have been improved by a small team of administrators telling clinical staff what to do. Command-and-control management would also have failed the Duke of Edinburgh's International Award Association, membership of which is entirely voluntary. Effort had to be put into ensuring that all those likely to be affected by the strategies being developed would have the opportunity to contribute to them. The International Award Association canvassed the views of its national authorities and independent operators. Individual coaching sessions were held with all the directors of the Harrogate Trust, not just those who thought of themselves as 'managers'. Similarly, the consulting teams had to work with their clients, learning from them, developing ideas in collaboration with them – a far cry from the hit-and-run strategy consulting clients have complained of in the past.
- *A balance needs to be struck between inclusion and speed.* Strategy (and strategy consulting) has moved a long way since the time when a strategic review took several months. Indeed, during the height of the e-business boom in 1998–99, afraid that competitors might overtake them, organizations went to the other extreme, formulating strategies in weeks, if not days. But compressed timescales had other flaws and often resulted in ill-considered plans that rarely returned a profit. The initiatives described here fall into the middle ground: small in scale and focused in intent, they were both completed in a short time, yet neither sacrificed the need to involve others.
- *The means are as important as the end.* The link between strategy and implementation has always been weak: mission statements that look good on posters fail to change behaviour; new business models prove unworkable in practice. It may be that, too often, we think

about 'a strategy' as an end in its own right. Perhaps clients and consultants have focused too much on the physical output – once the report has been written everyone sits back with relief, forgetting that is only the start of the process. In both the projects described here, the way that the strategy is developed is almost as important as the strategy itself. The process of formulating a strategy was used as an excuse to forge stronger links, between managers and clinicians at the Harrogate Trust, and between the International Award Association and its members.

STRATEGY CONSULTING: SMALLER, LEANER, FITTER

Strategy consulting was the main casualty of the downturn in the consulting market after 2001. Yet, as most consultants will tell you, strategy consulting has by no means disappeared. Certainly, with few organizations brave enough to commit resources to a full-scale strategic review, strategy consulting projects are smaller on average than they were 10 years ago, but the underlying reasons why clients find the input of consultants at a strategic level are as relevant today as they were during the boom years of the late 1990s.

The most important of those reasons comes through particularly clearly in these cases – the objective view that a consultant as an outsider brings to any situation. With no vested interest in the result and an ability to stand back from the day-to-day pressures that affect every manager, a consultant is in a unique position. As RightCoutts' work with the Harrogate Trust illustrates, the best consultants are also trusted confidants, able to address areas of fundamental concern to their clients. However, trust is equally important to the work of Capgemini with the International Award Association: if the consultants were to challenge the Association's accepted thinking, they could only do so from a position of trust.

Objectivity – the ability to see the wood for the trees – is a product of trust. But where does trust come from? This is a question that every consultant, walking through a client's offices for the first time, has to ask. It used to be thought that someone being interviewed for a job had around five minutes to make a good impression on the interviewer. Recent research suggests that it is really around 10 seconds – about as much time as it takes to say 'Good morning' and perhaps a few more words. Consultants face the analogous problem when they meet a new client: rapport has to be established instantly. Seconds are what the consultants from RightCoutts would have had when they first met the hospital directors, some of whom may have been sceptical about their role. The team from Capgemini would only have had seconds to establish credible ground rules for open debate and constructive criticism at the International Award Association.

Trust is not simply a case of personal chemistry though. In these projects, trust is also the result of joint participation, open communication and a shared investment in the work in hand.

- *Joint participation is vital.* It is obvious that success in both projects involved – indeed, relied on – input from the clients. Capgemini provided data to initiate internal debate, but the resulting conclusions could not have been reached without the Association's own staff being involved in the brainstorming sessions. Similarly, RightCoutts depended on its client explaining how the Harrogate Trust worked. In return, the consultants had to be flexible, tailoring the process to accommodate the issues that arose during the course of their work, rather than working to a preconceived plan. 'We developed the brief collaboratively,' commented the Harrogate Trust, 'and were able to focus on the most successful elements during the project. This required real flexibility and imagination from the consultants.' The days of the all-knowing consultant are clearly past: success here was the result of an equitable client–consultant relationship and mutual respect.
- *Open communication is very important.* A key part to that respect is the ease with which both parties are willing to exchange even confidential information.
- *Shared investment is required.* Most supplier–customer (and client–consultant) relationships involve only one-way investment – the buyer's. These projects were different because the consulting firms, too, were making a commitment. This is most obvious in the case of Capgemini, whose work with the International Award Association was carried out on a *pro bono* basis. The client's commitment here was not money, but time – a willingness by the Association's staff to put aside their day jobs in order to focus on more strategic issues. But there was commitment, too, from RightCoutts. Although being paid for their work, the firm's ability to win more work from this client and its broader reputation were both at stake.

SUMMARY – KEY LESSONS FOR MANAGERS AND CONSULTANTS

- The reputation of large-scale corporate strategy remains severely damaged by the false promises of the dotcom era. Instead, organizations are focusing their strategic thinking
- Bringing down the barriers within and between organizations may reduce one set of obstacles to change, but it creates another – multiple stakeholders. Successful change management involves confronting and reconciling, not bypassing, the different – sometimes conflicting – aims of those involved.
- Radical change can be easier than incremental change because it demonstrates the willingness of senior managers to resolve – rather than pay lip-service to – serious issues.
- Effective change management consulting follows Teddy Roosevelt's advice of speaking softly and carrying a big stick. In terms of its public interaction with employees, it needs to adopt innovative, even unexpected approaches. Behind the scenes, consultants have an important role to play in maintaining momentum and credibility.

CASE STUDY 6.1

CHANGING PEOPLE FOR A CHANGE

Inspiring change within large organizations often comes down to harnessing the will of key individuals. Goals, no matter how noble, remain abstractions until the people charged with achieving them take them to heart and act upon them. This project shows how well-planned and thoughtfully executed one-to-one personal intervention, particularly coaching, can reorient an organization in a time of massive opportunity.

The NHS was set up in 1948 and is now the largest organization of any type in Europe. Although the NHS is recognized as one of the best health services in the world by the World Health Organization, and widely regarded as the jewel in the crown of the British post-war state, the demands of modern healthcare are driving widespread improvements to the service.

The main tool used to date in getting more value out of the NHS has been the setting of targets. The NHS Plan, published in July 2000, is a detailed action plan for developing the service over a 10-year period. The plan defines a mass of measures for putting patients and people at the heart of the health service. As a result of the plan's implementation, patients will have more say in their treatment and greater access to information. New hospitals are being built, and more doctors and nurses trained and recruited. There will be net increases of at least 15,000 more general practitioners and consultants, 30,000 more therapists and scientists, and 35,000 more nurses, midwives and health visitors by 2008.

Patients' experience of healthcare will be impacted by shorter waiting times for hospital and doctor appointments, and cleaner wards, better food and updated facilities in hospitals. For example, waiting times for operations will fall from an existing maximum of 15 months to 6 months by 2005, and to 3 months by 2008. On the organizational side, there will be tougher performance standards for NHS organizations and better rewards for those who perform best.

However, by 2004 the government was signalling that targets do not, in themselves, guarantee improvement. As business managers know, it is the contribution that targets make to the cycle of management that gives them value. Targets that make sense to those who must pursue them and that contribute to broader goals act as directors of action and motivators of individuals. In the case of the NHS, according to an article entitled 'About Turn' published in the *Economist* (London), 14 February 2004:

> A recent analysis of the health service by the OECD found 'few indicators showing unambiguous improvements in outcomes over and above trend improvements that were already apparent before the surge in spending'. It said that targets can be achieved only if the incentives are right. Behaviour is affected only if service providers 'feel motivated to meet the targets'.

This case study shows how one management team's response to the modernization agenda focused on behaviours rather than numbers.

Change at the sharp end

The government's modernization agenda ripples out to every element of the NHS, including local delivery organizations such as Harrogate Healthcare NHS Trust. This trust provides acute, mental health and community healthcare to the population of North Yorkshire, primarily to the conurbations of Harrogate and Ripon. It employs over 1,700 staff in the region. Modernization triggered the appointment of the trust's chairman and chief executive, and the subsequent creation of a new top-level management team.

Furthermore, the opportunity to achieve a three-star performance rating for NHS Trusts in England for 2003 meant that the trust could apply for Foundation Trust status. Foundation Trust status shifts the balance of power in favour of the community, making the organization more customer focused. The Foundation Trust strategy devolves resources and decision-making to the front line of the health service, making it more responsive to people's needs and improving its accountability to those it serves. While the government believes that all NHS trusts will progress to Foundation Trust status over a five-year period, in the initial phase only trusts that achieve three stars in the annual ratings are eligible for change of status.

For Harrogate, becoming a Foundation Trust would require sensitive and strategic management within a challenging time frame. Miles Scott, the new Chief Executive, saw that the trust could use the external changes involved in the change of status to restructure the organization for the future. Scott recognized that it was vital to engage all those working within the organization in order to take advantage of the opportunity for change: 'We all understand how important the people side of change is and it needs to be more than just changing name badges.'

RightCoutts was engaged to support the organizational change process, with attention to both the executive team and the clinical team. The executive team included the chief executive and the directors of finance, HR, planning and performance, facilities, operations, the medical director and the chief nurse. Developing the executive team involved ensuring that every member was familiar and comfortable with his or her new roles and responsibilities.

The project's work with clinicians required the development of a general management perspective to augment their professional viewpoints. The changes involved in the NHS Plan require clinicians to manage resources as well as fulfil their specialist responsibilities. The trust therefore wanted its clinical directors to become more business focused, and to acquire the skills and knowledge needed to adapt their own processes while leading their teams through the period of change.

Hands-on change

The approach proposed by the project team aimed to draw together clinicians and general managers within the trust, working with individuals to assess their input to the work of the executive team as a whole. This approach allowed the trust's people to own the change process and influence its design, ensuring that its details met their needs and resulting in early buy-in. Working in this style demanded a shift in mindset for clinicians and general managers alike. Both groups had traditionally worked from the same agenda, but from different angles. Now the groups would share perspectives, appreciate each other's constraints, and develop solutions together.

RightCoutts' consultants began their work with the senior team by observing a working meeting, gaining a feel for how the team members tackled their responsibilities and interacted with each other. The consultants also conducted 360-degree appraisals by telephone in order to gain further confidential feedback on individuals.

The consultants then met with the directors on a one-to-one basis to discuss their needs. The team used psychometric tests in some instances to help identify areas for improvement. Personal development plans aligning individual needs to the trust's objectives were agreed for each director, ensuring that each individual had a precise, tailored roadmap for their onward development.

The team next put in place a programme of coaching sessions. The coaching sessions gave individual directors the opportunity to discuss their progress and to surface any issues associated with personal or organizational objectives. Sessions were held away from the client's work environment wherever possible. Off-site meetings helped build strong, committed relationships between executive team members and consultants, while minimizing any disruption to the daily flow of business at the trust.

Coaching is a high-value intervention, especially at senior levels of an organization. Supporting change in leaders often involves subtleties of attitude or behaviour, and finding and addressing such subtleties entails individual attention and sensitive management. Coaching enabled the project to address the organization's strategic goals and its leaders' personal capabilities in the same frame of reference. Strategy and individual action could be married, making the identification between the organization's mission and its leaders complete, intimate and robust. Coaching also helped the executive staff work more effectively together as a team. Dr Carl Gray, Executive Medical Director at the trust, says:

> The coaching has certainly helped me in my transition to a senior role within the trust. As a member of the Medical Director team you are set apart from your colleagues, who are sometimes looking for an authority figure to tell them what to do and at other times are seeking an advocate to argue their case. It's a difficult and challenging role for anyone to adopt, regardless of their personality type and the RightCoutts approach has given me confidence and a new perspective in my role from an early stage.

Chief Executive Miles Scott agrees that the coaching approach has made an impact throughout the organization: 'Everyone has got something different out of the RightCoutts coaching. Without doubt, the organization is making the progress I wanted to see – the sense is that coaching has been a helpful tool towards this.'

As well as its applied skills in personal and team development, RightCoutts brought a thorough, up-to-date understanding of the NHS and the changes it is undergoing. In particular, the team appreciated the diversity of work undertaken within a trust, and the multidisciplinary nature of its environment. The principal consultants and programme manager on the RightCoutts team had extensive knowledge and experience of working alongside clinicians and general management, and were specifically chosen to work on the project because of their backgrounds. Their backgrounds helped get the project off to a quick start, avoiding the need to explain NHS procedures, agendas and culture. This close alignment was an essential ingredient in meeting the needs of the trust in a very short time frame.

Reaching the stars

This was a highly visible project, with many hopes riding on its success. With a new executive team in place, there was naturally some pressure to make a meaningful impact on the life of the trust as quickly as possible. Furthermore, audit dates and deadlines for the achievement of three-star status provided a shared sense of immediacy throughout the project.

The project team had also to consider the positions and personalities of the senior managers they were working with. The trust's senior management team was working in an already well-performing, but very time-pressured, organization. Rapidly establishing the relevance and benefits of the project for the senior team and securing their buy-in was essential to the project's success. Tony Martin, RightCoutts' Programme Manager, says: 'Holding meetings at shorter intervals than normal and providing consultants who were dedicated to the project and its outcomes was essential. By taking the time to hold diagnostic one-to-one sessions with individuals as well as group work, we were able to truly engage people into the initiative.'

The project team's work with the trust was a key factor in the award of three-star status. Three-star status brings national recognition to the trust's excellence in serving the local community. As objective confirmation of the organization's good work, the new status had a huge impact on staff motivation and quickly became a strong factor in recruitment. The award has elevated the trust's image to that of an employer of choice.

Moving to 'hard' measures – those that match the indicators in the NHS Plan – Harrogate delivered the best waiting-time performance across the nation during 2003–04. In fact, the trust met NHS Plan targets for waiting times two full years ahead of schedule. The trust is now well positioned to attain Foundation Trust status. This will bring a new financial regime providing access to additional capital investment for building projects and materials, as well as drawing local people into the management team.

The trust has seen a marked change in the level of cooperative working among the senior management team. The success of the project has confirmed that this style of personal intervention can create great benefits within the trust. At the time of this writing, work continues to apply the approach at further levels of the trust's organization.

Coaching is a consulting technique that focuses on individuals and their core skills, behaviours and beliefs. This technique cannot be operated blindly, or according to formula. To risk an obvious pun, the Harrogate trust could only gain the benefits of coaching by trusting their consulting colleagues. This project is an excellent example of how personal commitment to the community and a willingness to change can be matched with national programmes that aim to improve the lives and well-being of millions.

CASE STUDY 6.2

RELEASING THE FUTURE FROM THE PRESENT

A classic review of an international organization nearing 50 years' service to young people is ensuring that half a million people will continue to develop their skills and challenge themselves every year.

We have heard less in recent years about the traditional mode of management consultancy, and it is tempting to think that the industry has changed thoroughly and irrevocably. Before the age of large-scale systems integration projects began, and managers turned their attention to defining change projects with strict ROI (return on investment) plans, management consultants were engaged for their skills in the areas of strategic direction setting, vision building and organization. Breadth and depth were valued, while specialist skills in systems or methodologies were secondary matters. The consultant was, more often than not, an informed, committed and engaged 'outside eye', bringing a range of experience to bear on the challenges of a well-established organization at a time of business challenge.

Capgemini's work with the Duke of Edinburgh's Award International Foundation is a timely reminder that the strategic challenges facing organizations have never gone away, and proof that a classic consulting intervention can bring long-term benefits. No amount of technology or rapid results methodologies can burn away the toughest questions at the leading edge of any organization: Where are we going? What do we mean to our customers?

Reaching young people

The Duke of Edinburgh's International Award is a self-development programme available to all young people worldwide. The programme aims to equip young people with life skills to make a difference to themselves, their communities and the world. More than 5 million young people from 111 countries have been motivated to undertake a variety of voluntary and challenging activities through the scheme. Over 520,000 young people worldwide are currently participating in the programme.

The Award operates on a national basis in 60 countries and there are 133 Independent Operators in a further 53 countries. The International Award is a generic title, and each National Award Authority (NAA) can choose its own title. The various national Awards include the El-Hassan Youth Award in Jordan, The President's Award in Ireland and The Source of the Nile Award in Uganda. In most NAAs the Gold Award is presented by the head of state.

The Award has three levels, bronze, silver and gold, each with different minimum starting ages and periods of participation. Each level has four sections:

- Service: to encourage service to individuals and the community through regular involvement in community projects, conservation work, voluntary work in hospitals or community homes or more specialized training such as lifesaving, first aid or rescue services.
- Expeditions: to encourage a spirit of adventure and discovery, understanding of the environment, and the importance of working together in a team with a common purpose. Expeditions may be made by foot, bicycle, boat or horseback, or in any equally challenging adventurous journey. Proper training and preparation, self-sufficiency, self-reliance and the exploration of new surroundings are the key elements. Participants frequently make their expeditions in countries other than their own.
- Skills: to encourage the discovery and development of personal interests and social and practical skills. There are over 200 hobby and vocational skills from which participants can choose, including photography, cacti growing, magazine production and metal work.
- Physical recreation: to encourage participation and improvement in physical activity. Participants are required to take part in some form of organized physical recreation and show individual progress. Most team and individual sports are included, such as football, athletics, archery, swimming and canoeing.
- At Gold level participants must also undertake a five-day residential project aimed at broadening their experience of living and working with others.

Originally launched in Britain in 1956, the Award programme quickly sparked huge interest in many other parts of the world, and its expanding internationalism was marked in 1988 by the formal establishment of the Duke of Edinburgh's International Award Association (IAA), with responsibility for the coordination and development of the Award worldwide. The IAA is made up of the National Award Authorities and Independent Operators of the Award.

The IAA is serviced by an International Secretariat based in London and managed by a Board of Trustees whose members come from many parts of the world. The Association is financially supported by the Duke of Edinburgh's Award International Foundation, a charitable company set up in the UK. This source provides funds for the core costs of the Association. Further funds are raised through charitable giving from individuals and corporations and from events held in different parts of the world.

The International Secretariat of the Association, comprising a secretary-general and a youthful team of 14 full-time staff, plays a vital role by:

- providing consultancy and support to members of the Association;
- assisting in coordinating their activities;
- maintaining international operational standards;
- promoting the Award to new countries and assisting with its establishment.

Due for review

With more and more countries joining the organization, and continuing growth in the numbers of young people entering the programme, the Award remains as relevant in the 21st century as it was in the 1950s. However, while successive new generations of participants were passing through the programme, the organization had maintained its fundamental shape and positioning. No fundamental review of the IAA, or the workings of the International Foundation (comprising the trustees and the secretariat), had been carried out for a decade, yet it was evident that during that time the world of young people and the organization itself had undergone many changes.

By 2003 it was time to take a thorough, professional look at the organization's strategy and operations in relation to its overall mission. The timing was apt, since Paul Arengo-Jones, the current Secretary-General (in effect the global CEO) was due to retire in a year's time and it was vital to specify the required profile of his successor before the recruitment process could start. The need to create the Secretary-General's profile in turn demanded a clear, up-to-date, agreed view of the aims and objectives of the organization and how they should be pursued and attained.

Financial stability had been achieved and maintained over the long period of Arengo-Jones's leadership. Extensive, energetic and creative fund-raising had ensured that the books were balanced. In more recent times a combination of external factors, including global recession and the events of September 11, caused a funding gap to appear. The funding gap was an added factor in prompting the decision to undertake a complete review of the organization.

The IAA decided that ideally the review would be undertaken by independent external consultants with global experience as well as in-depth knowledge of business strategy, finance, HR and organizational issues. The Association also wanted a team of consultants with a sound reputation and a world-class track record of advising major global organizations. This was not just a matter of practical qualifications: the Award's relationships with businesses and communities around the world form a key aspect of its presence, aims and funding opportunities. Capgemini agreed to take on the project on a *pro bono* basis, dedicating a small team of professionals keen to carry out such a strategic, all-encompassing project for an organization with a global span.

The IAA leadership decided from the start of the project that the Capgemini team would have complete freedom to go anywhere in the organization, talk to anybody, ask anything and see everything, including all documentation and financial records. The project's objective was to undertake a comprehensive strategic review of the organization's activities, structure and finances, identifying strengths and weaknesses and making appropriate recommendations for change. The team were asked to pull no punches in assembling their report and making their recommendations.

Laurence West, Capgemini's sponsor for the project, was impressed with the organization's open culture:

> The Secretary-General was very supportive right from the beginning, and we had excellent access. There were lots of currents of opinion, but the culture of the organization is that it's okay to have different opinions. The people there passionately believe in what they're doing. They were also keen to see how they compared to other organizations, including commercial ones.

Shaping the review process

The team divided the three-month review process into three phases. The first phase focused on gaining an understanding of the organization's current strengths and weaknesses, based on interviews, workshops, and financial analysis. The second phase addressed understanding stakeholder views and requirements through interviews with National Award Authorities, Independent Operators, donors, other youth organizations and trustees. This phase would also include identifying funding opportunities through strategic research and analysis. The third and final phase involved developing the organization's vision and mission through workshops and discussions with staff members and other stakeholders, and detailing how to implement them.

The team looked at all aspects of the organization's work including communications, branding, fundraising, corporate governance and finances. The team recognized the importance of seeking views from National Award Authorities and Independent Operators. These are the people who actually run the various Award schemes all around the world and who therefore have the closest appreciation of the organization's impact. The team interviewed a quarter of these key stakeholders in detail in order to discover which of the services provided centrally were of highest value, of medium value and of lower value. The project involved both one-to-one interviews and a series of group workshops, some of which were held at Buckingham Palace and Windsor Castle.

Paul Arengo-Jones recalls the largest workshop was held offsite at Capgemini's offices:

> All our directors, staff and regional directors were in for the annual regional meeting. We put aside one day for an offsite workshop where the consultants would tell us what they'd found out so far. We could all pose questions, there were breakout groups on different issues and we all reported back. We deliberately chose to have the workshop on neutral ground, and we had a facilitator for the day who was not involved with the project to maintain the objectivity.

Right from the start, the team stressed the importance of whole-hearted buy-in from each full-time member of the Secretariat's 14-strong staff. As with any review involving external consultants, staff members might have been worried about possible job losses or work restructuring. But, as Paul Arengo-Jones points out:

> The consultants handled everything very sensitively and diplomatically. They got everyone involved, so that nobody felt excluded. Once staff realized that they would be included and treated equally they all realized they had something to say. The staff sessions were once a week, and everyone was given specific tasks to do; for instance, researching a particular topic for the next session. It was very inclusive: it wasn't just someone in a corner, beavering away.

Capgemini's West adds that the consultants' external perspective was highly valued, which helped to build trust: 'People are inevitably influenced by their existing situation. We could add value simply by being independent and objective.'

The need for buy-in extended to the IAA's membership. Membership of the IAA is entirely voluntary, with the National Award Authorities around the world having complete freedom of choice as to whether or not they belong to the Association. The organization therefore has to take its members with it, and demonstrate continuing relevance to their aims and circumstances. Any proposals for change would have to be cogently argued, transparently rational and likely to be universally accepted. The organization could not resort to anything resembling a 'command-and-control' governance culture, an option that remains possible for even the most empowered commercial company.

A road map for the future

The team's report was submitted to the Board of Trustees on time in April 2003 following a 12-week schedule of interviews, workshops and analysis sessions. The report identified a number of fundamental strengths and weaknesses in the current pattern of operations, as well as some important opportunities for, and potential threats to, further development.

The report also proposed a reformulation of the International Foundation's statement of strategic intent. The revised statement would clarify and distinguish between its vision, its mission, and its overall strategy in achieving its mission. The report included a detailed picture of what the International Foundation would ideally look like in 2012, and outlined a three-phase programme of short-term, medium-term and long-term change to achieve this position.

A number of detailed recommendations were made in the report. Within three months of the report's delivery, the majority of the recommendations had been accepted in full and implementations begun.

The first outcome of the review was a strategy of regionalization, with four regions and full-time regional directors confirmed as the best structure for the future. The review recommended that the regional offices be enhanced to play a greater role in the delivery of the Award programme worldwide and in the maintenance of quality and standards.

The staff roles within the Secretariat would also be clarified. Alongside the ongoing development of the regions, clarification would result in a more focused and improved service to the IAA. Then a profile of the capabilities required by the new secretary-general to be appointed upon the retirement of Paul Arengo-Jones in 2004 would be developed. This profile would help ensure that the new appointment became a positive and logical step in the continuing development of the Association and its aim to remain as the foremost global Award programme for young people.

The report also addressed the marketing of the organization. Given that after 15 years the Association had matured into a global youth charity, the vast experience and capability of National Award Authorities and Independent Operators would be accessed to help others. At the same time the global brand (the 'global bird' symbol) of the Duke of Edinburgh's International Award for Young People needed greater exposure and marketing so that more support could be generated from governments and other funding sources for the development of the Award worldwide.

A quarter of National Award Authorities and a small but significant number of Independent Operators were interviewed by the team for the review process. Their feedback showed that these organizations valued the IAA's production of operational materials, especially those aimed at provisional NAAs. The interviewees also praised the advice and consultancy they received from London and from the regional offices. They appreciated the regular communication from the Secretariat, the regular *Award World* publication and the organization's annual report. Secretariat visits to participating countries were valued, as were international training courses and events.

The interviewees scored other services as being of medium value. These included promotional materials produced for participants, since the use of the English language in the publications limits their use in some countries. Lack of access to IT facilities presented some challenges to Internet and intranet use. Interviewees did not generally value the availability of IAA branded goods such as T-shirts, as most NAAs can produce these locally more cheaply than the IAA can.

A detailed action plan to implement the report's recommendations was prepared by the Secretariat in summer 2003. Paul Arengo-Jones estimates that around 70 per cent of the recommendations were adopted without change: 'Some of the suggestions were instantly acceptable, others didn't necessarily work for us as a charity.'

The first actions of phase one of the change programme include new fundraising plans with clearly specified targets. These plans are linked to a new events calendar and new communications material for donors. Detailed plans were also produced for the launch of a 'Young Fellowship' to bridge the age gap between those entering for the Awards and those sponsoring and supporting the scheme.

Further actions included the development during 2003–04 of a revised process for a rolling three-year budget. The new budget process includes involvement from all budget holders and is supported by improved finance and accounting procedures. Work began on the reorientation of the organization's annual report specifically to support marketing and fundraising requirements, and development of written job specifications for all staff to recognize reallocated roles, key objectives and training requirements.

Paul Arengo-Jones states:

> The strategic review was a most excellent and thorough piece of work. It provided us with an independent and objective analysis of our position and made clear which areas and activities were in good shape within our organization and which needed sorting. It was a wonderful catalyst for a whole series of changes which are now being put into operation with good effect. With the resulting new strategy in place, everyone here is now facing the future with renewed confidence. When I can hand over to my successor next year, it will be an organization headed in totally the right direction, and I can be confident that the Award will continue to thrive and succeed in the 21st century as well as it did in the second half of the 20th.

This project shows how even a broadly based international organization that has effectively invented its own business domain can benefit from an outside eye. Managers in the midst of a successful business that touches the lives of millions around the world are not always best placed to see how their organization could be improved and their services developed. As relationships develop in a distributed concern like the Duke of Edinburgh's International Award community, the way forward can easily become obscured by the minutiae of operations and the very maintenance of those all-important relationships. Capgemini were able to act as midwives to the future: bringing out the logical conclusions for the IAA's strategy from the organization's stakeholders. The team's success has released the organization's future spirit from its current experience – much as the IAA's 'global bird' icon symbolizes the freedom, growth and determination of the many thousands of young people who participate in the Award.

Capgemini's contribution must also be measured at the personal level. Management consultants have been accused of packaging their methodologies in the pursuit of repeatable and scalable engagements. The knowledge that is acquired in each project can be fed into the firm's methodologies, and the methodologies help to sell and structure future engagements. But consulting is not the application of formulae or the cranking of methodological handles. Consulting is a process carried out by people, with people, and for people. The IAA team was impressed with the personal commitment of the consultants assigned to this project. Their persistence and flexibility alike were valued by Arengo-Jones: 'The personalities have to gel well for it to work, because there is a degree of upset and suspicion at the start. The consultants were professional and energetic, but also brought a wealth of experience. They made themselves available – even in the pub after work!'

7

Technology exploitation

The four case studies in this chapter illustrate the extent to which IT and IT consulting have evolved over the last 10 years.

In the mid-1990s, it was the private sector that set the pace. A large-scale IT project might have required hundreds of consultants working with a much smaller team from the client side. Typically, it would have involved the implementation of new software that had to be tailored to meet the specific business needs and had to run on new hardware.

Today's IT challenges – and the pioneers responding to them – are vastly different. Three of the four organizations featured in this chapter are from the public sector; all are setting trends in the way in which they are using established technology for new ends. The scale and complexity of the projects are, if anything, greater. The technology used in London's congestion charging scheme involves cameras and software capable of 'reading' car registration plates. Drivers can pay their charge either via a network of electronic point-of-sale terminals in stores in and around London, via the Internet or via SMS text messaging. For the UK's Home Office, trying to bring together information on persistent offenders from a variety of independent agencies, complexity lay in the differences between the various organizations with different business processes, even between the ways in which those agencies counted offences. The problem the All England Lawn Tennis Club faced was almost the opposite: not so much getting information in from a wide array of stakeholders, but getting the information required to keep Wimbledon, one of the world's premier sporting occasions, out for spectators, players, television viewers, the press and officials. Every day of the two-week competition 120,000 statistics had to be captured and disseminated. Bradford Teaching Hospital NHS Trust depended on supplies of nearly 250,000 stock and a further 48,000 non-stock items. The trust relied upon a largely paper-based system in which each department had its own catalogue, orders took too long to fulfil, could not be tracked, and had to checked and corrected at many stages in the process. In this environment, there appear to be five hallmarks of success.

FIVE HALLMARKS OF SUCCESS

Making good use of tried and tested 'new' technology

Each of the organizations featured in the case studies in this chapter faced significant challenges. London's was the world's largest congestion charging scheme to be developed. The JTrack system for the Criminal Justice System involved the input of 43 police forces and 42 Crown Prosecution Service areas. The Bradford Teaching Hospital NHS Trust needed a system that would centralize procurement while simultaneously allowing clinicians to make requisitions as they moved around wards. But the solutions found did not involve state-of-the-art technology: instead, existing technology was used in new ways. SMS text messaging was one of the ways in which Transport for London (TfL) made paying the capital's new congestion charge as convenient as possible. JTrack provided the agencies involved in the persistent offenders' scheme with secure access to Web-hosted software. Clinicians in Bradford were given PocketPC devices enabling them to place orders through a wireless network. After the excesses of the e-business boom, organizations have focused their efforts on leveraging existing technology in innovative ways, rather than investing in new systems. The All England Lawn Tennis Club also used personal digital assistants (PDAs), to get information to important people likely to be roaming around the site – club officials, VIPs, and special guests – the first time that this technology had been used on this scale anywhere in the world.

Heterogeneity, not uniformity

Whereas the monolithic systems of the 1990s were predicated on the idea of bringing the disparate functions of an organization together by standardizing processes and centralizing control, the initiatives described in these case studies are indicative of a very different approach. Rather than trying to impose uniform technology on UK police forces, JTrack provided a secure, easy-to-use way to update and access information in a variety of formats to cope with the different business processes and counting rules used by the different organizations. Rather than try to make all central London drivers use one method of payment, JTrack allowed them to choose a method convenient to them, leaving behind-the-scenes technology to link everything together. Because each of these initiatives relied on the cooperation of a wide array of stakeholders, a top-down approach was never going to work. To encourage take-up, the different needs of potential users had to be worked with, not ignored.

Versatility and flexibility

Of course, taking a wide range of different requirements into account necessitates not only intense user involvement, but also an ability to respond to changes. None of these projects would have succeeded if those in charge had adopted a rigid approach, refusing to adjust the specifications as the project progressed. The congestion charging scheme was just too high profile for there not to be considerable political and media pressure influencing the form the final scheme would take. Bringing together so many systems and types of technology meant that mistakes were inevitable; lessons had to be learned. The Home Office concludes: 'Planning is essential to reducing risks and increasing the chances of success, but planning only takes you so far. After that, success is dependent on a flexible and cooperative approach which enables changes in scope and timescales to be accommodated and overcome.'

At Wimbledon, there was an issue with the number and varieties of use to which the match data could be put (players needed different information to commentators; online viewers wanted other information again). This was solved by having a single, central database from which a wide range of 'feeds' could be drawn.

Speed

But flexibility can be a double-edged sword: ensuring that the final system will meet a complex set of requirements increases the risk of delay. Too many changes can make a project seem never-ending. Yet all of these projects were completed to tight deadlines. PA Consulting Group used its Rapid Systems Development techniques and iterative prototyping in order to complete a pilot version of JTrack within just eight weeks. London's congestion charging scheme was implemented in two and a half years, one year less than an independent study had predicted it would take. It took the Bradford Teaching Hospital Trust only three months to pilot its new procurement system and assess the benefits. Like flexibility, speed plays an important part in building the credibility of a new system and increasing its take-up by users; if the people implementing a system are taking it seriously, then those supposed to use it will do so as well.

Multi-sourcing

The IT department of 10 years ago might well have expected large-scale projects to be undertaken by a single supplier, but it is rare these days for clients to 'single source'. The complexity of the work and technology involved means that it is increasingly hard for a single supplier to provide all the expertise required in-house: instead, they are more likely to focus on those areas of a project where their expertise is greatest and sub-contract other aspects to other specialists. Moreover, clients looking for world-class expertise – masters of one trade, rather than jacks of none – are better informed about which supplier excels in which area. Pulling together and managing consortia, especially where large-scale, complex programmes are concerned, has become a key skill for clients and consultants alike.

IT CONSULTING: LEANER AND FITTER?

For IT consultants, each of the five factors above represents a significant change in their way of working: indeed, to a large extent, IT consulting has had to reinvent itself since the late 1990s. Internet technology made it possible to link people in different organizations, using different hardware and software. Concerns about the speed with which the market was moving meant that companies wanted the implementation of new systems to take months, rather than years. The continuing failure of a large proportion of new systems to deliver the expected benefits depressed demand for them, and encouraged managers to find ways of using their existing technology more effectively. More attention was paid to the obstacles that prevent systems from being used effectively.

As these cases demonstrate, the new model IT consultant is very different from his or her predecessor. Instead of staffing complete projects, from project managers to junior programmers, the consulting firms involved here worked side by side with their clients. Deloitte's role in London's congestion charging scheme was to provide overall management and coordination of the 16,000 separate tasks and 20 separate organizations involved. In fact, Deloitte maintained only a relatively small number of consultants on the project full-time, choosing rather to bring in expert consultants only when they were needed. The firm also supplemented its use of consultants with a formal programme aimed at transferring skills from its consultants to TfL's own staff. PA's team worked with people from the Justice Gap Action Team and the other justice agencies, they did not supplant them. Similarly, at the Bradford Teaching Hospitals Trust, Atos Origin was there to facilitate the process of reconciling the potentially conflicting needs of users, not just to develop a wireless procurement system. Even at Wimbledon, where IBM fielded by far the biggest team (of the projects described here) in order to support the systems during the annual Championships, the main development team was only half a dozen people who worked closely with the All England Lawn Tennis Club.

The acid test for consulting though is whether it can help a client organization do what the client cannot do for itself. So where did the consultants add most value?

Part of the value they added was unquestionably technical knowledge. Given the speed with which new products come to market, it is hard for a client organization to stay abreast of developments, and even harder to maintain some understanding of how those developments may be being exploited in practice. For IT consulting firms, this knowledge is a critical activity, and one that is increasingly fostered by joint product development programmes and training initiatives between hardware and software manufacturers, and consulting firms. Consulting firms can achieve better 'economies of knowledge' than their clients. Because the cost of the investment a firm makes in technical knowledge is effectively spread across many clients, clients can access up-to-date skills more cheaply than if they had to build these skills themselves.

Another area where the help of consultants can be invaluable is where they are asked to act as honest brokers, arbitrating between the needs of different groups without having any self-interested axe to grind. It is often hard for organizations that are in the early stages of specifying complex systems to be able to step back and see the situation objectively.

However, perhaps the consultants' most important contribution here was momentum. With multiple stakeholders to consult, different technology platforms to integrate and significant cultural barriers to acceptance, the stage was undoubtedly set – in all three projects – for constant delay. While the congestion charging scheme had the advantage of being a completely new project, both JTrack and the procurement system at the Bradford Teaching Hospitals NHS Trust were developed alongside existing operations. Most of those involved in specifying the systems – the end-users – had busy day jobs: getting and keeping their attention was always going to be an uphill struggle when there were so many other, more immediate calls on their time. In each case, the consultants were able to provide the momentum and critical mass to keep the projects going. 'We could not have done this project without consultants,' said Derek Turner, the Managing Director of Street Management at TfL. 'Our confidence in Deloitte was well placed. Their passion and drive for this project helped it stay on track and deliver benefits to London.'

SUMMARY – KEY LESSONS FOR MANAGERS AND CONSULTANTS

- The best IT projects involve using recent, but still familiar, technology for new ends. Web-based and wireless technologies undoubtedly offer unparalleled opportunities to link people and organizations together, irrespective of their location or existing software. But technology does not have to be state-of-the-art for it to be used imaginatively.

- Finding ways to meet the often divergent needs of multiple stake-holders is a better guarantor of success than trying to override them. Users who think their interests have been neglected rarely have any desire to make a new system a success. However, the willingness to compromise and change has to be tempered with the need to get things done. Among organizations anxious to avoid the long-drawn-out implementation cycles of 10 years ago, the speed with which a system can be completed is crucial to management commitment, user acceptance and benefits realization.

- Old-style IT consulting would sit uncomfortably with this brave new world, and the last decade has seen significant changes in the way IT consultants work as a result. In place of armies of consultants that still haunt client memories from the 1990s, have come smaller teams, working side by side with client staff. While a small number of consultants play a longer-term coordinating role, the majority are used only when necessary, where the client lacks a particular skill.

- But it is momentum, above technical knowledge and working style, that clients still put at the top of their agenda when it comes to working with IT consultants. As projects become more complex, both in technical and human terms, the need to have some means by which energy is injected has become fundamental to success.

CASE STUDY 7.1

CLOSING THE NET ON PERSISTENT OFFENDERS

Tracking persistent offenders through a shared case-oriented system is part of an initiative to ensure that fewer criminals slip through the justice net. Multiple agencies and viewpoints have been reconciled in an application that ties together different components of the Criminal Justice System and delivers tangible results to the public.

Dealing with crime and its effects on the community is high on the agenda of any government. We judge the health of our society by our sense of personal security, and we judge society's development by the quality of its justice. Justice famously needs to be seen to be done. With the increasing sophistication of policing methods and the continued development of the law, those who manage to evade justice stand out as challenges to the system. Offenders who are not brought to justice offend the public's sense that we are in control of the social environment, and that the values we hold are universally honoured.

Recognizing the stubborn and highly visible nature of this problem, the UK Criminal Justice System created a strategy called Narrowing the Justice Gap. The strategy was to bring together all the agencies dealing with the problem of bringing offenders to justice, and particularly the most persistent offenders. Speaking at the launch of the strategy in October 2002, the Home Office Minister for Criminal Justice Reform Lord Falconer said:

> The CJS [Criminal Justice System] has halved the time it takes to deal with persistent young offenders from arrest to sentence. Building on this work, an early focus of Narrowing the Justice Gap is a strategy to clamp down on adult persistent offenders by bringing them to book for more offences and making them give up their life of crime. Home Office research shows that 100,000 criminals are responsible for half of all recorded crime and increasing the frequency of an offender being caught and convicted is the most effective single way of shortening their criminal career.

The strategy is implemented through the Persistent Offender Scheme, launched in February 2003. The scheme's aim is to target the most prolific adult offenders. These are individuals who have been convicted of six or more recordable offences in the previous year, together with other offenders identified by local police intelligence.

Progress had already been made in dealing with persistent young offenders. In 1997 the government announced its Persistent Young

Offenders Pledge to halve the time it takes to sentence persistent young offenders from the time they were arrested. The pledge was due for delivery by May 2002. The government calculated that in 1996 dealing with a persistent young offender took an average of 142 days. The pledge was in fact met by June 2001 when the time was cut to only 69 days, beating the government's target by 2 days. This performance has since been consistently sustained.

A key element of the new Persistent Offender Scheme was to be the introduction of a new IT tool. This new Web-based system, called JTrack, would easily identify for criminal justice agencies those prolific offenders who met the new persistent offender definition, and also allow police locally to flag up their persistent offenders. These offenders are responsible for a range of crimes, including theft, burglary, and crimes of violence such as robbery and criminal damage. JTrack would also enable these offenders to be tracked by the police and Crown Prosecution Service (CPS).

The police would be able to use the new tool in conjunction with local intelligence systems including the National Intelligence Model in order to identify and prioritize those offenders having six convictions in one year and other prolific offenders that need to be targeted locally. When these offenders are caught, the criminal justice agencies will give priority to their cases to ensure that they are brought to justice for as many of their offences as effectively and speedily as possible. This 'premium service' was already being piloted in the areas covered by the government's earlier street crime initiative and became a core component part of the Persistent Offender Scheme.

Lord Falconer went on to say:

> Too few offenders are brought to justice. In 2000–01 over 5 million crimes were recorded by police but in only 20 per cent were offenders brought to justice. The current size of the justice gap is unacceptable, we can and must do better. Narrowing the Justice Gap is a key measure of the effectiveness of the Criminal Justice System and a crucial indicator of success in reducing crime.

JTrack was to be an important driver for the Persistent Offender Scheme, and was intended to help spur further improvements throughout the justice process. Yvette Cooper, Minister at the Lord Chancellor's Department added:

> We have already made progress in cutting delays, in particular halving the time from arrest to sentence for persistent young offenders, but

over 50 per cent of trials still do not start on time. This causes unnecessary stress for victims and witnesses and increases the risk that cases may collapse completely. We are developing new measures to set out the timetable for trials, and provide incentives for defence and prosecution to get cases ready on time.

A new multi-departmental team called the Justice Gap Action Team (JGAT) was created to act on behalf of the three UK government departments responsible for overseeing the Criminal Justice System (CJS) in England and Wales: the Home Office itself, the Department for Constitutional Affairs and the CPS. In May 2002 JGAT asked PA Consulting Group to help create JTrack and deliver the system by 1 April 2003. A combined JGAT/PA team, working with all the relevant partner agencies, designed, developed and implemented the system in under six months. JTrack is now improving levels of collaboration between the country's 43 police forces and 42 CPS areas.

A multi-agency system

The first multi-agency application of its kind in the UK, JTrack is a Web-based system hosted on a secure network accessible by over 2,500 authorized users throughout England and Wales. The various agencies use the same set of information to manage crime and provide real-time management information. JTrack enables practitioners in the police and CPS to track the progress and results of cases from arrest to finalization in a consistent way, including not only persistent offender cases but also street crimes. Within four months of its implementation, there were already over 42,000 offences on the system. Work is under way to consider extending JTrack to other agencies such as the Probation Service and the courts.

The application mirrors the development of case-oriented systems in the business world. This type of system is a workflow response to the fragmented nature of the information held about an enterprise's customers. The focus of case-oriented systems is the progress of a piece of information-intensive work that requires the attention of a number of different specialists at different stages and in different organizations.

In the commercial environment, established organizations have traditionally suffered from fragmented views of their customers. Customer information is distributed among a range of different business systems, and aggregating data is cumbersome and expensive. Since businesses grow in response to market demand, it is natural that they develop systems in response to new opportunities, rather than for the purposes of improving overall management understanding of the customer base.

In the past, a company contemplating the launch of a new product would build a new system to support delivery of that product. Similarly, a company reaching out to a new market segment would design a new system for that business stream. At the same time company mergers and acquisitions frequently enlarge the number of logically overlapping systems in the organization.

One answer to this problem is to create a common view of the customer via a data warehouse or using a collaborative layer that brings together data from disparate systems. However, this approach tends to produce retrospective information, which may be excellent for business development purposes, but rarely helpful in serving customers directly. Customer-centric systems are therefore now built to support customer service under the banner of customer relationship management (CRM). CRM applications typically support call centres and other customer touch points where the initiator of any event is the customer rather than the enterprise.

Case-oriented applications solve the fragmentation problem in a different manner. The driver of this class of business systems is the standard work-in-progress that unites the various teams involved in pursuing the business goal. In a city planning office, for example, the central work-in-progress is the 'planning application'. This is a growing body of documentation incorporating plans, proposals, amendments, surveys, citations and consultations. The efficiency and effectiveness of the planning department depends entirely on its ability to manage the throughput of each case, ensuring that each dimension of the work is addressed in a complete and timely manner.

In the justice system, different agencies will measure their effectiveness in different ways, such as by offence, offender or case (which may have multiple offences and offenders). Part of the challenge of JTrack was to construct a system that could capture information in a consistent way across all agencies but present the data in a format that staff in agencies could understand.

Every case-oriented application calls for careful attention to the multiple complex requirements of the different teams involved on progressing the core work in progress. PA used its rapid systems development (RSD) methodology to capture requirements and deliver the project on time. RSD is an iterative technique that involves users and other stakeholders in the design and development of a system from day one. Consistent user involvement and application prototyping are at the heart of RSD, so the methodology ensured that all stakeholders' requirements were taken into account throughout the development process.

Threading the multi-agency web

The JGAT/PA team and its partner justice agencies quickly agreed the need to track persistent offenders across the criminal justice system so that all agencies could tackle them effectively. Agencies also required real-time access to consistent management information at both national and local levels so their performance could be effectively monitored.

There were, however, significant obstacles to providing the necessary information. First, the existing local case management systems could not track persistent offender cases across agencies, or provide consistent up-to-date local and national management information. Each system was an island of information.

Second, the only potential national source of management information was the Police National Computer. However, this system could not provide information where it was needed most – at the local level – since it was primarily designed as an operational system rather than a management tool, and had no reporting capabilities.

The team next found that the various agencies used different means of counting crimes. Some counted offenders while others counted cases that might involve several offenders and crimes. These inconsistencies made it impossible to measure cross-agency effectiveness, with no common method of measuring how successfully agencies were dealing with persistent offenders.

The fourth obstacle encountered by the team was located in the existing organizational schedules. Current strategic programmes to 'join up' the different agencies of the Criminal Justice System would not deliver for at least three to five years. The Persistent Offender Scheme needed a solution by 1 April 2003, the formal start of the scheme and the date from which its performance targets would apply. The team would somehow have to square these conflicting timelines.

Fifth, the team had to deal with an absence of key performance indicators (KPIs). Because of the deadline set for the project, the new solution would need to be built while KPIs for the Persistent Offender Scheme were being defined. The time constraints also ruled out some of the standard approaches to systems development in a complex environment. PA's Andrew Hooke explains:

> Developing a system to track persistent offenders was a gap in the market, as it were. This system is bringing new information into the process. At the feasibility stage you normally look at making enhancements and linkages to existing systems. But because we were driven by the time frame, only a bespoke system, built from scratch, would do. Then we'd

need to ensure the appropriate linkages with other systems as part of ongoing maintenance work.

Lastly, a poor track record of IT delivery within the Criminal Justice System had made local users understandably cynical about new IT initiatives. They were unwilling to commit to using new systems, and JGAT had no powers to force them to do so.

Overcoming the obstacles

Meeting the project's deadline was the key determinant in the team's choice of approach. The team used PA's RSD techniques to develop the system through an iterative prototyping process. RSD made it possible to have a version of JTrack ready for piloting within just eight weeks. Working with selected police and CPS users, the development team subjected this first pilot version of the system to intensive review, testing and redevelopment.

The team then exploited existing communications networks to make the system accessible to all agencies without the delay inherent in implementing a new IT infrastructure. JTrack was hosted on the Criminal Justice Extranet (CJX), a secure national infrastructure. This was the first time that the CJX had been used for such an application.

Although identifying the CJX as a route to delivering the system was a distinct benefit to the project, obtaining the required hosting permission within tight timescales was a challenge in itself. Any system has to be formally accredited by the Police Information Technology Organisation (PITO) prior to its use on the CJX. However, since the CJX had not been used for a cross-agency system, there was no clear accreditation path. The team worked closely with PITO and secured accreditation in under six months, an impressive turnaround given the vast scope of the system.

When it came to measuring business performance, the team had to make JTrack flexible enough to accommodate the different counting rules used by the police, the CPS and other agencies, while providing the consistent means of measurement required by the Persistent Offender Scheme. JTrack was therefore designed to use offences as its core measurement unit, but offers the ability for users from different agencies to view and input information in the way they are used to, whether by case or by offender.

The team also recommended that JTrack be designed to track street crime cases, and thereby replace local tracking systems. The system was built with these requirements in mind and all street crime areas have subsequently migrated to using JTrack.

To make the system as flexible as possible in use, the team gave JTrack many optional elements that can be turned on and off to suit different users. For example, the system can be used to track local priority groups of offenders, as well as the nationally defined persistent offender and street crime groups, thus meeting both national and local performance reporting requirements.

JTrack can generate a range of performance reports at divisional, area and national levels, as well as enabling areas to compare their performance with other areas. In addition, users can easily and flexibly download subsets of the database to undertake their own performance analysis. PA's Hooke stresses that communicating the local and national benefits of the system was crucial to developing a system that would be usable, and used:

> You have to look at the system from at least two dimensions. The first is meeting the government's requirement for a central view and measuring progress in meeting national initiatives. The second is that you've got to provide something of use to local practitioners. The position is: I'm not coming here with a centrally driven initiative – my primary aim is local management information that will help you manage your business. Then the local people take more interest, they begin to buy into the project, and they're more ready to build the KPIs.

The RSD methodology helped the team respond to changing user requirements during the project's life cycle. The Persistent Offender Scheme was changing as JTrack was being built. Halfway through the development, it was decided that the Persistent Offender Scheme needed extra flexibility to allow for local definitions of persistent offenders. RSD enabled the team to respond quickly to these developments, while safeguarding core functionality and respecting delivery commitments.

The system was developed using Web technology and XML, a means of creating, storing and processing self-describing data. This architecture makes JTrack easy to maintain and enhance.

The methodologies and technologies chosen by the team ensured the technical capability and quality of JTrack. But even the best-designed systems can founder in the face of user disinterest. Intensive user involvement was critical if JTrack was to be accepted by its diverse user base spanning 43 police forces and 42 CPS areas. Fortunately the RSD methodology allows users to drive the direction and scope of the development process. The team established a core group of users who, together with Home Office and CPS national representatives, helped to define how JTrack would work and look, down to the level of individual page layouts. In this way the team ensured that from day one JTrack's design was informed by the real needs of users.

Working closely with the system's target users allowed the team to define extra features that increased JTrack's usefulness to local users. For example, the system includes an interface with the Police National Computer so that it can transmit details of persistent offenders to JTrack every month. This feature enables users to track offenders not only in their own area but also in adjacent areas. While the representative users effectively drove the development process, the team kept all stakeholder groups abreast of progress and helped them prepare to connect to, and make effective use of, the system. As the go-live date approached, the team trained more than 1,500 users, completing the process within 10 weeks. This training played an important role in convincing local users that the system could help them in their work.

As the cases flow, the justice gap closes

JTrack was ready for roll out by December 2002, just five months from the start of the formal development project in July and a month ahead of schedule. Take-up of the system was enthusiastic. All areas were connected to JTrack and had started to use it by 1 April 2003. As of 1 July 2003, there were 2,358 users and 42,960 offences on the system.

In August 2003, JGAT commissioned a review to evaluate the first few months of the Persistent Offender Scheme. Initial reaction to JTrack was that it was a good system. The majority of users found it straightforward and simple to use. Managers were beginning to take advantage of the rich and comprehensive data now held on JTrack. In particular, several areas said that JTrack was a valuable management tool for tracking local priority offenders.

JTrack is, of course, not an end in itself. Its true value lies in its contribution to the overall process of reducing crime rates, bringing more criminals to justice and so building greater public confidence in the justice system. JTrack is helping progress towards these objectives by providing a real-time tool that coordinates the agencies' efforts and provides shared visibility of actual progress. JTrack is encouraging effective joint working at a local level. For the first time, agencies in the criminal justice sector are able to share common data with one another. While accommodating each agency's preferred ways of working, JTrack provides consistent local and national measurement. Users can now compare their performance regarding persistent offenders and street crime with achievements in other parts of the country. Performance data is now available daily and monthly for all areas. Previously this information was either not available at all, or was at least six months out of date.

The team's achievement in bringing the system to delivery in such a complex organizational environment is recognized by those within the IT community. The Head of Information Systems & Technology at Durham Police says:

> This has been one of the smoothest IT projects I have been involved with for a long time. PA's contribution was key to this smoothness. By using the firm's own flavour of rapid applications development, PA managed to reconcile different needs, opinions and worries by centring the project on the production of a usable system. This allowed the team to progress issues constructively and demonstrate progress through successive iterations of the system, rather than tackling a cumbersome process made up of meetings and documentation.

PA also demonstrated a highly valued attribute of the best consulting practices: the ability to go beyond the formal scope of the project when needed. John Kennedy, JGAT's project manager, recognizes that making the system available on the existing network was a major plus point: 'PA also provided support above and beyond remit by helping us select the hosting provider and successfully negotiating CJX accreditation.'

Significantly, the system's contribution to the fight against crime is also recognized at the sharp end of policing. A detective inspector with Hampshire Police says: 'This is the first system where volume crime offenders are captured in one net. Each area now has the opportunity to pick the most prolific offenders and concentrate on dealing with them proactively and effectively.'

It is fitting that a network of cooperating agencies has been able to use Internet technologies to help close the net on the UK's persistent offenders. As a result, the criminal justice system is on its way to meeting its target of bringing 1.2 million offences to justice by 2005–06.

CASE STUDY 7.2

GREAT JOURNEYS AND SMALL STEPS

The Mayor of London's ambitious plan to unclog the city's streets trig-gered one of the world's most complex and pressurized projects. The targeted use of practical methodologies and a can-do attitude got the work done on time, and London's traffic is flowing once again.

Roads form one of the modern world's scarcest and most fought-over resources. While the fuel that powers our vehicles is continuously won from the earth with ingenuity and care, often miles from where we live and work, the roads we drive on do not expand to match our appetite for travel. Road scarcity is no more pronounced than in the world's great cities, where accommodation may grow vertically, but surface transportation is constrained. Old cities with peculiar, evolved street patterns fare worst from the relentless onslaught of traffic. London's millennial traffic crawled at the same average pace achieved by horse-drawn carts a century earlier, and vehicles typically spent half their journeys waiting in queues. The impact of slow-moving traffic on the environment was particularly obvious in London's new tradition of summer photochemical smog – 'peasoupers' to rival the fogs its clean-air Acts had banished from the winter scene in the 1950s. And road congestion was calculated to cost the city's business community some £2 million every week.

The concept of charging for road usage has been circulating in pol-icy circles since at least 1951, when economist Milton Friedman co-wrote an essay in which he proposed charging road users a fee 'in proportion to their use' of the highway. While this proposal is per-fectly in line with free-market thinking, its political implications made decision-makers steer clear of it. Pricing road usage as a means of manipulating demand clashed with the ideals of personal liberty represented by car ownership. Governments had invested in the development of the automobile industry and in roads infrastructure through general and specific taxation. To bar drivers from the road system they had paid for was, for generations, a step no politician was willing to take.

Ken Livingstone, the first elected Mayor of London, made the con-cept of congestion charging for the central London area a major ele-ment of his campaign for office. Livingstone had shown during his leadership of the now defunct Greater London Council (GLC) that he was not afraid to apply pricing mechanisms to the city's trans-port system. The GLC's 'Fares Fair' scheme of the mid-1980s for the

Underground system was ruled illegal, but not before causing a measurable improvement to services. This time around, the pricing mechanism had been cleared by central government in 1999. The Mayor's Transport Strategy of July 2001 promised a central London charging zone by February 2003.

The objectives of the overall two-and-a-half-year plan were to:

- reduce traffic levels by 10 per cent to 15 per cent;
- reduce congestion by 20 per cent to 30 per cent;
- generate net revenue for investment in public transport;
- achieve a habitual shift from private to public transport.

From an academic theory that horrified elected representatives to a working scheme on the ground, impacting (and even impeding) the lives of millions of Londoners – within two years. Could it be done? The complexity of the task created one of largest and most publicly scrutinized risk management challenges the world has ever seen.

A sense of volume

Deloitte was hired to programme manage the creation and roll-out of the congestion charge scheme. The firm's team would work closely with management at Transport for London (TfL) and sit above the many other service providers needed to deliver congestion charging, and be involved right the way through to delivery. A key responsibility was technical assurance of all the various elements being procured and deployed for the scheme. The team was therefore acting as a source of continuity for a programme containing many diverse elements as well as performing a quality assurance role. The programme management challenge can be summed up in a handful of numbers. Deloitte designed eight work streams articulating over 430 projects, representing more than 45,000 separate tasks needed to deliver the scheme on its set launch date of 17 February 2003.

The scale and complexity of the delivery responsibility becomes clear when we appreciate the physical, political, and cultural dimensions of the scheme. In the first place, the congestion charging zone would cover an area of 21 square kilometres, containing some of the most obscure road patterns built. The zone would create a new entity on the map of London, and impose a new border. Many thousands of vehicles would flow across this permeable barrier every day, and each would have to be accounted for.

An occupying power might simply impose the charging scheme on the citizenry, in the historic tradition of roadblocks. But this scheme was being implemented by London for London. There would be an 18-month consultation process, running from the announcement of the strategy right up until the last practicable minute prior to launch of the scheme. The consultation process was designed to include presentations, public meetings and public exhibitions. In the event the debate also continued in the local, national and international media. A legal challenge from Westminster City Council (WCC) also led to the scheme's consideration (and approval) in the courts. Communication with London's many stakeholders was crucial to the success of the scheme, both during its development and ultimately for its smooth operation after launch. The resulting public communications exercise was the largest seen in the UK since the 'Ask Sid' campaign for the privatization of British Gas.

Tollbooths would have added to congestion rather than reducing it, and electronic methods for charging vehicles were nowhere near ready for market. To make the scheme work, a network of more than 600 enforcement cameras, both fixed and mobile, would have to be installed. These would be sited at 174 access points on the zone's boundary as well as at roadside sites throughout the zone. Camera images would be fed to interpretative systems that would in turn cross-refer to databases of payments. Taken together as a system, the monitoring element of the scheme became Europe's largest camera and telecoms procurement contract.

The scheme's designers estimated that around 200,000 vehicles would use the zone each day. Each single instance of a vehicle crossing the zone's boundary would be monitored and checked against its payment status. The technology needed to read vehicle registration plates and relate them to vehicle databases had already been proven in the 'ring of steel' around the City of London. However, the business processes and systems needed to take payments from drivers had no single working precedent that could be scaled up to the new challenge. Making it easy for Londoners to pay was paramount to the scheme's design. Although there would be penalties for those who refused to pay, the primary purpose of the congestion charge scheme was to influence road usage rather than generate defaulters. In order to make the payment options as broad and inclusive as possible, a wide number of methods were introduced including via SMS text messaging. No one could predict how many people would use this latter channel. In the event 12 per cent of users chose to pay in this way at the start of the scheme, rising to 19 per cent within three months.

The scheme also entailed the use of building an EPOS (electronic point of sale) retail terminal network running in over 200 central London stores. There would be a further 1,500 outlets within the orbital M25 motorway, and more than 7,000 other locations throughout the UK. More than 100 self-service payment machines would be located at destination car parks. Fleet operators would have their own post-payment solution.

While the pricing mechanism proposed by Friedman provides the central rationale of the congestion charging scheme, the project would also involve a number of micro-measures to further improve traffic flow. The project created the largest traffic management scheme in Europe, designed to ensure that traffic flows at its maximum possible speed and volume while minimizing any negative effects at the boundary of the zone. In Westminster alone, the initiative generated a clutch of management mechanisms including automatic traffic monitoring sites streaming real-time data on traffic volume and speed, new bus routes with new double-length 'bendy' buses, and a mass of new road signs and markings. The London Traffic Control Centre (LTCC) was set up by TfL to provide real-time information on traffic levels around the capital.

Monte Carlo in London

The project was delivered not by developing new technologies, but by using proven technologies in innovative ways and on a scale never seen before. The main challenges to the project's success therefore lay in the mix of activities, their interdependencies, and the unpredictability of their interactions. Deloitte saw risk management as the key theme for the programme's successful delivery through to launch.

Monte Carlo modelling is an analytical technique for solving problems by performing a large number of trial runs or simulations. Solutions are inferred from the collective results of the trial runs. Another way of defining the technique is as a method for calculating the probability distribution of possible outcomes. The name Monte Carlo was coined during the Manhattan Project of World War II, based on the similarity of statistical simulation to games of chance.

The team used Monte Carlo techniques to model the risks in the programme's costs and duration. This approach enabled the team to visualize the project's potential outcomes and direct attention to likely hotspots before they flared up. Pertmaster and @Risk software (a product of Palisade Corporation) were used to run the simulations and analysis for both cost and duration factors. Further analyses were run during the evolution of the implementation plan so that the team could understand the critical risks around key milestones. The results were fed directly into management actions to mitigate failures.

As the project progressed, risk management was used as a major communication tool, especially prior to the launch. Deloitte consultants developed a bespoke risk database with a Web-based front end, so that risks could be captured centrally but communicated and managed remotely by each appropriate team.

The project team worked with the 33 London boroughs, particularly those with roads in or around the boundary of congestion charging, to mitigate the impact of changing traffic patterns. This involved coordinating approximately 400 traffic-related schemes. As well as formal methods of risk management, the team used a direct, hands-on approach that Deloitte's Chris Loughran calls an 'invasive' programme management style. He explains the approach in this way: 'A passive style of programme management focuses on evaluating what people achieve, not what they do. The invasive approach involves looking inside the black box and assessing the processes. It does sound painful... but it's really a combination of carrot and stick.'

Such a technique needs to be used with sensitivity. Deloitte ensured that access to documentation and the right to audit outcomes and processes at key stages were written into every supplier contract.

Complementary skills and shared views

The complex nature of the congestion charging scheme meant that a large number of different specialisms were required at different stages of the project. For example, specialist engineering firms were involved in the design of traffic management systems, while networking experts were needed to design the communications structure between the traffic cameras and the data centre.

While the individual components of the solution were proven technologies, their combined use was novel. Orchestrating the delivery of the overall programme therefore presented some unique challenges to the team. Loughran says: 'There were some core methodologies that were tried and tested, but they only went so far. This was a large and multi-disciplinary programme – from public contractors to the funding of complementary traffic schemes, through to cameras and enforcement arrangements. There was no "cookie cutter" set we could use.'

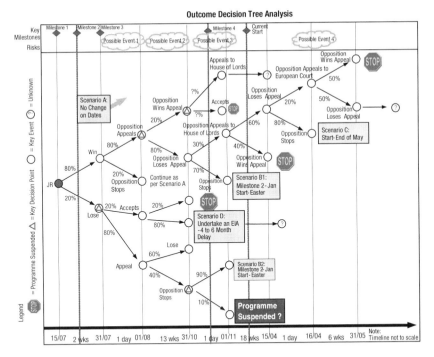

Figure 7.1   *Outcome decision tree analysis for contingency planning (Williams and Parr, 2004)*

Deloitte therefore had to deploy a flexible, multidisciplinary team to match all the specialisms involved in the delivery that the client could not provide from within its own staff. With the responsibility to assure each element of the implementation, Deloitte needed to deploy experienced professionals as and when they were needed, with each individual hitting the ground running. Loughran estimates that of all the many Deloitte people who have been involved with the project over almost three years, only five have been with the programme continuously. Sharing the project's scope, direction and issues was therefore crucial for continuity through time as well as for the current completeness of the management view.

A current, comprehensive picture of the project's status was provided by a programme strategy chart, a device introduced to the management process early on by Deloitte. The chart enabled the TfL/Deloitte team to track individual work streams while maintaining a sense of the programme's overall shape. The chart also acted as a focal point for the reporting, analysis and actioning of all progress, making it a proactive engine of the project's advancement.

Day-to-day management of the programme was further bolstered using a Business Severity Forum. Programme managers, client and suppliers met daily to review the current issue log. Current problems and their status were brought together from all work streams so that the joint team could agree on the severity and priority of each. The team could then address the most significant issues in the correct order, protecting the critical path of the programme. In this way the principal stakeholders maintained a live, accurate and objective watch on progress. Potential show-stopping issues were identified, communicated, prioritized, fixed and retested in a very rapid cycle.

Breaking the wave

The primary challenge faced by TfL was to develop a politically acceptable and operationally practical policy for a project without precedent, in an environment full of uncertainties. It was difficult to predict the response of the public and key stakeholders. Intense media interest meant that every decision was challenged.

While London would wake up to congestion charging on a set date, the programme team introduced as much as possible of the new scheme ahead of its formal launch. The 'big bang' planned for 17 February 2003 was preceded by careful foundation work. The preparation for the start date was spread over six months to reduce last-minute activity by the public. The team was keen to avoid what the team called a 'bow wave': a sudden rush of registrations that might swamp the systems. Residents and other discount holders were able to register for the congestion charge scheme well in advance of its launch. Incentives were introduced for early registration and discount applications.

A thorough testing strategy meant that the scheme had been run in trial mode for some considerable time prior to launch. Elements of the scheme's implementation could readily be tested in isolation. For example, live data capture and analysis from the network of cameras could be tested and tweaked without any charging mechanism being in place. Loughran says: 'We couldn't stop London – but we could capture live data from the cameras and test that. We could test the plate recognition routines and so on. So the go-live was not really a single event.'

The only element of the scheme that could not be tested ahead of the go-live date was public reaction. Three days before the launch, the Mayor predicted there could be difficulties. Most pundits predicted utter chaos. As no traffic management scheme of this type and scale had been implemented before, no one knew for sure what would happen. With the world's media watching, day one was critical to the success of the congestion charge. The team geared up for the antici-pated storm by modelling a range of potential scenarios and putting the necessary processes in place to deal with them if they occurred.

In the event, even the most hostile of observers had to admit that the big bang was remarkably quiet, as traffic died back, payment systems worked as planned, and London went to work.

Assessing the outcome

All major milestones of the scheme were achieved to plan – including the concept design, procurement, technical design study, building and testing – against a timescale described by observers on a scale from 'challenging' to 'unachievable'. The congestion charge quickly improved central London's traffic congestion issues, with a measur-able increase in passenger numbers on buses and trains:

- Initial traffic levels entering the zone were immediately reduced by 25 per cent, pulling back to around 20 per cent after the first two months.
- Congestion plummeted by over 30 per cent during charging hours.
- The number of vehicles driving within the zone fell by 16 per cent.
- Journey time on a round trip to and from the zone dropped by 13 per cent.
- Around 100,000 people were paying the congestion charge on a daily basis (excluding fleets).

In its report *Congestion Charging*: *Six Months On* (23 October 2003), TfL summarized the scheme's performance to date, including these achievements:

- Traffic data, payments data and survey information all pointed to new settled patterns of travel.
- Traffic delays inside the charging zone had now reduced by about 30 per cent, which was towards the high end of TfL's expectations.
- Drivers in the charging zone were spending less time in traffic queues, with time spent either stationary or travelling at below 10 kilometres per hour reduced by about one quarter.
- Journey times to, from and across the charging zone had decreased by an average of 14 per cent. Journey time reliability had improved by an average of 30 per cent.

- Traffic management arrangements had successfully accommodated traffic diverting to the boundary route around the congestion charging zone.
- About 60,000 fewer car movements per day were now coming into the charging zone. TfL estimated that 20 to 30 per cent of these had diverted around the zone; that 50 to 60 per cent represented transfers to public transport; and that 15 to 25 per cent represented switching to car share, motorcycle or pedal cycle, or other adaptations such as travelling outside charging hours or making fewer trips to the charging zone.
- Public transport was coping well with ex-car users. Extra bus passengers travelling to the charging zone were being accommodated by increased bus network capacity.
- Excess waiting times (an indication of the time that bus passengers have to wait above that expected if the route was operating as scheduled) had reduced by over one third on routes serving the charging zone, partly as a consequence of reduced congestion and increased bus services.
- Congestion charging was expected to generate £68 million for the financial year for spending on transport improvements, and £80 million to £100 million in future years.

There have also been numerous intangible benefits to London as a result of the scheme, including the following:

- Pollution has been reduced.
- Noise has been reduced.
- Buses now run more reliably, with shorter journey times, resulting in improved timetabling.
- Road safety has improved.
- Emergency services are reporting improved response times.

The first anniversary of the charge's introduction was marked with the announcement that TfL had towed away or clamped 255 vehicles, while 40 persistent offenders had had their cars crushed.

The success of this project is principally due to collaborative effort. Deloitte provided a multi-disciplinary team of consultants to work with TfL in fully integrated teams. This worked so well that senior TfL management commented that Deloitte team members were indistinguishable from their own staff.

Commitment to the project was extremely high. Everyone involved recognized they were involved in a project that would have a significant impact on public policy around the world. Through the TfL/Deloitte team's dedication, a genuine 'can do, will do' culture developed. The collaborative style of teaming also paved the way for a smooth transition from the project team to TfL staff, who assumed responsibility for managing the service provider after the project went live.

Deloitte's key contribution to the project was its versatility. The ability to provide the right mix of professionals at the right time while maintaining continuity in the core team ensured that TfL had the support it needed at each point. While the larger consultants can all claim extensive portfolios of skills and experience in their work-forces, applying those qualities successfully in a real project situation is not always a given. The factor that helped above all to engage Deloitte's capabilities in this project was the symmetry between the attitudes of colleagues from the consulting firm and its clients. Loughran says: 'Our flexibility comes from being in a high-profile, high-pressure environment. It's what we're used to. There's no standing on ceremony, people are "can-do". They get the job done. But this characterizes the client too. We had very comple-mentary styles.'

Derek Turner, former Managing Director of Street Management at TfL, says that the consultants' involvement was crucial to the pro-gramme's success:

> We could not have done this project without consultants, and our con-
> fidence in Deloitte was well placed. Their passion and drive for this
> project helped it to stay on track and deliver benefits to London. The
> days are gone when a consultant borrows the client's watch to tell him
> the time.

Ken Livingstone, Mayor of London says: 'This is the most talented group of public servants that I have ever worked with.'

Congestion charging has had a long political journey from abstract concept to concrete realization. TfL and Deloitte have ensured that millions of smaller journeys will now be less painful for London and its citizens and businesses. This is the way that the circulation of the 21st century metropolis will be reinvented.

CASE STUDY 7.3

MOBILE TECHNOLOGY AS ENABLER AND ENFORCER

Taking a procurement solution to the pockets of decision-makers has saved this organization time and money while preparing it for the coming generation of mobile healthcare applications. But the key aspect of this case is not technology: it is the combination of enforcement and empowerment that is ensuring the promised benefits of a streamlined supply chain really do happen.

In 2002 Bradford Teaching Hospitals NHS Trust embarked on a comprehensive supply chain re-engineering programme to streamline its processes, reduce supply spend and operating costs. The project took almost 18 months to complete, involving as it did every part of the organization, from clinical staff through to those working in the hospital's delivery bays. The project has produced significant savings in purchasing costs as well as substantial product standardization and consolidation of the trust's supplier base. Process efficiency has been improved while clinical risk has been reduced.

All these benefits have been achieved within a cultural change in the way that clinical staff think about purchasing. The responsibility of buying the stocks that the hospital needs to treat patients has moved as close as possible to the people who use those stocks. They can now order supplies from personal, mobile devices, cutting through the long paper chase that used to apply. As a result, the hospital's performance is becoming faster, cheaper, safer and more accountable. The project also lays the foundation for further advances in the trust's processes.

The Bradford trust spends in the region of £53 million every year on supplies. The items it buys cover nearly 250,000 stock and 48,000 non-stock items ordered from a catalogue of 10,000 different product lines. Stock items are typically the day-to-day items used on the wards and departments and are managed by a team of materials managers, whereas non-stock items are more ad hoc and can include special devices, such as implants, that must be ordered uniquely by a qualified clinician for each patient that needs them. While non-stock items make up a numerical minority in the overall shopping basket, these items often have a high value in both money terms and their contribution to treatment of patients.

Atos Origin's David Whatley observes that in many NHS trusts there is a tendency to move many items into managed stock in order to simplify the procurement and logistics process. However, a procurement process for non-stock items will always be needed. Bradford took the path of migrating as many stock items as possible to materials management, while empowering clinical staff to order non-stock items with a user-friendly and accessible procurement system:

> There's nothing new here in the principle of what we've done. But we are the first to put the ability to place an order quickly and efficiently in the hands of the people who need to make that order. Materials management works extremely well for the high-volume, low-value items used on a day-to-day basis: it is easy to set re-order limits and define stock replenishment days. However, it is not appropriate or cost effective to have infrequently used and high-value items sitting on the shelf until they are required. This can have a significant impact on cash flow and reduce wastage as items go out of date. For example, a clinician is never going to pick up a £15,000–£20,000 pacemaker off the shelf. We needed a system that could cope with both non-stock and stock items without burdening clinical staff. Moreover, problems can arise because even Materials managers, who are responsible for replenishing stock, are not aware of the day-to-day fluctuations in ward activity. As a result, valuable clinical staff time can be spent looking for stock in other wards if an item suddenly runs out due to out-of-pattern consumption.

The paper chase

Prior to Bradford's supply chain project, there was a paper process for procurement which resulted in multiple hand-offs, re-work, and time spent chasing orders, especially as more than 10 per cent of paper requisitions were illegible, incomplete or incorrect. The typical errors produced by sloppy or faulty paperwork and the lack of up-to-date catalogues were overordering, incorrect ordering and late delivery.

The overall procurement process was slow, with some requisitions taking up to 11 days to reach the purchasing department due to delays in approval and internal mail and then 2 to 3 days to process the order. Firefighting took up a great deal of time that could have been better spent with patients. Some requisitioning staff reported that they spent up to two and a half hours each week trying to sort out supply-related problems to ensure that they had the correct items for an operation or course of treatment. Most of these problems were not caused by any inherent complexity in the products being ordered or difficulties at the supplier end, but were due to the poor quality of the requisitions themselves or even because paper simply got lost in the system.

Staff had responded to the endemic slowness of the procurement process by habitually submitting 'urgent' orders to try and accelerate the process. This practice would delay the order stream while blurring the sense of truly urgent orders, thereby helping to devalue clinical prioritization.

The trust also had to deal with multiple paper catalogues covering the mass of supplies available for requisition. Paper documents are notoriously hard to manage. They replicate with abandon, but are hard to cull. Each department had its own catalogue of items that it would use for regular orders, but these documents were frequently out of date. Even more seriously, many of the departmental catalogues in use did not conform to the trust's policy.

Many organizations have identified the potential costs in staff members buying 'off-catalogue'. If the organization has struck a deal to buy, say, stationery at one price from one supplier, then 'maverick buyers' who use a competing catalogue, perhaps by accident, can end up overpaying for their goods. In the case of a clinical environment, the risks of off-catalogue buying are even more serious, as Whatley explains:

> Where a trust doesn't have control over its purchasing, staff can order items that they're not qualified to use, or that aren't compatible with the equipment or drugs that are going to be used. You sometimes hear of a clinical incident where somebody used something they weren't trained to use – but what that means is that somebody bought the wrong thing. Different departments are trained to do things in different ways, so it isn't cost-effective to encourage too much substitution. There's a cost in training people to use different products. Not everything is like, say, a cotton wool ball, where there can be an advantage from standardizing. But even then the significant saving comes from reducing the processing costs, not getting a cheaper priced product.

The supply chain project reduced the number of items that staff were able to order from 15,000 down to 10,000. However, the trust did not have an effective means of controlling how the new, consolidated, authorized catalogue was used. Whatley says: 'Technology helps enforce the right decisions. Without this control, you're just buying the wrong things more quickly.'

Once a paper requisition had been submitted, it was difficult to find out where it was or its status. This added to the time spent chasing orders and also resulted in staff resubmitting orders in case they had been lost, only to end up with a duplicate order later on. Delivery confirmation was slow and sometimes non-existent, resulting in delays in payment and adding to the time staff spent chasing departments for delivery notes. In addition, the trust had no effective management information with which to manage the supplies process.

Atos Origin therefore worked with the trust to implement an e-procurement solution that would eliminate paper and automate the procurement process throughout the organization. The goals of the project were to increase the quality of ordering, reduce the time spent by clinical staff handling supplies and speed up the delivery of goods. At the same time the new system would enforce the trust's purchasing policy and procedures. The trust's chosen procurement processes would be in effect glued in to the system that staff would have to use if they wanted to order any item. The technical requirements for the system included its ability to integrate with a new Oracle Financials installation that was being implemented at the same time, and be amenable to integration with certain supplier systems in the future.

The system would therefore act as a single gateway to procurement for all suppliers, all products and all staff. This was a business-centred approach that avoided inefficiencies represented by the potential alternative of installing suppliers' systems for procurement. Whatley says: 'We produced a solution that's supplier-agnostic. Very often a supplier will say, "Use our system to buy our products." But any supplier system will only address part of what the trust's people need.'

The target user group for the system was large and diverse. The trust wanted to put the power of procurement directly in the hands of responsible staff, whatever their technical specialism or role in the supply chain. Bradford has around 400 designated requisitioning and approval staff in more than 100 departments spread across several sites, with supply requirements ranging from basic stationery to complex medical equipment. The profile of these staff varied throughout the trust. They included both clinical and non-clinical staff, deskbound workers and completely mobile workers, those who were computer literate and those with no experience of computers, and people working on trust sites and in the community.

The trust wanted to limit the number of people who could raise clinical requisitions to designated clinical staff familiar with the products and responsible for their use. This policy reduces clinical risk while making people aware of the costs of the materials that they use. Bearing in mind that clinical staff rightly consider their priority as spending time with patients and not ordering supplies, this requirement posed several challenges to the team.

First, how would they persuade clinical staff to use the system? Clinical staff will always be responsible for raising requisitions for clinical items, but typically they are inclined to scribble their orders on pieces of paper and hand them to office clerks to create the requisition. This saved them a few minutes in creating the requisition, but invariably they spent time later on chasing and sorting out problems due to illegible, incomplete or inaccurate orders. We all have a tendency to put a higher value on present time than future time, especially if we work in highly pressured environments with multiple demands for critical decisions.

The team therefore needed to demonstrate to staff that getting the order right up-front would significantly improve the process, while presenting a solution that made it easy for them to get it right first time. The system would have to be quick to access and navigate. Raising requisitions, tracking them and receipting them would need to be fast, simple and intuitive. The system would have to be accessible to staff that did not have access to a PC or whose work required them to be mobile. Ideally, the system would require minimal user training.

The second challenge was the issue of effectively enforcing the organization's purchasing policy and procedures. As a result of standardizing its product set, the trust had significantly reduced the number of products that staff were entitled to use. However, without an effective control mechanism, the trust would find it difficult to realize the benefits. Whatley says: 'We can save 3–7 per cent of supply chain costs for an NHS trust by these means. The technology underpins that, and makes sure you get the actual cost savings.'

A solution called WANDER™ procurement

Atos Origin and Bradford analysed these requirements and constraints, and decided to pilot an e-procurement solution that was mobile enabled. Mobile applications, which use pocket or handheld devices connected wirelessly to corporate or public networks, are becoming increasingly popular in enterprises with large populations of mobile workers. However, such applications are usually costjustified by their impact on the productivity of a specialist group of workers, such as engineers who fix equipment in the field, or salespeople. In such cases, mobile technology helps to spread the benefits of corporate information systems to the periphery of the organization, where people have typically had poor access to enterprise systems. There is no doubt that mobile applications have become fashionable in recent years – if only among systems developers.

Bradford was not interested in using mobile technology for its own sake. Instead, the team recognized that the mobile platform addressed the project's varying needs in an optimal manner. In the first place, providing the application via a wireless network would mean that staff would be able to access it wherever they were on site, regardless of their sedentary or mobile work style. Second, the small screen size and reduced processing power of mobile devices has the beneficial effect of enforcing simplicity on applications developed for them. The team decided to use PocketPC devices, which run a simplified variety of Microsoft's Windows operating system and integrate well with other systems. The PocketPC operating system is very easy to use – users require virtually no training. The devices are sold as consumer items, and therefore enjoy low cost and easy supply.

Finally, the team recognized that mobile applications are becoming increasingly popular in the health sector and that a wireless network deployed for e-procurement could be used by other clinical and non-clinical applications. The mobile e-procurement system – now dubbed WANDER™ – would demonstrate the use of mobile technology in an application that touched every department and grade across the organization. Unlike organizations that introduce mobile applications for specialist teams and then frequently find that they have duplicated functionality and technology spend in several areas, Bradford would enter the wireless world with a truly corporate system that supported a high-profile business process. Future mobile applications would be more likely to use WANDER™'s infrastructure and reuse its development strategy, thus saving unnecessary redevelopment and the creation of disconnected and incompatible systems.

WANDER™ allows requisitions to be raised quickly using trust-approved catalogues. If the requisition requires approval it is automatically presented to the designated approver who is notified by e-mail, otherwise it goes straight to the purchasing department. Purchasing staff then process the requisition and send the order to the supplier. Staff can go online at any time and establish the status of the order and when it is due for delivery. When the item is delivered, the person responsible for receipting can call up the purchase order and confirm delivery against the item. The accounts payable team is then able to check that the item has been delivered before paying an invoice.

WANDER™ therefore automates the entire procurement process, and with its e-mail notification capability it also drives the workflow. Mobile access means that delays in inputting, approving, ordering, querying or receipting requisitions are removed. Now the ordering function can fit efficiently into the stream of events with which each staff member is dealing. It is an elegant solution to the trust's desire to make its clinical staff responsible for their own supply needs which also has the virtue of creating a seamless collaborative process among the many individuals involved in procurement.

Pilot and launch

The team decided to pilot the solution before rolling it out across the organization. The pilot phase would enable the team to assess the effectiveness of its technology choices and iron out any problems with functionality or usability before WANDER™ became the mandated route for all the trust's purchasing activity.

The trust worked with Atos Origin to map the desired procurement process in terms of stages, outcomes and user permissions. The team then selected two pilot areas with varying user requirements. These were the ENT (ear, nose and throat) theatres and the paediatric outreach department. A wireless network was installed and connected to Atos Origin's Managed Service Centre, where the application is hosted, via the national NHS.net network. User permissions were installed so that relevant functions were accessible by authorized users. Finally the standard catalogue items were loaded into the system.

People with responsibility for requisitioning, approving, purchasing and receipting supplies were given up to two hours of training. The training session described the rationale for e-procurement and the benefits of wireless mobility within the trust. Staff were also shown how to use the PocketPCs with which they were issued. The training session was used as an opportunity to make staff appreciate the source of their existing purchasing problems in the paper process and how the automated solution would eliminate these errors once and for all. The team was pleased to note that the very first transaction made on the new system via a PocketPC was from a paediatric nurse with no prior experience of computers.

The pilot lasted three months, during which time the team monitored progress and made minor improvements to the system following user feedback. The trust's supply chain board then judged the pilot a success and gave the green light for its extension to a further 30 areas and 150 users. This extended pilot phase lasted from July

2002 to January 2003 when it was agreed that WANDER™ would be rolled out across the entire organization. The trust-wide roll-out commenced in August 2003 and more than 700 staff now have access to the system every day.

Faster and better

The team has been able to measure the improvements brought by WANDER™ and noted particularly how the system has accelerated the procurement process. Speed translates very readily to improved quality of care and greater throughput, which are two of the most important variables used to assess a trust's performance.

The elimination of paper has eradicated errors and the need for re-work. Requisition accuracy has increased from 90 per cent to 100 per cent. Meanwhile the time from raising a requisition to presenting it to the supplier has reduced by up to 90 per cent.

Clinical staff are now able to spend more of their time caring for patients rather than concentrating on administrative tasks. Andy Sykes, a team leader in ENT says: 'The whole requisitions process now takes 2 to 3 minutes whereas, previously, paper-based requisitions could take anything between 15 and 20 minutes.'

The time spent chasing orders has also been reduced due to the elimination of errors and the ability to track orders. For example, staff can now see if an ordered item has been delivered but not yet receipted at its final destination, and if necessary retrieve the item from its current location. Previously delivered items could be held up within the trust's sites and staff would not know they had actually arrived within the organization's control. Deliveries now arrive more quickly at the places they need to be.

The compliance with the trust catalogue enforced by the system has reduced clinical risk while sustaining the benefits achieved through the earlier rationalization of the supply chain catalogue. The wireless mobile capacity of WANDER™ has extended the supply chain to people that would otherwise continue to use paper methods or have to disrupt their work patterns to find a workstation. The team has also confirmed that it is considerably easier and faster to train staff to use the mobile device than desktop PCs.

The benefits WANDER™ offers for the future include the value of its wireless infrastructure as a platform for other clinical and non-clinical applications. The trust is also now well placed to create strategic relationships with suppliers by encouraging them to interface with WANDER™. This puts the trust in the driving seat: rather than electing to take systems created by different suppliers, the trust can ask suppliers to match their e-commerce offerings to the data standards and functional attributes of its organization-wide procurement system.

The final benefit that WANDER™ has brought to the organization is a subtle one, but nonetheless of significance. The provision of a simple, mobile, reliable and policy-conformant application for procurement throughout the trust speaks volumes about the organization's belief in the importance of getting purchasing right, and in empowering its decision-makers to drive the supply of the items they need in order to treat patients. By investing in e-procurement in this very visible and personal way, the trust is demonstrating that what people buy is core to how well the trust performs, both as an economic entity and as a collection of dedicated professionals. Rose Stephens, the chief nurse and director of hospital services at Bradford, is convinced that this solution is having a real impact on the trust's work:

> WANDER™ is a simple, practical tool that lets us get on with the job
> we joined the NHS to do — caring for patients. It is a great example
> of how technology helps us cut administration and do our jobs better.
> The greatest benefit we have seen from the supply chain project is in
> managing our clinical risk. We are seeing real clinical benefits by
> focusing on a standard range of core products.

Mobile applications are still at an early stage of development, and most that have been developed to date have been aimed at niche tasks or attractive vertical markets such as estate agents or engineers. The Atos Origin team saw that mobile technology could be readily tamed and put to the service of a core corporate function. They chose the mobile channel for delivery because it matched what the trust needs in terms of accessibility, usability and personal responsibility. But the team's technology insights were joined by an appreciation of the challenges facing NHS trusts, especially with regard to purchasing policy. Procurement is one area where it can be easy to throw technology at problems without exploring the context of those problems. A paperless solution may appear to be the obvious answer to slow, error-prone manual processes, but applying a standard commercial solution would not have been optimal for this situation – and could even have been dangerous. The Atos Origin's team experience in clinical settings is driving the firm's formulation of strategy for NHS clients, resulting, for example, in a passionate belief in the support of efficient and accountable non-stock supply rather than a wholesale shift to commercial-style materials management.

That the firm has also made the trust an effective host for other mobile applications is an incidental bonus, but one that will ensure that the organization continues to meet its commitments to the community, staff – and clinical excellence.

CASE STUDY 7.4

WHEN SMALL BUSINESSES GO GLOBAL

For IBM, its 15-year involvement with Wimbledon has seen several generations of technology transition from the laboratory to the marketplace. Its recent work at the All England Lawn Tennis Club has been a useful proving ground for its 'e-business on demand' strategy, aimed at helping small players make big hits when they need to.

For two weeks every year, millions of armchair tennis fans pray for the rain clouds to avoid southwest London so that they can avidly follow the fortunes of the world's greatest players at the game's most prestigious event. There is little that consultants can do to alter the weather, but consultants from IBM, who have been working with the Wimbledon organization for 15 years, have consistently applied technology to improve the experience of the annual Championships for players, organizers, broadcasters and spectators alike. In recent years the two partners have proved how technologies can transition from the laboratory to the business environment.

Despite the size and fame of the annual Championships at Wimbledon, the All England Lawn Tennis Club is actually best classed as a small business – albeit one that grows to much larger proportions every June. The challenge for the IBM Global Services team based at Wimbledon is that of ramping up the information facilities of a small business to meet the intense demands of the Championships, while not committing the organization to expensive services it does not need at other times of the year. Dealing with a peak of demand that is regular in timing but unpredictable in size has helped IBM develop its 'e-business on demand' offering, and thereby help other small- and medium-sized enterprises (SMEs) to rise to similar challenges.

Tennis is a global sport that has grown in popularity over the past decade. While the facilities at the All England Lawn Tennis Club have grown to keep up with this demand, there will always be a finite number of people who can attend as spectators during the two-week Championships at Wimbledon. Now the world's largest annual sporting event, 'Wimbledon' signifies the grass game to millions of people across the world. During the event, there is a high demand for information from around the world and around the clock. Fans want to follow the matches, the players and the buzz of the event. Some of them will find their needs served through broadcasting networks, while others will want to interact in a more personal way. The Club needs to meet the surging demand for information relating to the event in a way that embodies the Wimbledon experience of quality and attention to detail.

The goal set by the Club with IBM and its suppliers is to ensure that all of the stakeholders involved in the Championships have the information they require to enhance their overall experience of the event. The stakeholders include in-ground spectators, television viewers and the online audience. Players and coaches are also key stakeholders, and their satisfaction with the available information services is a growing component of their overall appreciation of the event. The press, broadcasters and commentators make up another key constituency, as do the officials of the Club itself.

From point played to data displayed

The Championships' information flow begins with shots played on the courts of the Club. Just as efficient information systems located within mainstream businesses aim to capture data at the point of creation, and to capture it only once for whatever uses it may be put to, so the Wimbledon team collects data on each shot as it is played. A group of 48 tennis specialists use laptop and handheld devices to record every detail of every game. These recorders are often players of considerable skill and achievement in their own right, and they use their knowledge of the game to collect and categorize the data correctly. The 'show courts', or those which are televised, have their match statistics captured in real time and streamed to a local area network (LAN). The outside courts do not require real-time statistical information so details for these matches are captured using an IBM Workpad and uploaded into the central database after each match.

The team captures around 120,000 statistics on every day of the event, and these are stored in a central database. The database in turn feeds a number of users. For example, scores and detailed statistics gathered from courtside can be displayed by the BBC as a graphic to support television coverage of the match and commentators' analysis. The distinctive graphics have been designed over several years by the All England Club and the BBC, guided by IBM consultants in graphics design. Any combination of over 90 graphic elements can be called upon at any point in a match. The systems generate the required graphic, tie in the data and display it to the BBC producers, ready for live transmission at their discretion.

In addition, each commentary position is equipped with a system that gives detailed analysis of the current match by player, match fact or set. This system provides a wealth of information for the match commentators, adding hard factual evidence to their own expert match analysis.

Some foreign broadcasters also need match statistics in real time to augment their coverage. The project's central database is replicated to individual data repositories as and when any updates occur. This means that any internal design changes required to the database, or changes to information required by an individual client, can be made independently of each other. This approach facilitates change across the client base and removes the need for discussion and compromise within a complex change management process. Each broadcasting client gets, in effect, a tailored service while the underlying data remains identical and authoritative for all users.

BBC Interactive uses this facility to provide key match statistics to users of its digital TV service. This service gives the viewer the opportunity to choose from any of the show court matches in progress and to view the key match stats alongside live coverage.

The team has also attached its data streams to a match information display (MID) within the ground. The MID is a large screen that displays up-to-the minute scores on matches in progress, enabling anyone on site to see the latest information at a glance. Other information can be displayed such as player biographies and animated display sequences plus general announcements from the Club. A second display was added in 2003.

Looking beyond the ground and the broadcasting community, the team also uses the data it collects to drive its public Web site. The 1995 Championships Web site was the first global sporting event to be put on the World Wide Web and since then the online audience has grown exponentially. In 2003 the site had over 4 million unique users generating 231 million page views and 27 million visits. The average time spent at the site by visitors, sometimes known as 'stickiness', was 2 hours 11 minutes.

A key element of today's www.wimbledon.org is the real-time scoreboard that shows scores correct to within a few seconds of the point being played. In 2002 the scoreboard was also voice-enabled in five different languages.

Other elements of the Web site include interactive cameras known as 'Slamcams' which can be controlled by the users. There are also full player biographies and historical match highlights. The site also streams Radio Wimbledon and The Wimbledon Channel, a daily live studio presentation, with eight hours of video, match analysis, features about what is going on at Wimbledon, plus player and celebrity interviews. The site also contains an online store.

While the Web has become a key focus of the team's service to its global audience of interested individuals, the team has also branched out into other delivery channels. Information can be supplied by SMS (text message) to mobile phone users, and to special WAP (wireless application protocol) pages to phones with browsers. There is also an interactive TV service.

Serving the players

The Club's determination to meet the players' needs helps explain why, year after year, the top players in the world return to play at Wimbledon. The players are not only attracted by the challenge of playing on grass and the uniqueness of the All England Lawn Tennis Club experience, but also the other services that the Club offers the players, making their stay a more fulfilling experience. Information is an increasingly important part of this experience.

The team's information service to players begins the moment a player leaves the court. A detailed player report is generated at the end of each match. This report details the match broken down stroke by stroke and point by point in the areas of a player's game. The player can see at a glance how he or she performed in terms of service, attacking play, defensive play, winning shots, unforced errors and forced errors. The report is delivered within a few minutes of the match completing and is waiting for the players when they return to the changing rooms.

The 30-page player report gives an accurate representation of how a player won or lost the match and used in conjunction with the full match video it is an invaluable coaching tool. Players and coaches often request other player reports to review for any potential areas of weakness in their opponents' game, showing just how reliant on detailed analysis the modern top-level game has become.

The Club introduced Internet, e-mail and word processing facilities for players and their support teams a number of years ago and by 2003 was providing 15 workstations to meet their needs. However, mobile facilities look set to subsume some of the functions of these static facilities as the team's wireless service expands.

Within the Wimbledon organization, information support for the period of the annual Championships has grown into a sophisticated system much relied upon by club staff, players, coaches and members of the media. The Club's intranet Wimbledon information system (WIS) contains more historical content than the public Web site and has more video content of key matches played during the current Championships. WIS has similar content to the Web for match statistics and player information, with additional information for people who have access to the ground facilities.

In 2002 the team produced a version of WIS optimized for PDAs (personal digital assistants) called Pocket Wimbledon. This application gave hospitality guests, Club officials and VIPs access to real-time scores throughout the site via a PDA enabled with GPRS, a packet data network service for mobile phones. This was the first time this combination of technology had been used on this scale anywhere in the world. The following year the team made a version of Pocket Wimbledon available beyond the ground to anyone with a connected PDA. This version of the application took 20 or so elements of the main site and optimized them for the mobile user. IBM's Mark McMurrugh says: 'The idea is to help people have continuity of a quality service whether on TV, mobile or Internet channels.'

The development of Pocket Wimbledon 2003 and the team's attention to its role within a multi-channel world is an indicator of how information services are evolving to exploit the growing number of available platforms, and how services can be tailored for each channel without losing coherence. As an analogy, we can see how members of the eBay auction community use the Web to research their initial bids or mount their sales but use mobile alert services to keep up with the progress of auctions. An event such as Wimbledon has a similar mix of 'sit down' and 'keep up' activities: fans may want to watch a package of highlights and expert commentary in the evening, but keep up with scores or breaking stories during the working day. In many workplaces where it would be unacceptable to have a television set tuned to a sporting event over a long period, it may be acceptable to have a window opened at www.wimbledon.org.

The team also enhanced its mobile service for users within the Wimbledon site. Wireless hotspots were added to key locations so that users could access Pocket Wimbledon through a high bandwidth channel as well as through the somewhat slower GPRS service. The higher bandwidth allowed the team to add canned video segments to the mobile service. The team also added interactive maps to help users find their way around the site and access the Club's services.

McMurrugh envisages that enhanced mobile services of this sort will become available to the general public in time, but that high bandwidth mobile applications are some way off being mainstream: 'There will be a slower progression to the public domain. But eventually anyone will be able to have a seat on Centre Court or Court Number One.'

Clearly, the transition of technologies and systems from closed communities to wider populations is an underlying theme of IBM's work at Wimbledon. However, McMurrugh stresses that while Wimbledon acts as a showcase for IBM technologies and skills, much of the team's work focuses on how SMEs can exploit the capabilities of bigger organizations when they need to.

All year round

IBM fields a team of more than 180 people at Wimbledon during the annual Championships to support the applications and over 600 items of IT equipment. During the year the team reduces to an on-site team of three to six people providing consultancy, project management, technical and administrative support. However, the organization's two weeks in prime time requires an annual cycle of activity to ensure its success. Reviewing the year's performance and planning goals for the subsequent event begins in September. By December the plan is set for the year ahead, including any enhancements to existing systems, new pilots, or transitions of exiting pilots to full production. New systems, enhancements, integrations and transitions are developed between December and March. March sees a major test of the entire suite of applications and all the required hardware. April is scheduled for a second round of testing if required. April and May are taken up with final developments and enhancements so that set-up can commence in June. After the Championships have ended, it takes the team a week to break down the systems. 'Then we spend a month recovering,' says McMurrugh. This business cycle finds an echo in many seasonal businesses, particularly in industries geared around major trade shows. Many companies also match their activity to buying seasons (as in the fashion industry) or sales seasons (as in consumer goods).

The team at Wimbledon may be focused on the annual Championships, but it also has to support 'business as usual' for the Club and its members. McMurrugh says: 'We want to maintain the same level of innovation and productivity at the Club as in the Championships. Where technology can make life easier for everyone, the Club is interested – but neither of us is interested in technology for its own sake. There has to be a real business need.'

So, for example, the team has created a court booking system for the Club to replace its 'lovely embossed book'. Members can book courts online, or book via the telephone with the Club's secretary operating the system for them. It may not be a complex system when compared with the applications developed for the Championships, but this application increases the quality of service to the members and plays directly to the Club's mission.

The long-term nature of the relationship between the Club and IBM is a major benefit to both parties. Year-on-year learning is key to the evolution of the Club's information services. Jeff Lucas, IT Director of The All England Lawn Tennis Club, says:

> Our team becomes stronger and stronger every year, as we develop a deeper understanding of each other's objectives. There is a lot of synergy between the Club and IBM in terms of how protective we are of our brand values, and in the way we like to evaluate everything thoroughly before making a decision.

Extra power on tap

IBM markets 'e-business on demand' as a set of services, but it is more of a business principle than a product. The concept is to create a flexible, scalable information systems environment that meets a customer's peak needs without requiring the overheads and infrastructure of a constant solution. The on-demand principle gives customers access to more power as and when they need it by aggregating and balancing diverse customer needs across a large installed base of equipment. In this way, SMEs can have virtual access to a large-systems environment on a serviced basis without making any capital investments of their own.

The All England Lawn Tennis Club has around 100 staff and 400 members, making it, for 50 weeks of the year, a small business. Then the demand on the organization's Web site jumps from a respectable 2,000 visitors per month to a peak demand of 250,000 concurrent users. More than 1.3 million people access the site every day during the annual Championships. The team can rise to this challenge because it can immediately tap extra capacity from the on-demand environment. Server 'farms' around the world can provide the extra capacity within seconds and with no interruption in service.

This 'pay for what you eat' model lets smaller organizations share in the economies of scale in computing made possible by global networks. It is also a compelling model for larger organizations that may have to deal with sudden surges in demand on their systems. McMurrugh cites news organizations whose Web sites attract sudden peaks in traffic when major world events occur, and companies involved in new product launches. While Web site usage provides the major public example of the on-demand response, surges are beginning to apply to other usage scenarios, particularly in the area of mobile applications where the need for teams to access corporate systems 'on the run' can lead to bottlenecks.

For Lucas, the simplicity of the on-demand principle is a key benefit:

> We are aware of what e-business on demand is, and it's very important to the All England Club that our Web site is able to cope with whatever demands it is placed under. One of the strengths of IBM is that they can deliver the technology we need, as we need it, without complex re-negotiations or re-writing programs.

Wimbledon is more than a showcase for tennis, and its IT services are more than a showcase for hardware, software and networks. The team at Wimbledon has developed much of the management thinking that goes with successful information delivery in a multi-channel world, from the collection of primary content through dissemination of data to different clients and on to responsive management of capacity. IBM is proving at Wimbledon that small businesses can go global when they need to.

8

Outsourcing

Outsourcing has come a long way from the days in which organizations saw it as a way of washing their hands of a problem and cutting costs into the bargain. Once primarily a defensive strategy – shedding non-core work – it is increasingly becoming a means by which organizations can make radical changes.

SECOND-GENERATION OUTSOURCING

Although the need to minimize costs still plays an important role in the decision to outsource, all three of the organizations featured in this chapter were seeking additional benefits. The Medicines and Healthcare products Regulatory Agency (MHRA) wanted to use new technology to share information more effectively while complying with increasingly stringent regulatory demands. It also looked to outsourcing as a means of improving the procedures by which medicines are approved, not simply to automate the processes it has traditionally relied upon. The UK's Vehicle and Operator Services Agency (VOSA), responsible for overseeing a range of vehicle safety and licensing operations, needed to ensure that its IT infrastructure could keep pace with its rapidly evolving role. Similarly, Sainsbury's Supermarkets was seeking to reverse a decline in margins and saw outsourcing as a way of making radical change to existing processes and systems and to improve business performance. 'Technology change impacts people and processes too,' said Richard Wildman, from Accenture, which worked with Sainsbury's on this project. 'We had to ensure that large-scale change could occur without disruption to Sainsbury's service levels. It was like sailing a ship while you're still building it.'

This is true for all the outsourcing projects nominated for an award from the MCA. Contrary to popular myth, good outsourcing projects are more likely to be focused on generating revenue, improving customer satisfaction and raising productivity than many other types of consulting.

However, the greater the scope of outsourcing, the greater the challenges involved. Not surprisingly, flexibility has become something a holy grail. With too many stories of companies who, having outsourced, found themselves trapped into paying over the odds for changes to rigidly defined contracts, the need to be able to accommodate change was uppermost in the minds of all the companies featured here. The MHRA needed an open-ended outsourcing contract so that new processes could be accommodated without paying premium charges. VOSA had already outsourced its IT infrastructure, only to find that it could not keep up with the level of change taking place in the business. With a workforce distributed across a network of offices, VOSA was not just interested in flexibility but in scalability. It needed a new outsourcing contract that could provide a high-level framework into which different initiatives could be slotted.

Inherent in flexibility is the idea of preparing an organization for the future, giving it operational resilience in the face of uncertainty and change. Under its contract with Sainsbury's Supermarkets, Accenture is not only taking over the operation of existing systems but is overseeing their wholesale replacement, building Europe's largest consumer database, updating buying, merchandising systems and supply chain systems and providing new HR and financial systems to support the company's 1 million employees.

Another feature of these cases is the speed with which the projects were expected to yield benefits. Because of their scale and scope, outsourcing contracts typically last for between 5 and 10 years – far longer than an 'average' consulting project. Of the first generation of contracts, many have become mired in arguments about the quality of service provided. With most of their efforts focused on running established systems and processes, outsourcing companies found it hard to identify the areas for improvement. Although still at a preliminary stage in its planning process, the MHRA (formerly the Medicines Control Agency) needed to realize the benefits of its decision to outsource within two years, if it was to meet its business objectives. There simply was not enough time to develop the detailed definition of the outsourced service typically required in such cases.

Flexibility and speed are both made possible by a new approach to the client–outsourcing supplier relationship. Clients are rightly cynical of much of the talk around 'working in partnership' with their suppliers. All too often, experience suggests, companies pay lip-service to this ideal without any real conception of how they are to deliver it in practice. Key to each of these three projects was the extent to which conventional customer/supplier barriers were overcome by innovative, risk-sharing contractual terms. Whereas VOSA's first outsourcing contract focused wholly on the immediate services to be provided, its deal with Atos Origin ensured that the relationship would be measured in terms of broader business goals. Neither of the conventional models for working with private sector suppliers would have worked in this case. A traditional contract would have been too rigid, but the obvious alternative – a Public Private Partnership (PPP) – was primarily designed for greenfield construction projects, not the renewal of existing information technology. With this in mind, VOSA produced a document stating its budget and its objectives; suppliers were invited to bid for specific business propositions designed to achieve those objectives, but the actual process by which they did so was not prescribed. Atos Origin also adopted performance measurements that reflected VOSA's goals, rather than via compliance to a traditional service level agreement.

Ensuring the commercial goals of clients and suppliers encouraged the high degree of openness and sense of team spirit common to all the projects in this chapter. The alignment of Atos Origin's corporate goals with those of VOSA was mirrored by ensuring that people from the two companies worked together. As Nigel Shenton, Head of IT at VOSA explained, 'Our teams are badgeless. At the top level we're working to coordinate a number of initiatives, some of which don't even involve Atos Origin. The end-user is the same, so it's critical we work together to turn these into a coherent programme of work.'

FROM ADVICE TO DELIVERY

Outsourcing is big business for the consulting industry. 2001–03 has seen a significant shift away from more traditional consulting services towards outsourcing and outsourcing-related work. Philip Geiger is a Board Director at the IT consulting firm, Xayce:

> You only have to look at the number of outsourcing announcements by blue chip companies in the last few months to appreciate that the time is fast approaching when a lack of appreciation about IT and business process outsourcing (BPO) would be akin to ignoring the impact of IT in the 1960s. Clients expect their consultants to understand the many facets and implications of BPO. The upside is that this represents a significant opportunity (and

one that will close as clients acquire the experience to do it themselves); the downside is that you won't be able to ignore BPO. You could get away with that for a while, but – ultimately – clients won't want to talk to you.

From the supplier point of view, the case studies in this chapter typify two distinct sectors of the outsourcing industry.

Independent advice

PA Consulting Group's role was to advise the MHRA throughout the outsourcing process. It worked with the Agency to convert a high-level strategy into a practical set of requirements and to draw up a proposition that balanced the MHRA's need for flexibility with the commercial interests of potential bidders. Much depended upon establishing the right governance principles from the outset, upon being clear about how risks would be shared, and upon ensuring that the relationships involved did not deteriorate into confrontation. As the scale and complexity of outsourcing continues to grow, this independent, in-between role looks set to become ever more important.

As this case demonstrates, success will be determined by the extent to which a consulting firm can play the role of an honest broker, helping to create working relationships where all sides stand to gain. Commercial acumen and a broad knowledge of how other deals have been constructed are also prerequisites here: PA was able to add value to the client because it had seen where other contracts had succeeded or failed and apply these lessons to the challenges facing the MHRA.

Delivery

Accenture's work with Sainsbury's begins with a consulting premise – how best to improve business performance – and translates this into practical changes to systems and processes. While advising its client on how to achieve those improvements, it is also responsible for making them happen. Thus, while PA's role was to develop a commercial framework within which other suppliers could work, Accenture's work with Sainsbury's includes implementing new systems, exploring the use of new technology, and re-engineering the way Sainsbury's and its suppliers work collaboratively. Atos Origin, too, was responsible for the delivery of the outsourced service, working side by side with VOSA's own staff across a wide range of operational areas.

Clearly, both firms' track record in delivery is fundamental to their success here, but it was the use to which this experience was put that makes these projects outstanding examples of this kind of work. Neither firm was satisfied with the conventional relationship between client and outsourcing supplier: both set out to create environments in which more time would be focused on achieving the client's business objectives, and less on debating the minutiae of the contract. Success in this sector of the outsourcing market will primarily stem from the supplier's attitude.

That advice and delivery are being undertaken by different firms is significant. While 10 years ago it might have been possible for a single supplier to fulfil both of these functions, to give advice and to be involved in delivering the service, most clients now see the two roles as mutually exclusive. A firm that sells delivery services cannot be expected to offer independent advice on who is best positioned to deliver a service, because it has a vested interest in the outcome. By contrast, a firm that focuses on delivery is likely to be better positioned when it comes to offering in-depth knowledge about a particular technology. Both roles have their place in the market, but clients want suppliers to be clear about their position.

However, both models illustrate the extent to which organizational boundaries are changing – and this is one of the reasons why a more open, collaborative and flexible relationship is so critical. To be effective, outsourcing advisers and suppliers have to function as though they were part of their client's organization, sharing common objectives, making decisions on their behalf, and developing a similar culture.

Ironically, the greatest measure of successful outsourcing is the extent to which a process appears to be in-sourced.

SUMMARY – KEY LESSONS FOR MANAGERS AND CONSULTANTS

- Successful second-generation outsourcing projects are not predicated solely on the idea of cutting costs. Organizations are turning to outsourcing as a way of getting access to new technology, of replacing cumbersome processes with more streamlined, efficient ones. The resulting projects tend to be larger in scale and more ambitious in complexity.
- The keys to transferring responsibility successfully to external suppliers are:
  - contractual flexibility;
  - speed;
  - providing an incentive for clients and suppliers to work together through contracts that share the risks and rewards;
  - establishing an environment of openness in which people from each side work together as equals.

- The supply side is dividing into two distinct, mutually exclusive approaches. Some firms are taking an advisory role, assisting clients to find their way through the commercial pitfalls of large-scale, complex deals. Others are positioning themselves primarily as service providers, making changes to and running a client's processes and systems. From a client's point of view, transparency – being able to tell one type of firm from the other – is essential.

- However, overall success is dependent on clients and suppliers overcoming the conventional 'them and us' distinctions true of many commercial relationships.

CASE STUDY 8.1

EVOLVING THE OUTSOURCING MARKET

Outsourcing deals are becoming more creative as organizations tackle increasingly uncertain requirements. Working with experienced deal-makers is one way of ensuring that organizations get the greatest flexibility and commitment from their partners.

The strategic use of outsourcing enables organizations to focus on their core business, leaving specialists to provide ancillary services. It sounds simple, but many outsourcing deals fail. Offshore and global deals in particular have proved much tougher than anticipated, and the 'one size fits all' contract approach has largely failed. PA believes that organizations need to look beyond the use of out-sourcing simply as a means of achieving savings, and to consider outsourcing in the round. Innovative outsourcing arrangements can deliver competitive advantage, increased stakeholder value and world-class services.

The outsourcing supplier market is constantly evolving as it matures. Innovative deals help to augment the capability and diversity of the market as new business models are proven contract by contract. One deal between suppliers can vastly alter the services the market can offer to clients, changing organizations' options at a stroke. PA's close involvement with groundbreaking outsourcing deals ensures deep and current knowledge of what the market has to offer, while its projects contribute to the very development of the market.

In the case of its work with the Medicines and Healthcare products Regulatory Agency (MHRA), PA's consultants had to deal with two qualitatively different challenges: an existing information management strategy, which had yet to be translated into practical terms, and a commercial environment constrained by capped annual budgets. To meet the strategy, challenge, the PA team had to take the work of one set of information systems professionals and transition it faithfully for the use of another team. To meet the commercial challenge, the team had to rethink the way public sector organizations enter into long-term supplier relationships, reconciling the economic constraints of the MHRA with the formal rules of public procurement and the goals of outsourcing suppliers.

An information business

The MHRA's role is to safeguard public health by ensuring that medicines, healthcare products and medical equipment meet appropriate standards of safety, quality, performance and effectiveness, and are used safely. On the medicines side, MHRA is the UK's licensing authority for pharmaceuticals, responsible for the licensing of medicines before they are brought to market and whenever products are issued in new versions. The agency regulates clinical drug trials, issues safety warnings, ensures compliance to standards of pharmaceutical manufacture and wholesaling, and sets quality standards for drug substances through the British Pharmacopoeia, the authoritative source for drug information. It evaluates approximately 1,000 product applications and up to 20,000 variations of existing licences annually. In addition, the agency deals with around 75,000 adverse drug reaction notifications every year.

Like many contemporary organizations, the agency has discovered that it is primarily in the business of information. Its status as a trading agency means that it funds its activities entirely from sales, rather than from a central government budget. The agency charges fees to the pharmaceutical companies whose products it regulates. However, these fees are fixed by HM Treasury. The agency does not have the option of raising its income simply by raising its fees. Fees are in any case politically sensitive, and make a poor target for revenue growth. Drug developers are naturally wary of paying high or unnecessary fees to regulators, while the government-mandated fee scale could be impacted at any time by wider industry controls.

MHRA's latitude for improving its revenue is focused on the professional interpretation of the information it collects in order to perform its primary role for the industry and the public. As a nexus of drug data and an employer of highly skilled and knowledgeable industry professionals, the agency is ideally placed to aggregate, analyse and disseminate information relating to the pharmaceutical sector. It adds value to its input data through professional interpretation, thereby creating marketable intellectual property. The terms of reference for the organization allow and encourage this activity, so long as any information products and services created by the agency are genuine, non-competitive and open. As well as having a commercial market value, such products and services also benefit wider public health, being used by, for example, the NHS in its planning activities.

Paper exercises

The organization had traditionally worked as a paper-intensive business. Submission documents would arrive from pharmaceutical companies and be copied to the various teams who needed to work on their several sections. Although some systems had been installed to help with the work, these had been designed for the use of different departments. These systems also required substantial rekeying of incoming documents. While around half of the agency's staff were technical specialists drawn from disciplines such as medicine and pharmacology, the other half were administrative staff.

Apart from this huge administrative burden, reliance on paper was limiting the speed with which submissions could be processed, and imposing overheads in terms of storage costs: the MHRA has a statutory obligation to retain much of the information it receives. At the same time volumes of applications were continuing to rise as pharmaceutical companies sought to enlarge their product portfolios, leverage new discoveries and target new diseases.

MHRA recognized that it needed a fundamentally new way of operating, based on electronic sharing of information. In this way it could speed up the decision-making process, helping itself to meet the demands of the pharmaceutical marketplace, while still complying with strict regulatory obligations and accommodating new operational demands and any government and EU initiatives. Electronic working would also slash the costs of working with, managing and storing paper records. In addition, modernized information services could stimulate a wider market for the agency's services and so generate additional revenues.

Recognizing that the organization's core business was information, the chief executive commissioned an information management strategy. This articulated the agency's information environment, and illustrated how information resources underpinned the commercial rationale of the organization. However, the information management strategy did not in itself implement any information management capability. The agency needed to find a partner who could make the vision an operational reality. With the pressures of commercial management at work in the business on a daily basis, it also needed to move quickly.

Outsourcing was the obvious solution, but the manner in which this could be achieved was far from obvious. To meet its business objectives MHRA needed to see benefits within two years – half the time such a project would normally take. However, the information management strategy was currently defined at too high a level to take to market and the agency's business plan would not allow for the three or four years needed to develop a standard requirements specification. Yet suppliers would need enough detail not only to develop the system but also to identify the business process changes needed to realize its benefits.

PA stepped in to perform two critical functions for the MHRA. First, the team needed to produce a defined set of services that could be used to attract and measure bids from third party systems houses, using the high-level information management strategy as input. Second, the team had to define and manage a procurement process to make the best possible deal to implement and maintain the resulting technical road map. As PA's Graham Beck says: 'Private sector companies can't respond to a vague requirement. We would take the high-level position to a level of requirements [specification] sufficient for the outsourcing market to bid for. We would take it out of the clouds, make it priceable.'

Down from the clouds

PA installed a team of systems design specialists to add detail and structure to the existing high-level strategy. The team included information architects and network specialists, process analysts and database gurus. A mix of skills at the logical and physical levels of systems development helped to anchor the 'clouds' of the high-level strategy and relate it to the capabilities of current technology. MHRA appointed a team to the project, so that PA's specialists had full access to the business throughout the project.

Much of the work involved analysing the data and uses from different organizational perspectives. This helped to break down the divisions created by the existing legacy systems, which had stranded information sets on departmental islands. The existing systems forced staff to hold frequent exploratory meetings with each other as they attempted to create bridges. One team would share its interpretation of a document with another's view, and together they would attempt to synthesize their understanding and set direction for the next stage of resolution. It was a cumbersome process fraught with opportunities for duplicated effort and omissions. The organization lacked a single coherent view of current work in progress that could be accessed and shared across functions, and was unable to predict with certainty how long any piece of work would take to complete.

The analysis took into account the different uses MHRA makes of common data at different stages in its work. The team also explored what type of users needed access to the data, and how they would prefer to view and manipulate it. The result was an information management architecture of sufficient detail to communicate with potential suppliers. The architecture stated what the agency needed in enough detail for suppliers to respond with how they would meet those needs. The PA team did not specify the technical strategies, designs or platforms to be used by the eventual supplier, since these are precisely the areas of individual competitive expertise that produce cost savings and quality benefits from the outsourcing market.

While the information architecture represented a static definition of the systems portfolio needed by the MHRA to service its mission, the PA team also developed a complementary, dynamic view of the business context in which the new information capabilities would operate. New systems would not produce benefits without new business processes to feed, support and exploit their functionality. The open nature of the information architecture encouraged new ways of thinking about the agency's processes. An end-to-end, workflow-based view of the organization's activities soon emerged. The new systems would allow incoming cases to be categorized and interrelated on their entry to the organization. New cases would immediately be visible to those who needed to see them, and viewable in the extent and format required by each discipline. As agency staff worked on each case, its knowledge base would be automatically augmented. Detail would no longer be duplicated, lost in the cracks between departments or accidentally misinterpreted. The information architecture's business-based structure would facilitate faster throughput and more flexible methods of working. It would also bring the benefit of helping to release the hidden value of the agency's data. With professional staff now able to collate and analyse their wealth of data, they would be able to create valuable new information products for their markets.

Outstanding outsourcing

MHRA's requirements of its potential suppliers were sharpened by PA's work on its information architecture. While this created an objective base against which suppliers could be measured, it was not the only factor to be managed in the procurement process. As well as needing hardware, software and integration services, the agency needed a partner who was willing and able to help it exploit its intellectual property. With a limited budget available for securing the optimum arrangement, the deal's financial engineering was also crucial.

The agency needed its outsourcer to work with it in a very open-ended way to define the new systems and processes, and share the risk throughout the contract. Risk-sharing is not an option that a traditional outsourcing contract would usually consider without charging huge insurance premiums to cover its costs. PA therefore worked closely with the MHRA to design a new kind of outsourcing contract that allowed for variation in planned expenditure. The contract would share risk between MHRA and the outsourcer without unacceptable cost overheads for either party. Rigorous governance processes would ensure that the agency stayed firmly in control throughout the projected 10-year life of the contract.

PA produced a commercial proposition that was attractive to bidders, yet recognized that, because the requirement was not yet fully defined and therefore contained acknowledged ambiguities, the contract could not be priced in a conventional manner. The deal was structured around risk-sharing, in a manner that allowed the agency to control expenditure without the need for insurance. For each year of the contract, the requirement and cost detail of each project within the programme would be defined and agreed by the two parties on a project-by-project basis within overall affordability. Once a project was agreed, any resulting actual under- or overspend is shared by both parties on a pre-determined, capped basis.

Effectively, the agency's budget is fixed in any one year. If, during the year, pre-agreed projects deviate from plan, the agency and its outsourced supplier decide jointly on how they will redirect their investment. The variance from plan is shared equally between the two parties. If a review shows an underspend, the agency can choose to invest in further actions on its information management agenda. If, on the other hand, the parties find an overrun during the year, they can rein back, taking an equal hit. Graham Beck says:

> When traditional outsourcing arrangements go wrong, they don't have the proper governance [procedures] in place. The client thinks it's all down to the contractor and that they'll get on with it. But now you've got a third party running the core of your business. You can't let them run riot, nor can you tie them down. So there's a degree of play in the arrangement. It's got great flexibility.

PA approached the search phase of the procurement process in a commercial style that helped to cut down on the time needed to create the right deal and that attracted the right kind of responses. Informal approaches to the market were made, keeping the agency's identity anonymous and presenting an outline of the requirements and constraints of the likely contract. Although the procurement process was run through the mandated OJEC (Official Journal of the European Communities) regime, as an independent party, PA could undertake non-prejudicial market soundings to test the feasibility of some of the commercial scenarios under consideration without revealing the identity of the client.

Designing an appropriate commercial framework required unusual openness from the agency when discussing such areas as budgets with all the stakeholders. The spirit of openness was fostered by PA's collaborative approach. PA worked closely with MHRA and its lawyers, Simmons & Simmons, to design and evaluate a number of possible commercial solutions for the proposed outsourcing contract.

Thanks to the 'market warming' resulting from PA's previous informal soundings, interest was high and 23 formal responses were received; the average quality of bids was exceptionally good. Five bidders were invited to negotiate and three responded with a formal bid. The ultimate winner of the £50 million strategic outsourcing contract was Accenture, who were able to demonstrate the required expertise in systems building and infrastructure installation alongside experience in helping clients market and sell information products and services. The 10-year strategic outsourcing contract was agreed in December 2002.

The outsourcing deal was subject to several kinds of official scrutiny: the OJEC tendering process, the Department of Health formal review process and HM Treasury. PA drew on previous experience of such processes to help the agency move through each phase as smoothly as possible. For example, when negotiations entered a single-supplier phase, the agency had still to be able to demonstrate that the deal would meet 'value for money' criteria, in order to satisfy its overseers as well as itself. PA resolved this issue by developing a control 'reference bid', with figures based on what it would cost the agency to effect the step-change required in-house. The reference bid gave the agency a second set of figures against which to evaluate the supplier's proposition and gain greater understanding of the associated cost drivers.

Moving ahead

The agency was able to move from high-level strategy to contract signature within 18 months. Such a timescale is unprecedented for a government agency, and even in the commercial arena, three to four years would be more normal. In addition, the innovative nature of the contract provides a model for other organizations to adapt. Its main features are:

■ For each year of the agreement, baseline expenditure was set in the contract – effectively a joint budget for the MHRA and the supplier.

- All budget underspends and overspends were agreed and shared; risk has been spread and is the responsibility of both client and supplier alike.
- The contract encompassed financial profiling to match the agency's business strategy and flexibility to deal with the impact of known and unforeseen change.

MHRA will see its operating costs improve by 20 per cent through the lifetime of the contract. Other benefits extend beyond the agency to the UK economy and public. For example, re-engineered processes for licence applications and more streamlined post-licensing analysis will enable better information to be more effectively provided to the pharmaceuticals industry and the healthcare profession. An independent study suggests that NHS hospital costs relating to adverse drug reactions could be reduced by about 25 per cent, saving some £26 million per year.

The implemented information management strategy is enhancing the MHRA's ability to fulfil its regulatory and advisory responsibilities. The Agency is also better placed to deal with:

- the ever-increasing volume and complexity of regulatory requirements, including those emanating from the EU;
- pressure from the pharmaceutical industry's greater product diversity, technological modernization and improved throughput of medicines applications and changes;
- meeting central government e-business targets;
- the need to share information with other government and EU bodies;
- wider provision of information on medicines.

As well as achieving this range of tangible and intangible benefits, the project also illustrates the transforming power of independent consultants collaborating with professionals from the business. From the outset, agency and PA staff worked side by side. The project's core team consisted of agency and PA staff in approximately equal numbers. PA's Beck says: 'This assignment demonstrates just how effectively government bodies can modernize themselves through focused use of private sector expertise to complement their own.'

PA was able to analyse and understand the MHRA's business, but also to use its own independence and knowledge of the evolving outsourcing market to get its client the best possible deal. The agency devolved its non-core concerns to its partners, and thereby strengthened its commitment to the information business over which it must demonstrate mastery and competitiveness. A culture of partnership, mutual respect, creativity and commitment to clarity allowed an innovative deal to be successfully created in a challenging timescale – and helped to advance the cause of outsourcing that little bit further.

CASE STUDY 8.2

OUTSOURCING FOR OUTCOMES

An agency with a growing real-time information business has designed a novel partnership agreement around measurable business outcomes instead of lists of systems. The new method of defining the client–supplier relationship is adding absolute value and flexibility to each partner, and showing other organizations the way forward in an inherently unpredictable world.

The Vehicle and Operator Services Agency (VOSA) is one of four UK government agencies responsible for improving safety and environmental standards on the roads. The agency also aims to reduce vehicle crime. VOSA was formed on 1 April 2003 with the merger of the former Vehicle Inspectorate (VI) and the Traffic Area Network (TAN) divisions of the Department for Transport. The agency employs around 2,800 staff, 1,700 of whom are based at operational sites around the UK. VOSA's customers include companies from the road haulage and public service vehicle (PSV) industries, as well as the relevant trade associations and vehicle manufacturers. VOSA also oversees garages that perform MOT tests on vehicles, and the general public. The role of staff is very much hands-on. VOSA people can be found at the roadside and at weigh stations, checking vehicles and communicating with their drivers, as well as at over 90 specialist test stations around the country.

Much of VOSA's day-to-day work is concerned with ensuring compliance with commercial operator licensing requirements. The agency's licensing activity targets road safety and environmental improvements, while helping to safeguard fair competition. In practical terms, VOSA's obligations translate into a number of transactional and monitoring processes. These include the processing of applications for licences to operate lorries and buses, and registering bus services. VOSA is responsible for operating and administering testing schemes for all types of vehicle, including the supervision of the MOT testing scheme. VOSA is also responsible for enforcing legally defined drivers' hours, roadworthiness and licensing requirements, and provides training and advice for commercial operators. Lastly, VOSA has a key role in investigating vehicle accidents, defects and recalls.

The agency's powers include a power of last resort to impound vehicles that are operating illegally, ie outside the licensing regime. Impounded vehicles are taken to a secure compound where they remain for 21 days. The impounding period enables the owning companies to comply with licensing or safety requirements without endangering the public, and also allows for an appeal process.

VOSA's proactive approach to its responsibilities include Operation Mermaid, a joint police/VOSA national targeted check of goods vehicles coordinated by the Metropolitan Police. The checks are carried out at some 45 locations throughout the country. During 2003, VOSA vehicle examiners checked 6,222 vehicles and issued 651 immediate and 819 delayed prohibitions for mechanical defects. Meanwhile VOSA traffic examiners checked 4,636 vehicles for traffic offences such as abuse of drivers' hours, overloading and hazardous substance infringements.

During 2002, VOSA worked with Atos Origin to create an innovative outsourcing partnership covering a nine-year programme of work. The two parties built a commercial agreement that ties an element of Atos Origin's reward into the agency's ongoing business performance. 'Shared risk, shared reward' has long been a mantra for partnering organizations in the purely commercial world, but applying such a concept in a public–private setting is unusual to say the least.

VOSA's responsibilities are set to grow in line with the continued rise in road traffic of all kinds. At the same time, the nature of the work is becoming increasingly complex. New types of vehicles, operators, licences and road usage patterns add to the growing challenges. With the pace of change increasing, VOSA found itself constrained by traditional outsourcing arrangements that failed to accommodate shifting business requirements.

For example, if the number of staff based at an office changed, then the relevant core services arrangements had to be amended accordingly. Each modification had to be scoped and costed separately, resulting in huge amounts of work for both VOSA and its suppliers. The cumbersome services regime seriously hindered the agility the agency needed to adapt its presence and capabilities on the ground. Information systems presented the bulk of the problem. Nigel Shenton, Head of IT at VOSA, says: 'We had found that rigid outsourcing arrangements were making it difficult to evolve our IT infrastructure in line with our business needs. We wanted to structure a relationship that would offer more commercial flexibility.'

A new service model

Traditionally, IT services for the public sector have been procured by awarding a contract to the supplier who best meets a statement of requirements developed by the business. This seems a very sensible approach: define what the business needs, then select those who can meet the requirements at the best price and service levels. But this approach relies on the assumption that requirements are known ahead of implementation, are known in their entirety, and are fixed for all time. Increasingly, few of these attributes can be guaranteed for any information system.

Although it is a relatively young industry, the IT community can point to a number of services that have become commodities. Payroll, for example, has been operated as a standardized, unchanging class of service since the earliest years of its deployment in enterprises in the 1960s. More recent examples include software packages for accounts, or customer relationship management (CRM) systems. Desktop systems and packaged enterprise systems have well-defined operating requirements, maintenance schedules, upgrade paths and integration options. Services targeted at these kinds of applications can be provided readily to an agreed standard via a service level agreement (SLA), which acts as a scope and set of terms. In these traditional situations, planned applications are known and unlikely to change in detail, allowing a schedule of work to be planned well in advance.

For longer-term partnerships, where the future applications portfolio, service levels and schedule of work were potentially unclear, problems quickly arose. A number of high-profile delays have resulted from failures of contractors and government agencies to agree changes to scope (and the corresponding charges) in the middle of large-scale projects. The delays have led in turn to overspending and disruption to service for the public sector, and damaged relationships with suppliers.

The Private Finance Initiative – and more specifically the Public Private Partnership (PPP) – was devised to address these issues. Through the PPP, a private contractor would design, build and operate (DBO) a facility such as a prison or a hospital. This arrangement gave the contractor freedom to innovate, while transferring the risk of project delay and overspend out of the public sector. For the contractor, the prospect of a predictable long-term revenue stream together with complete control over the design and build of the facility made for attractive deals.

However, the PPP model rarely works for soft projects such as large-scale information systems and consultancy projects, where the DBO cycle is often iterative. Computer systems rarely exist in greenfield situations, with the majority of new systems being required to interface with existing systems or replace existing systems. At the same time existing infrastructure, including equipment, buildings and networks are usually transferred to the new outsourcing supplier.

Applying PPP to the IT services market demands a level of creativity to bypass its origins in heavy-duty construction.

The key determinant of success in new systems development is the extent to which a system can respond to changing requirements. While the IT profession has tried in the past to constrain the change cycle to a period of requirements gathering and then a schedule of post-implementation upgrades, experience of the ever-shortening change cycle suggests that most business systems need to be built to absorb modification as a constant pressure, rather than a periodic event.

In other words, applications are increasingly being architected for inherent flexibility. This can mean that the platform on which the application is deployed changes, or its core database technology is replaced, or its access methods are widened to include access from mobile devices or automated transactions with systems owned and operated by other parties. Traditional contracts necessarily specified items such as platform and interfaces in very strict terms. These are expensive items, and the choice of one option over another has substantial implications in terms of hardware, software licensing, software development and systems support activity.

Tying down the IT options creates excellent financial visibility. But it also closes out opportunities. Where a system's every feature is described in a contract, discovering the cost of moving to a new technology, justifying the business case and amending the contract accordingly can cause the opportunity to be missed. The IT business cycle changes much more quickly than the standard contract renegotiation process.

In the organizational setting, the inevitability of changes to contracted services means that every contract atrophies over time. Just as every new vehicle begins to depreciate in value the moment it leaves the dealership, so every commercial services contract begins to corrode as business change impacts its rationale.

Introducing commercial flexibility

VOSA's response to this situation was to shift away from detailed requirements of how systems were to be delivered to what they were to deliver for the business. At the beginning of the procurement process VOSA produced a statement of partnership outcome requirements (SPOR) for all the potential bidders for the outsourcing contract. This statement clarified the strategic outcomes that VOSA was seeking, and enabled bidders to focus on the real business needs of the agency rather than a mass of pre-defined solutions.

VOSA stated up-front their budget for the services together with a set of expectations from the new contract. Potential contractors developed a number of business propositions aimed at enhancing VOSA's business in line with the SPOR statement. Transition from the existing supplier to winner Atos Origin took place over Christmas 2002 and live service began on 1 January 2003.

The flexible partnership struck between VOSA and Atos Origin shares risk and reward so that each organization is left free to focus on what it does best. All projects are fixed price; the risk of cost over-runs attributable to them is borne by Atos Origin, while VOSA is required to meet a set of obligations to ensure that the projects proceed to plan. Project costs are incorporated into a managed service payment profile which, while penalizing any late delivery, is not designed to be unduly harsh or destabilize the partnership.

Project successes are assessed by published key performance indicators (KPIs) that measure the business benefit delivered by each solution as it beds into VOSA's operations. The risk of failing to achieve the KPIs is borne by both parties. As the projects are performed by business consultants, systems integration experts and managed service staff, the realization of the business opportunities presented by new technological advances are integrated into each proposition.

Shifting back to the example of car maintenance contracts, we can compare the VOSA/Atos Origin partnership with traditional outsourcing deals by looking at how services can be expressed in terms of customer benefits. While a traditional maintenance contract might specify that the garage will provide an oil change every 40,000 miles, a VOSA/Atos Origin-style contract would assert that the garage will guarantee the car's trouble-free performance throughout its lifetime.

Atos Origin's Simon Albutt says: 'Our experience with VOSA has proved that if the scope of a project is expressed in terms of a desired business outcome, and we are empowered to choose the most appropriate method of implementation, then we can manage risk effectively.' Atos Origin is free to decide the level of resources put into any particular project. If the team does not apply enough resources, it shoulders the burden when the project goes off-track. If the team oversupplies in any one area, it can scale back on preventive maintenance. The ability to match and trade variances across projects is made possible by the size and diversity of the IT portfolio at VOSA, and by the length of the contract.

The shared risk and reward approach also means that traceability and accountability within the organization improve dramatically.

One example is the provision of knowledge management services, the success of which is measured by 'dwell time': the amount of time users spend looking at a page of information from the knowledge management system. The system maintains details of known vehicle faults and developing trends, such as a spreading method of falsifying tachograph readings. 'Obviously we're not in control of how long users spend looking at the information,' says Albutt. 'But we believe that if we keep the system relevant and up to date, we can ensure that it makes a real difference to VOSA's business.'

Underpinning the partnership is a commitment to offer a consistent business focus rather than one based on technology. The terms of the contract mean that any deviation from pursuit of VOSA's business objectives will result in neither party reaping the potential benefits of the risk–reward arrangements they have devised.

Badgeless teams

Building an effective and enduring partnership requires seamless working at all levels of both organizations. VOSA has consistently organized work in joint teams across the agency from the Partnership Board to the Partnership Leadership Team and throughout the operational areas touched by IT. Albutt is clear that this style of operational partnership is not for show: 'It's particularly important that we work alongside client teams if we are to be measured against their performance.'

The partnership has enabled each organization to evolve beyond the traditional lines of customer and supplier to a more integrated way of working. Nigel Shenton agrees that the blurring of organizational 'home' is a key part of the partnership's effectiveness: 'Our teams are badgeless. At the top level we are working to coordinate a number of initiatives, some of which don't even involve Atos Origin. The end-user is the same, so it's critical that we work together to turn these into a coherent programme of work.'

The governance structure devised for the partnership enables the team to monitor progress across projects, with a clear process for managing and escalating risks. Interdependencies are identified so that the team can prioritize and focus resources according to need as issues develop. A weekly 'dashboard' showing the status of key measures is produced in Microsoft PowerPoint format.

'The governance arrangement we have with Atos Origin has been a model for managing complex programmes of change more efficiently,' says Nigel Shenton. In fact, this model marriage has been so well received that the same disciplines are being adopted by all VOSA projects regardless of whether or not they are IT related.

Technical and business innovation together

The VOSA/Atos Origin partnership agreement provides a framework into which a range of technology initiatives can fit, many of which serve the needs of a highly distributed workforce and IT estate. Key requirements for the business are flexibility and scalability, so the systems architecture is designed to evolve to meet future business and technical initiatives. For example, one of the business propositions identified during the procurement process was to support VOSA's key business objective to increase the numbers of defective vehicles stopped at the roadside. The Targeted Enforcement Programme aims to increase the effectiveness of spot checks by enabling VOSA to target time and resources on people most likely to offend rather than on random drivers. VOSA and Atos Origin have collaborated to design and implement a package of new business processes, intelligence information and training for enforcement officers in order to meet the objectives of the programme. A key enabler is a state-of-the-art handheld devices that will convey real-time information to enforcement officers at the roadside.

The deployment of mobile devices to the roadside is a good demonstration of the alignment of business goals with technological capability. Such an initiative is rarely visible at the initial planning stage of an outsourcing contract, and amending an existing contract to embrace the project could fatally erode many of its business benefits. VOSA's commercial architecture lets it drive critical business information systems forward without loss of momentum. Meanwhile, Atos Origin's flexible technical architecture ensures that new functionality will continue to be welcomed in the VOSA operational armoury. Albutt says: 'When we signed the contract, VOSA effectively transferred significant risk to us. In turn we have the flexibility in the way we deliver services. Overall, our relationship with VOSA is characterized by trust.'

VOSA's Finance and IT Director, Jeff Belt, echoes these words, and adds that the partnership acts as a signpost to other agencies: 'The partnership model is giving us the freedom to work together for mutual benefit. This contract is fixed for a substantial period of time. What we're doing with Atos Origin is building a model for outsourcing services in the future.'

VOSA is now set to get the information systems it needs for its future growth, while Atos Origin is incentivized to make those systems work. Outsourcing contracts have traditionally been about the letter of the law: this deal manages to encapsulate the spirit of partnership in a practical mechanism that is as much about relationships as it is about technology.

CASE STUDY 8.3

GEARING UP FOR RENEWED BATTLE

Replacing a long list of failing systems and plugging key information gaps has provided Sainsbury's with a platform for reinvigorated competitiveness.

Food retailing is one of the most fiercely contested sectors in the modern business world. For those who succeed, the prizes are immense. There were more than 100,000 independent grocers in the Britain of the 1960s, but only 20,000 were left by the end of the century. Concentration of the industry has continued to drive ever-greater numbers of purchases through the main chains. Criticized for encouraging out-of-town developments that disadvantage people without their own transport, supermarkets have returned to the high street with neighbourhood stores. Each store group continues to add to its offer: clothing, coffee shops and credit card accounts are as much a part of contemporary supermarket shopping as the smell of freshly baked bread and the gleam of fresh produce. But behind the inducements to shop, and the efforts to nurture customer loyalty, is a technological arms race. Customers may not necessarily see the weapons being deployed on their behalf, but the weapons are real nonetheless.

Sainsbury's is one of the UK's largest and most successful grocery retailers, but it has slipped some way from its historic heights. Established in 1869, the company now has 16.2% of the UK market, with more than 535 stores, 238 filling stations and 145,000 employees serving 13 million customers per week. As well as its prominent food stores, Sainsbury's runs a bank.

During the 1990s, Sainsbury's faced stronger, consolidated competitors that fell into two categories: those that emphasized value, like Tesco and ASDA/Wal-Mart; and those that based their offers on quality and service, like Waitrose and Marks & Spencer. Sainsbury's market position fell between these two markers. This strategic problem registered as a downward trend in sales and while Sainsbury's profits continue to be large in absolute terms, the company is recognized to have fallen behind its competitors.

In 2000, with its share price falling and a 23.3 per cent decline in operating profits, the company recognized something radical needed to happen to improve its performance. Business as usual was not working, and small fixes made at random would not address the fundamentals.

Radical change was led by CEO Sir Peter Davis. Davis and the Sainsbury's board saw three areas that needed fundamental change. These were:

- stores and customer service;
- supply chain performance and efficiency;
- IT capability.

The company wrapped these areas into an umbrella initiative called the Business Transformation Programme. The board set six key strategic objectives for the programme:

- Establish a differentiated market position and deliver sustainable shareholder value.
- Dramatically enhance the customer shopping experience through a clear understanding of target consumers and of each store's operating model and service drivers.
- Create a step-change in customer shopping experience through a radical change in the roles of store managers and their teams.
- Remove complexity and drive up effectiveness by taking out all processes and activities that do not add value to the customer experience or to shareholders.
- Create a high-performance organization and infrastructure that is rigorous, nimble and customer-centric, where quality is not negotiable.
- Leverage new capabilities and opportunities in e-commerce, business-to-business and business-to-consumer channels, maximizing the synergies of the group.

In short, the company aimed to transform all its vital business operations and to accomplish the overall transformation, the board believed its underpinning technology systems also required radical change. The company's technology infrastructure had failed to keep pace with the demands of a truly customer-oriented business. Systems were isolated from each other, and unable to share information. Introducing amendments to systems was painful and time-consuming. Above all, the existing systems portfolio did not support a more flexible attitude to running the business. It may be an overused and often vaguely used word, but Sainsbury's needed to re-engineer its *platform* for doing business and therefore outsourced its IT transformation to Accenture.

Focusing on the customer

Sainsbury's overriding goal was to make the customer the heart of the business. A joint Sainsbury's and Accenture team created a series of projects to deliver superior and differentiated service to Sainsbury's shoppers. The programme was designed to impact every aspect of the shopping experience at Sainsbury's through the intelligent application of IT.

The first project saw the development of a customer data warehouse and customer value management (CVM) application. The system became one of Europe's largest consumer databases with information on more than 13 million shoppers. The data warehouse provides insights into what customers buy, when they buy and from which store. This data drives key retail marketing and trading decisions, in particular the mix of products supplied to each local store. Granular profiling allows the CVM application to develop customized marketing campaigns, has cut down the planning, analysis and execution of campaigns from months to days and has delivered a massive reduction in data processing costs. The system has also enabled Sainsbury's to target product development better in response to customer demand. Improved customer segmentation is yielding increased mailing volumes and increased response rates to campaigns.

The new customer information systems immediately clarified the existing fragmented customer view, but they did not generate any new raw data of their own. With the aggregated customer information platform in place, the team could now turn to stocking the warehouse with further and better data. The team worked to transform the company's existing reward card loyalty programme into a novel national multi-company loyalty programme known as Nectar. Launched in September 2002, Nectar was Europe's first multi-partner loyalty programme and quickly became the UK's largest loyalty programme with more than 13 million active users.

Nectar enables customers to earn better rewards, faster. Cardholders can collect and redeem points with partner companies including BP, Barclaycard and Debenhams's department stores. From the point of view of its partner operators, Nectar acts as a gateway for acquiring customer intelligence. Individual shopping preferences registered through Nectar are fed directly into the Sainsbury's customer data warehouse to provide further insights on buyer preferences. These insights in turn help shape customer offers both in the direct channel and in-store. With the success of Nectar, the company has added around 1 million additional customers to its direct marketing campaign population.

The team now needed to ensure that customer information would flow to all the appropriate parts of the organization. Accenture developed a customer information system for Sainsbury's to collect data from all touch points including the customer contact centre and in-store customer service desks. The system provides a consolidated picture of all formal customer interaction with Sainsbury's. As a result, service representatives can view a history of every interaction a customer has had with the company and respond more effectively. The system has enabled customer service representatives to resolve an increased number of customer enquiries during the first telephone call, driving down costs and improving the company's image.

The customer service desk representatives at each store also have access to Connect, the company's new knowledge management system. Connect provides answers to all frequently asked questions, which are now fully documented to expedite customer response time and ensure consistent handling.

Meanwhile the team conducted a complete upgrade to the Sainsbury's-to-You home shopping Web site, delivering a scalable, more flexible site better able to accommodate future transaction growth. The site has already allowed Sainsbury's to expand orders per week by over 300 per cent, and the system now has the capacity to handle significant future volume growth. All the site's key performance metrics of sales, customer satisfaction and retention have improved.

At the back end of the operation, the team has implemented a new dynamic routing engine for booking home deliveries from the Sainsbury's-to-You site. The routing engine constantly optimizes the daily delivery schedules. When a customer requests available delivery times the engine calculates the economic viability of delivering to that customer, taking into account all other deliveries scheduled for that geographic area. This strategy allows Sainsbury's to decrease costs by clustering deliveries and to increase service levels by adjusting average road speeds and doorstep times. The result is an accurate route plan with achievable delivery times, leading to a decrease in late or missed deliveries.

In each of these projects, technology has been applied to improve Sainsbury's understanding of its customers so that it can serve them better, now and in the future. These projects demonstrate how customer information has developed from a nice-to-have feature lobbied for and funded by marketers to a central plank of today's business operations. Knowing the customer is directly shaping the offers made to him or her. Knowing how to get customers into stores, and deliver the goods and services they need, is the next factor in Sainsbury's transformation.

Changes in store

Sainsbury's was keen to reinvigorate the customer experience. The company continued to explore new store formats and generate new ideas for customer interactions. But away from the models and plans the team faced a major obstacle to implementing in-store change: the systems used to make financial transactions with customers. Sainsbury's had 12 different electronic point of sale (EPoS) systems, a situation that impeded the delivery of uniformly high levels of customer service and made systems upgrades difficult to plan and implement, and slow to roll out. To make the whole system simpler and more cost-effective, the team standardized EPoS systems throughout more than 700 outlets including supermarkets, gas stations and convenience stores. The EPoS system from Retalix and NCR was selected and installed over a 13-month period, rolling out to 18 stores per week at peak. More than 14,000 EPoS checkouts were standardized and 100,000 employees were trained on the new system to provide a seamless service transition in all outlets.

The business benefits resulting from the new system were huge, enabling Sainsbury's to deliver a competitive service offering and realize immediate reductions in the total cost of operation. The single platform structure paved the way for future systems changes, including a self-checkout application.

To keep store features fresh, the team created a template for a 'store of the future'. This site would serve as a model for innovation for the entire store network, and exploit technology as much as possible. The Hazel Grove store, located just south of Manchester, was chosen for this role. It was designed around the wants and needs of actual shoppers, with requirements captured through surveys and focus groups. The results were articulated in three sharp customer statements:

- 'Get me out of here!'
- 'Inspire me.'
- 'Make it fun for me and my kids.'

For customers who want to move quickly through the store (the 'Get me out of here!' group), Hazel Grove includes a Quick Shop that stocks 2,000 essential products and has 'countdown parking' that allows for 20-minute stays and alerts customers when time is up.

There is also a Sainsbury's-to-You pick-up area for those who want to pick up online shopping items without leaving their cars. The store has served as a public trailblazer for the retail marketplace and was named *Retail Week* magazine's 'Retail Launch of the Year.' Customers also rate the store favourably. Eight out of ten customers surveyed report they are 'extremely satisfied' with the new environment. Within its first six months of operations, Hazel Grove was twice the company's top-performing store.

Store formats can be designed to meet particular customer preferences for service, but if the right mix of staff is not in place in those stores then products will not sell as effectively as planned. To manage the scheduling of more than 100,000 total store workforce, a joint Sainsbury's/Accenture team selected the TempoSoft scheduling solution. The application provided a full range of labour planning and scheduling capabilities, matched the company's technical architecture and could be deployed at scale. Sainsbury's TempoSoft implementation was to be the largest of its kind in Europe.

To ensure buy-in from store personnel, the TempoSoft system was integrated with local employee programmes. The scale of the project meant that the solution required extensive testing to ensure that it would work with all of the integrated systems. The TempoSoft solution required the most up-to-date employee information and was designed to link with a new Oracle/Workbrain HR system to avoid costly double entry of information. The system also linked to the data warehouse and the time and attendance systems, providing a 360-degree view of employee information. TempoSoft went live in 480 stores in April 2003 and contributed to an improvement in front-end service levels. Staff scheduling mismatches have decreased significantly, allowing resources to be redirected to areas of critical need, further boosting customer service levels.

Honing trading capabilities

The ability to buy the right products, distribute them to the right stores and sell them at maximum profit is critical to any retailer's performance. The team quickly recognized the need to update buying and merchandising systems substantially, and chose Marketmax planning systems to support range and space planning functions. The application enables traders to plan which products to place in individual stores and shows how the products should be positioned for optimum sales. The insights provided by the system are generated by information from the customer data warehouse and from a new trading data warehouse.

The team conducted extensive testing alongside existing and new-release merchandise management systems before the first release of the product to users. The Marketmax solution has given Sainsbury's a unique opportunity to simplify and overhaul its entire product range.

To handle the merchandising around Sainsbury's products, the team chose the Retek Merchandising Systems (RMS) tool to help the trading community drive sourcing, pricing, promotion and stock management operations. Using the consolidated data in RMS, traders can make better decisions about range, space, promotions and pricing by supplier and by store.

The integration of Marketmax and Retek RMS has had a huge impact on Sainsbury's operations, enabling faster and more efficient demand forecasting and store replenishment. The systems are additionally supported by Retek Demand Forecasting (RDF) and the Advanced Inventory Planning (AIP) system. Together, RDF and AIP enable Sainsbury's to calculate accurately the demand for every single product across its entire range and plan the appropriate store orders to meet inventory requirements. The sophisticated replenishment engine within the system allows the company to run a highly efficient supply chain. The system also allows Sainsbury's to predict accurately what customers want and respond accordingly. While these systems work silently behind the scenes, better product ranging and availability have made a great impact on customer service.

To give Sainsbury's a competitive edge in its development of new products, the team installed a collaborative product development (CPD) solution. This application enables Sainsbury's internal teams to collaborate effectively with a vast array of stakeholders, from product development people, chefs, manufacturers and third-party suppliers, to lawyers and marketers. Through the CPD system, all parties in the development process have access to the same information. This makes collaborative working easier and makes better use of resources.

The new regime introduced by CPD triggered other business changes, including training of employees and a communication programme to ensure that all involved parties across the supply chain were fully briefed. Training was delivered online and linked to a 24-hour helpdesk. Another part of CPD is the Idea Bank: a repository of ideas relating to new product development.

All private-label Sainsbury's products, representing some 40 per cent of all goods sold, are now developed on the CPD platform. Time-to-market has been cut by 50 per cent and development costs are down 30 per cent. Life cycle revenues for new products are expected to rise in the region of 20 per cent. Peter Strode, Sainsbury's business-to-business coordinator, says: 'CPD has changed radically the way we develop products. It has taken the strain out of managing the masses of information across a wide network, and has freed us to focus on quality and innovation instead.'

Rebuilding the supply chain

One goal that all of the Business Transformation Programme projects strive for is simplification. Nowhere has this been more apparent than in Sainsbury's efforts to re-engineer its supply chain. Retek Demand Forecasting (RDF) was implemented to manage the supply chain, supported by Infolink software to detail the progress of future deliveries. These two applications plus new warehouse management systems from Manhattan Associates are key to enabling Sainsbury's to implement the core of its supply chain initiative: four automated warehouses, the largest of which is 700,000 square feet.

The re-engineered supply chain process starts when pallets are received from suppliers and put on to a conveyor system. Cranes take goods to a reserve location where they are later chosen by 'pickers' based on store demand and fed through another conveyor belt. Products are then sorted and loaded in 'family groups' with other products from related store areas. This sorting cuts down on handling as products are taken directly off trucks and placed on their appropriate shelves.

By Spring 2004, the new network was servicing 60 per cent of Sainsbury's total network volume, allowing the company to close less efficient facilities and achieve significant savings. The smooth operation of the warehouses is only part of the story; Martin White, Supply Chain Director of Sainsbury's says: 'Systems are at the core of our new supply chain, but the success comes in connecting our people with these changes.'

To manage the 'last 50 yards' of the supply chain, the team designed and implemented Shelf Availability Monitor (SAM), an in-store system that provides critical information on sales patterns of each individual store. Through point-of-sale data capture, SAM monitors what a store would expect to sell against what it is actually selling. Where discrepancies appear, SAM highlights problems that may relate to shelf availability, or to service and staffing issues. In the first five months after its implementation Sainsbury's gained more than £22 million in extra sales, in addition to increasing its on-shelf availability by half a percentage point.

Connecting to knowledge

Sainsbury's has more than 145,000 full-time employees working in retail outlets, warehouses and corporate offices. The team developed a sophisticated yet easy-to-use knowledge management system to gather and organize the collective experience of all of the company's staff. Connect is a portal using Vignette's Epicentric technology on the Web front end together with a document management system and search engine. The application allows staff with diverse and unpredictable needs to access the information they need when they need it, and in a format that makes the information instantly usable. Connect holds information on the status of different company projects, provides links to critical online technical resources and hosts discussion forums. The portal is also used in-store to centralize business-critical applications like labour management spreadsheets and retailing procedure documents.

Finance also received an IT boost. The team developed a suite of financial systems that allows for greater control of reporting, accounting and project management. The applications include an enterprise reporting application based on Microstrategy and a project accounting application based on Oracle Financials.

The IT support organization's infrastructure was also upgraded in the course of the Business Transformation Programme. The local area network (LAN) infrastructure was renewed and Microsoft Office suite and e-mail delivered to more than 3,000 users. The head office was moved to a fully equipped desktop environment.

Finally, to drive down costs and improve effectiveness in the area of HR, a payroll system built around solutions from Oracle, WorkBrain and Rebus solutions was implemented to give staff self-service access to their own personal information. This cuts down on the paper trail traditionally associated with personnel issues. Head office staff can use the system to undertake a variety of tasks from making claims for variable payments such as mileage, to booking training courses and updating personal development plans. The system is additionally used by stores to manage staff holidays and absences.

Savings and earnings

Sainsbury's Business Transformation Programme has modernized the company's information systems capability, and given it a stable platform for renewed vigour in its highly competitive sector. The benefits to date have been measurable as cost savings. After the company launched the programme, it's primarily achieved six consecutive half-year profit improvements, increased the dividend paid to shareholders and grew its sales. The company expected to realize cumulative cost savings of £710 million by March 2004.

The struggle for excellence in the supermarket rarely pauses. The team at Sainsbury's is now looking to reap top-line benefits from the use of technology, as further systems projects target increases in sales volumes and values. The Business Transformation Project shows eloquently how information technology has become a core part of business survival. Perhaps the biggest change the team has achieved is an enduring readiness for change.

9

Electronic trading

Information is the life blood of a joined-up world. Yet, successive initiatives – knowledge management, e-business – have failed to deliver a free flow of information to those who need it in many, if not most, organizations. Old challenges remain, as the projects described in this chapter illustrate.

Take-up is critical: how do you bring disparate, disorganized sources of information together without creating cumbersome, bureaucratic processes that deter potential users? The four case studies in this chapter faced the following challenges:

- With the general public seemingly ever more apathetic about the democratic process, e-voting is high on most governments' agenda. Could the Office of the Deputy Prime Minister (ODPM) use alternative channels to increase levels of inclusion, engagement, and participation? Then, having provided a multitude of possible voting channels, the ODPM had to ensure there was no possibility they could be abused, with one person voting in several different ways. Only technology could provide the answer to this.
- Behind the scenes, it is technology integration that matters most. As a result of a string of acquisitions, BAE Systems had inherited several enterprise resource planning (ERP) systems used for procurement and these were cutting into the savings the company hoped to achieve via electronic trading.
- The Neighbourhood Renewal Unit was faced with the prospect of trying to get hard data on successful urban regeneration initiatives to a wide range of people who might find it useful – local residents as well as public agencies.
- As one of the world's largest insurance brokers, every piece of correspondence is important to Aon. Shifting this from physical to

electronic format was not just a matter of technology; there was also a 300-year heritage of doing business face-to-face and a long-standing suspicion of change.

PULL NOT PUSH

The first generation of knowledge management and workflow systems opted for the stick, rather than the carrot, approach. Compliance was everything: once systems had been developed, people had to be made to use them. This is not a strategy that would have worked for Aon, the ODPM or the Neighbourhood Renewal Unit. The ODPM could not force people to vote, anymore than Aon could have forced everyone to use its new electronic document management systems for all their correspondence. The Neighbourhood Renewal Unit could not argue the benefits of consistency (as Aon could have done), because its initiative was not intended to change what people do, but to provide them with an invaluable source of information on which ideas were more and less likely to work in practice.

One way of encouraging more people to engage with government is to offer them a variety of possible channels, allowing them to select one that is convenient to them, rather than demanding that they go to a polling station in person. SMS text messaging and the Internet both offer alternative ways to vote, and the ODPM is also experimenting with digital television, telephone, and multilingual touch-screen systems in kiosks. Those less comfortable with technology can vote by post, with the counting done electronically. Perhaps it is not so much the range of options here that matters most, rather the choice and convenience it gives the consumer. Choice engenders a sense of control and that, in turn, creates a sense of commitment. Convenience simply makes it easier. As with the ODPM's e-voting initiative, take-up of the Neighbourhood Renewal Unit's knowledge management portal was partly going to depend on making the relevant people aware of its existence – considerable time and effort was therefore invested in designing and building up the portal's brand. But this was balanced by the careful consideration that went into establishing exactly how the information could be most effectively presented, so that potential users were not deterred by the volume of material available. Six months were spent in consulting more than 2,000 prospective users and in developing prototypes that could be tested out in practice. The content, too, had to be right – authoritative but accessible. Interactive features – discussion forums and e-mail updates – were added in an attempt to increase the portal's 'pull' factor.

As those involved with workflow automation at Aon put it, it was not just a case of getting the technology ready for the business, but of getting the business ready for the technology. Good, consistent and regular communication with future users was supplemented by more innovative initiatives, such as a dedicated 'familiarization' area, which allowed people to see what the final system would look like in practice.

GETTING THE TECHNOLOGY RIGHT

Electronic trading is necessarily about moving information across systems, allowing (at a corporate level) organizations to exchange information quickly and accurately, and (at an individual level) people to access common sources of information easily, irrespective of where they are based or, indeed, of the type of technology they prefer to use. This means that electronic trading projects depend as much on integration between systems as they do on particular applications, the vast majority of which are imperceptible to the people using them. What can look like a common point of entry for different groups of people can, in fact, be more like spaghetti behind the scenes.

It was certainly something like spaghetti that BAE Systems faced as it sought to link its 32 different ERP systems together in order to improve its procurement processes (most of which, not surprisingly, were still done manually). The solution was obvious – a single procurement gateway – but how would it be connected to everything else? The system would have to translate data from the procurement gateway into formats that could be used by the other systems, and vice versa. Similarly, voting channels cannot be treated independently: the only way to avoid fraud is to ensure that they all update one central database. 'Pull' from the users' point of view therefore has to be balanced with behind-the-scenes push: standardization, simplification and centralization.

TECHNOLOGISTS, COORDINATORS AND BRIDGES

From the projects described in this chapter, it appears that consultants have three distinct roles to play when it comes to implementing electronic trading initiatives.

The first, not surprisingly, relates to the technology itself. Part of the role of Unisys, in working with the ODPM, was to advise on which technology to use and how to make it work in practice. Knowledge of state-of-the-art developments and new applications was clearly an essential component in making this work. Similarly, CSC Computer Sciences' work with BAE Systems depended on expert knowledge of how complex and disparate legacy systems could be linked together in practice.

That complexity gives rise to the second role. In environments where there are likely to be multiple hardware and software suppliers (as Unisys found with e-voting), as well as multiple internal stakeholders, coordination is critical. When the Neighbourhood Renewal Unit hired PA Consulting Group to help with the development of its portal, the consultants' role was as much about creating a structure that people would want to contribute to and to use. Having helped with the process of selecting the right technology suppliers, Impact Plus worked with Aon to integrate the vastly different streams of work involved in moving their staff from paper-based processes to electronic systems.

However, perhaps the most important role the consultants in these cases play is as bridges between the 'pull' and 'push' aspects of electronic trading. As with PA's work with the Neighbourhood Renewal Unit, part of their role is balancing technological simplicity with having sufficient, high-quality content to appeal to a diverse group of potential users. As with CSC's work at BAE Systems, part of their role is to bring together different platforms and systems without constraining the business.

SUMMARY – KEY LESSONS FOR MANAGERS AND CONSULTANTS

- The first generation of organizations that have tried to 'manage' knowledge have found that people could not be compelled to use the new systems – and, without constant updating, the systems languished. Focusing attention on usability, convenience and people's experience in using a system is more likely to increase take-up.
- Flexibility at the front-end has to be balanced with clarity and single-mindedness behind the scenes.
- Consultants can provide help in coordinating stakeholders and suppliers, as well as expert help in terms of the technology selected, but their key role is to provide a bridge between the front and back office.

CASE STUDY 9.1

PIONEERING MULTI-CHANNEL VOTING

Helping 300,000 citizens pilot new voting channels required careful attention to communications and tight control of project tasks.

Voting procedures in the UK have not fundamentally changed in the last 100 years. During that time the UK has resisted every mechanical form of voting machine, and while the nation has avoided any controversy caused by 'hanging chads' or other troublesome artefacts of voting machinery, it has paid the price in expensive, labour-intensive and time-consuming election processes. While the world at large has struggled to eliminate paper from its daily business, democracy in the UK still relies on individuals using pencils to make crosses on ballot papers at local polling stations. Selected schools, community centres and other local amenities are closed to normal business during each polling day. Fleets of vans carry metal voting boxes to centralized venues for counting by hand. If someone were paying for this unwieldy and outmoded process, it would be reformed with all due speed. And of course someone is paying – the taxpayer. Although the current e-election pilots are not designed to demonstrate value for money, this will be a major consideration in the government's future modernization programme.

The government had made explicit commitments to implement electronic service delivery across all public services, setting a target of 100 per cent availability of services electronically by 2005. As part of this drive for modernization of the relationship between the citizen and government, voting could not be left behind. The government commissioned e-election pilots to test UK citizens' appetite to vote by whatever means reflects their lifestyle. E-voting would therefore be a very visible plank of e-government. Unisys's Phil Cheetham sees e-voting as an inevitable development: 'Citizens can bank online and shop online, and all other government transactions are being enabled online, so the voting system shouldn't be left behind.'

A government-backed report published by De Montford University in May 2002 confirmed emerging public support for the idea of Internet and telephone voting, but warned that the government would have to help educate those electors who were less confident with new technology if an electronic General Election could go ahead in the future. The report also endorsed the government's policy of trialling e-voting in local elections, through 'multi-channel' voting, which offers voters a range of options including the traditional polling station and ballot box. Electronic voting had been used for the first time in the 2000 local council elections, and helped lift voter turnout in some areas. However, postal voting had proved the most popular voting method, almost doubling turnout in some places where it was piloted.

The government committed to extending the pilots, with a view to considering an e-enabled general election after 2006. The local government minister, Nick Raynsford, said that the government was keen to make the electoral process 'more relevant to modern life', but warned that 'any changes to the voting system must be properly researched to ensure that they are of real benefit to the public, as well as incorporating effective safeguards against abuse'.

The De Montford report had in fact raised public concerns over secrecy and security, with possible threats from viruses, power supply disruption, hacking and limits to system capacity. People feared that the risks inherent in large commercial online systems could transfer to the electoral arena. Technology could be used to improve the voting process, but maintaining public confidence in the integrity of the process needed to be the highest priority in any new approach.

The job of managing the UK's Electoral Modernization Programme is funded by grants to a number of local authorities and managed by the Office of the Deputy Prime Minister (ODPM). The ODPM was created in May 2002, with responsibility for policy on housing, planning, devolution, regional and local government and the national fire service. It also takes responsibility for the Social Exclusion Unit, the Neighbourhood Renewal Unit and the Government Offices for the Regions.

Unisys and its partner, Election Systems & Software (ES&S), were appointed in March 2003 to deliver multi-channel voting systems to the citizens of South Tyneside, Chorley and Rushmoor Councils in the May 2003 local elections. The combined electorate of the three areas was more than 300,000 people. Unisys and ES&S were also contracted to provided data hosting services for a further five local authorities whose 'end-user' election services were managed by BT.

The pilot options

Multi-channel voting covers a number of different methods for registering votes, not all of them high-tech. In an all-postal ballot, for example, the local authority posts ballot papers to all those registered to vote. Usually included with the ballot paper is a 'Declaration of Identity', which the voter and, in some cases a witness, are required to sign.

'Early voting' is the name given to an extension of normal voting hours. Confusingly, early voting can also include polling stations closing later than usual, or even remaining open for additional days. Where polls are open for additional days, councils can use mobile polling stations, located at convenient sites such as supermarkets and train stations. Early voting is regarded as a novel voting channel, even though it is only a procedural variation on the traditional voting arrangement.

However, electronic methods also have a part to play in the improvement of traditional voting methods. 'E-counting' is a means of automating the counting of paper ballots either by scanning the paper directly into a computer as an image or printing bar codes on the ballot paper next to each candidate's name for scanning.

In Internet voting, electors are each supplied with a unique security code. They log on to the voting site and enter their code. The system then checks their eligibility to vote and displays the voting information for the relevant electoral ward. Telephone voting uses automated response systems, familiar from commercial helpline services, to register votes while the SMS or text messaging option exploits the popularity of this method of communicating from mobile phones. Voters are sent a personal identification number (PIN) and a pack listing the names of the candidates standing in their ward and their corresponding candidate numbers. Voters then send a text message, including their PIN and the identifier of the candidate they wish to vote for, to the telephone number supplied with the voting pack.

Piloting the alternative channels

The three pilots each used a different mix of technologies to deliver new voting choices. In South Tyneside electors were able to vote via post, the Internet, touch-tone telephone, as well as via SMS text messaging and multilingual touch-screen kiosks in six locations around the city. Postal votes were counted electronically rather than manually. The voting period was from 15 April until 5.00 pm on 1 May with the exception of the SMS option, which closed 24 hours earlier.

Chorley citizens were able to vote by post with electronic counting, by Internet and touch-tone telephone from 18 April until 9.00 pm on 1 May. Citizens in Rushmoor combined voting at traditional polling stations on 1 May with Internet voting from 25 April until 9.00 pm on 1 May.

The e-voting pilot schemes had four objectives. The first objective was to make voting more straightforward for the public by offering simple methods for registering their votes. The second objective was to make elections more accessible, by making it more convenient to vote and by making voting more attractive to people currently less likely to vote. The third objective addressed the behind-the-scenes aspects of elections, by making the administration of elections more efficient and cost-effective. The final objective of the schemes was to maintain or even increase the level of security at elections.

The Unisys project team also added a management objective to collect and analyse operational information in order to assess the scalability of each method for subsequent pilots and potentially a General Election. The focus of the data analysis was to help future elections to be run more efficiently and resources to be deployed more effectively. The team also wanted to discover how long it took for the local authorities to become familiar with the technologies used in the pilots. This information could then be fed into the planning and milestones for future e-voting pilots.

The government required every supplier in the e-voting pilots to demonstrate innovation. The team were therefore given considerable freedom in how they managed and delivered each pilot. The pilots were set in areas with diverse demographic characteristics. The project was further complicated by the fact that each technical solution was different and the voting periods varied across the areas.

The three pilots were implemented using Unisys TEAMmethod™ project management methodology. TEAMmethod™ is a formal approach to designing, implementing and maintaining information systems organized in four phases: Strategy and vision, Planning and road map, Deployment and review, and Validation. Several components of this flexible methodology were implemented including acceptance, quality and testing. A primary focus was placed on strong management of risks and issues.

The centralized ES&S software application was installed at a secure Unisys data centre in Milton Keynes and contained records of all registered voters and their voting activity. The application was based on an Oracle database and Oracle 9iAS server. All the source code was reviewed by an independent testing authority to ensure that it complied fully with European coding standards. Centralization of the e-voting systems meant that there was no technical disruption to the systems environments of the three authorities.

A team of experienced project managers was placed with the local authorities to work in delivering the elections. A central management function and project office managed the team. A centre of excellence including skills for election delivery, the solution and its technology and processes was formed to support the local authority pilot project management. A round-the-clock helpdesk, with communication channels through to the local authorities and the centre of excellence, was put in place to address any queries from voters.

Dealing with the issues

Expanding the voting options available to electors is not simply a matter of installing the right technologies. Indeed, the technologies used for the pilots were all proven solutions that had been used in a range of commercial environments. The public were not going to be guinea pigs for new technology solutions. The team's concern was more focused on how the alternative voting channels would be delivered, so that the technologies could yield their expected benefits and the performance of the pilots could be adequately assessed. Changing electoral methods is about influencing behavioural changes and determining which mechanisms have the greatest impact on turnout and cost-effectiveness.

The first issue the team faced was the various local authorities' familiarity with the technologies being applied in the pilot. Some officers were concerned about the consequences for public confidence if a channel failed during the 'live' voting period. The twin spotlights of government scrutiny and public opinion were firmly on the pilots and any glitches would be magnified in media coverage. It was vital for the team to keep the authorities constantly up to date with project developments and to take them through each stage of the process at an appropriate pace. The authorities needed to feel that they were in control of the pilots, and that the technology tail was not wagging the democracy dog.

Having chosen the channels to implement, the local authorities needed to agree the voting processes and the look and feel for each channel. For Rushmoor, where the Internet was the only novel channel being provided, designing the voter experience was a relatively simple process. The team created a set of templates for the process and walked colleagues from the authority through the screens. Each screen was then laid out to meet local preferences, with the content and style of each screen documented, implemented and agreed. At South Tyneside there were five channels to implement including e-counting, Internet and SMS text messaging. The designs of all these channels were completed and agreed in the same open and collaborative style.

With the channels correctly tailored for each voting area, the team then turned to the task of ensuring that each local authority team had enough support to deliver the pilots. A central support team was rapidly formed and briefed on the project's goals, timescales and predicted challenges. This team developed into a lively, supportive community linking the different pilot sites and disseminating knowledge among them. The cross-fertilization between the different pilot areas meant that potential obstacles were identified across the community as soon as they arose in one area. Solutions could also be conveyed to the wider team before the problems were even encountered. In this way a virtuous cycle of learning and improvement took root during the pilot exercises themselves. This inductive learning was an additional bonus to the knowledge the team expected to gain at the completion of the pilots, when overall performance could be compared to traditional methods.

The third issue the team faced was voter awareness of the pilot channels. The team developed a 'Voter Outreach' campaign to increase the public's awareness of the new technologies being made available for the upcoming elections.

Wider awareness campaigns were run in each area to reinforce the personal communications packs and encourage voter engagement with the pilots. In Chorley, the team worked with Chorley Borough Council to devise and deploy a 'voting at your fingertips' marketing campaign. This campaign targeted several communications channels simultaneously in order to ensure complete coverage of the local area in the key period of the run-up to the elections. The team ran a local press campaign to make sure that relevant stories were published regularly before and during the election period. The team also designed an advertisement to run on the main local radio station throughout the 12-day voting period. Posters using the distinctive 'voting at your fingertips' logo were placed at a selection of prominent roadside billboard sites, and posters highlighting the voting channels, voting period and helpline number were displayed in community sites such as doctors' surgeries and post offices. Finally the team ran an open day on the middle Saturday of the voting period. Sited in Chorley town centre, the open day event allowed voters to ask questions face to face with team members and acted as a lively reminder of their voting options to passers-by.

Central to each pilot was a 'voting pack' containing all the information about the channels available in each voting area. Every elector within each constituency received one of the packs, ensuring that no one would be excluded from the alternative channels by accident or lack of access to general information sources. The pack was practical as well as informative, containing simple step-by-step instructions for voting by each voting method. A helpline was also set up so that any citizens with questions about voting channels or procedures could call one central number and have their queries answered personally and in full.

The authorities were highly aware of their leadership position in trialling the new voting methods. Chorley's Deputy Returning Officer Martin O'Loughlin says: 'By increasing the choice of Internet and touch-tone we are making voting even easier. Britain is ahead of most countries in moving to e-voting and Chorley is leading the way nationally and now internationally.'

The team identified and tackled all these issues within the context of a fundamental constraint: the project's timeline. The timetable for delivery was short and non-negotiable. For the delivery of a voting system to be operational in mid-April when it was ordered in mid-March, the project had to be tightly managed so that there were no delays in any stages of the project. Regular team briefings meant that issues were overcome almost immediately. The immovable timeline was a helpful constraint on the project, guarding against any potential for 'scope creep' or the addition of extra options. According to Cheetham: 'There was no time to dwell on problems, we had to fix them.'

The Unisys consultants on site at each local authority were integrated as part of the election project teams and participated in regular project meetings and status reporting. Where specific areas of expertise were required, the appropriate representatives were called in for those meetings.

Reporting to the central management structure spanning all the pilots was done by weekly status reports. These reports included risk and issue logs. Weekly meetings were attended by at least one person from each local authority site. A teleconference link was made available for anyone who could not attend in person, but this was rarely used since most team members felt the value of personal attendance.

Unisys also worked in close partnership with the ODPM throughout the election period and afterwards, regularly discussing and advising on issues relating to service levels, detection of attempted security breaches and the progress of the various public awareness campaigns. The team also worked collaboratively with other government agencies including the Electoral Commission. The team's practice was to maintain an 'open door' policy for all stakeholders in the project, inviting attendance at internal project meetings as well as site visits to our project sites.

Over to the count

When the voting is over, the counting begins and the shape of the public's democratic decision emerges. With the end of the elections the project team was able to measure the uptake and performance of each pilot channel to see how voters had expressed their preferences for the way they vote.

Analysis by the Electoral Commission showed that the overall level of user awareness and comprehension of the voting methods being tested were high, with 77 per cent of those interviewed during the election and 88 per cent interviewed afterwards confirming that they were aware of the new voting arrangements. Analysis also showed that voters were appreciative of the alternative channels. Independent MORI polls reported that respondents felt that the convenience of e-voting channels was on average 'very good' (40 per cent) or 'fairly good' (27 per cent). Those who said that the channels were neither better nor worse than traditional channels totalled 8 per cent, 7 per cent said the new channels were 'fairly poor', 3 per cent 'very poor' and 14 per cent had no opinion. Opinion polling also revealed local variations in voter responses, with three-quarters of respondents to the Electoral Commission's MORI poll in Chorley saying that the new voting methods made the process of voting better.

On the technology side of the project, independent security tests carried out on the electronic channels failed to penetrate the security of any channel. The team could also find no evidence that the alternative voting procedures led to any increase in electoral offences or malpractice.

The team refuses to mistake 'soft' benefits for measurable effects, but it does point to several outcomes it believes make a significant contribution to the progress of the electoral system. For instance, voting turnout is influenced by a number of factors and politicians frequently disagree about why numbers go up or down at different elections and in different areas. The impact of e-voting on turnout is particularly hard to assess as there is so little historical data. However, as with the 2002 local elections, the turnout for Chorley in 2003 (49.81 per cent) was substantially greater than historic turnout figures for traditionally run elections in the borough (32 per cent). Meanwhile, South Tyneside's Council Leader Paul Waggott says: 'These e-voting methods have made this a very different election. The experiment has been a success as it has doubled the number of people voting than at traditional ballot box elections.'

A further 'soft' benefit of the pilots has been the increase in local authority experience in running e-voting systems and their associated communications and support programmes. This should help increase the level of efficiency and reduce implementation costs for future e-voting pilots while reducing reliance on external agencies for help in implementation.

The team also notes that the cost profile of e-voting is not yet mature enough to judge in terms of standalone value. As in any new technology-dependent process, e-voting requires up-front investment that takes time to pay back. The expenditure needed to provide one-off pilots for individual authorities was borne by the ODPM. The provision of telephone and Internet voting did lead to a significant increase in expenditure over the normal cost of traditional elections, mainly for the provision of the hardware and software needed to support the new channels. Deploying this technology over a number of years and on a wider scale will provide further operational evidence to inform the assessment of the long-term cost of implementing e-elections.

There were no e-voting pilots in the 2004 local elections. The Electoral Commission advised that the simultaneous European Parliament elections would make the 2004 elections complex enough without additional voting channel trials. However, Cheetham says: 'It's clear that e-voting works and that it should be expanded in future years.'

Unisys collaborative work with its partners in the local authorities shows that careful preparation and attention to detail can make alternative methods of voting simpler than the time-honoured practice of folding paper slips into boxes, and can help to improve the reach and effectiveness of our democratic process. The consulting firm was able to centralize systems provision for all of the pilot areas it served, saving the public from duplicated costs and avoiding disruptive work at the local authorities involved. In addition, Unisys was able to hold together the different strands of activity in each voting area, thereby providing a local focus for each authority without distracting management attention from their ongoing concerns. Detailed expertise in the various novel channels and their technical deployment would not be found in complete or up-to-date form in any of the authorities, so access to a full range of skills was important to each area's e-election.

Crucially, Unisys acted as a conduit of learning, both geographically and historically. Alerting different teams to issues already encountered reduced the numbers of errors and delays encountered across the election as a whole, while the lessons learned from the exercises will be used to improve elections in future years. Good consulting firms act a little like living libraries, helping to transport knowledge across the miles and years. This valuable experience may pay further dividends for the company and its partners as pressure mounts for publicly traded companies to move to e-voting. Phil Cheetham is convinced that e-voting will soon become the new tradition: 'This was a challenging project because of the timescales and the complexities. But citizens and customers were delighted, and there's real zeal for continuing the pilots. The ultimate [end] will be the General e-enabled Election.'

CASE STUDY 9.2

COLLABORATING SYSTEMS DRIVE DOWN COSTS

Getting BAE System's procurement systems to talk sense with the industry's online trading environment is anticipated to make the company £20 million in cumulative savings. The flexible method the company used to streamline procurement will also spark further savings throughout the business as it is applied to a growing number of business processes.

BAE Systems employs more than 90,000 people worldwide, and generates annual sales of around £12 billion. The company designs, manufactures and supports military aircraft, surface ships, submarines, radar, communication tools, guided weapons and avionics equipment. The company operates in an economic and political climate where customer value is all-important and public scrutiny intense. This is big business: service agreements with governments and airlines are measured in the billions of pounds and product life cycles are measured in decades. It does not automatically sound like a great candidate for an e-commerce solution.

Some managers bridle when they hear the term e-commerce. The hype surrounding business-to-consumer e-commerce during the late 1990s led to some best-forgotten projects as organizations tried desperately to join the Internet revolution. While the leading e-commerce players such as Amazon and eBay have gone from strength to strength, smaller players have fared less well. Existing businesses that went online frequently did not generate the revenues they expected, and sometimes overspent on expensive Web sites that added little to the bottom line.

However, e-commerce is now silently and unobtrusively delivering significant recurring benefits to businesses around the world. These successes are in the category of business-to-business systems, and in particular applications for online procurement. Cost-effective procurement is a vital part of managing service delivery costs, so engineering paper transactions out of the process can generate substantial value.

Exostar is one such business-to-business solution. It was founded by BAE Systems together with other industry leaders Boeing, Lockheed Martin, Raytheon and Rolls-Royce as an online trading exchange for the aerospace and defence industry, linking up manufacturers, suppliers and customers. Exostar provides an online, collaborative trading system where data and component designs can be shared with suppliers, contract agreements exchanged, and parts sourced and purchased electronically, saving considerable sums of money compared to paper-based trading. Exostar's user base includes over 300 buyers in 20 different countries and more than 12,000 suppliers worldwide.

Businesses can gain instant benefits from using online procurement as a means of buying standard supplies such as stationery or furniture. Most businesses now use online sources for purchasing items that can be readily listed in catalogues. However, Exostar goes beyond the typical catalogues. Exostar members can use the system to share design documents with each other, allowing companies to collaborate on the products they are seeking to create or consume. In this way users can craft their own deals. Furthermore, once such a contract has been agreed on Exostar, the two parties can complete all their purchasing functions with each other through Exostar. In effect, Exostar provides a standardized environment in which parties can do business with each other from concept through to delivery.

Electronic trading links existed in BAE Systems' industry prior to the launch of Exostar, but these relationships carried a small proportion of transactions. Exostar created a new, open, global channel for electronic transactions that would drive much more business online. The implications for trading partners' systems were profound, not least at BAE Systems itself.

BAE Systems had inherited a host of different Enterprise Resource Planning (ERP) systems as a by-product of a series of mergers and acquisitions. Each business area had its own ERP suite used for procurement. These different procurement systems with their varying functions, standards and platforms did not form a natural electronic trading strategy for the company. The legacy base was also driving escalations in the business's operational costs. The costs of duplicated functionality and lost opportunities for efficiencies caused by the non-availability of a unified trading environment within the company were felt to be large, though hard to compute. BAE Systems estimated that 99 per cent of its purchase orders and invoices were still being processed manually. Given the scale of its global operations, and the leadership in electronic trading it had provided with the co-founding of Exostar, the company saw a massive opportunity to reduce costs and improve stakeholder value. The result is a streamlined procurement platform calculated to generate cumulative savings of £20 million by 2010.

Tasking the team

A BAE Systems/CSC Computer Sciences Corporation team was formed to enable the business to trade and exchange procurement information effectively and efficiently, both within the business and with external partners. Exostar would provide the 'pull' for the project, while the unacceptable costs of the legacy situation provided the 'push'. BAE Systems and CSC would work closely together throughout the project, sharing the business goals and involving each other as integral members of the design, development and deployment teams. BAE Systems' e-Business lead Andrew Mossop says: 'The project success was all about working together as one team. [BAE Systems] and CSC worked closely together to deliver the final solution that removed non-value-added tasks from the procurement process.'

CSC's Mike Burz adds that BAE Systems' long history with CSC was an important factor in the project: 'Over the years we'd proved to them time and again that we deliver state-of-the-art solutions that benefit them financially. And so they trusted us to come up with an innovative solution to this e-commerce problem.'

The team was asked to design, develop and deploy a solution that would enable each ERP system to connect to Exostar. The solution would include:

- establishing the connections between the ERP systems and Exostar;
- collaborating with BAE Systems' dedicated e-business team to develop a business case and secure buy-in from the key stakeholders within the business units;
- promoting the use of the newly developed solution for other e-business applications, such as e-Finance, e-Sales, e-Sourcing and e-HR, within BAE Systems worldwide.

The team defined and evaluated three different approaches to meeting the project's goals. The first option was to create a centralized procurement system to replace the plethora of existing systems throughout the business. This would have the benefits of standardizing procurement processes within the company and removing the legacy burden. However, it would also be an expensive approach that would expose the business to critical risks. The diverse procurement processes fitted the businesses they served, and defining a single, universal replacement system might not be possible without fatally compromising some areas of the business. Building a system that offered the full flexibility needed by the company's operational units would essentially have entailed rebuilding the functionality manifested by Exostar, albeit in an in-house setting rather than a sector-wide context.

The second option was to implement a set of point-to-point solutions, where each of the existing ERP systems was connected directly to Exostar. An operational relationship would be designed and coded to give each legacy system a 'private line' to Exostar. While this was a more viable and less risky approach than the first option, it would add to the complexity of the company's legacy systems. Each relationship would have to be hand-crafted, and there would be no opportunity for sharing data or functionality among the relationships. The team would have to build and maintain a unique bridge for each legacy system, without being able to share any building materials or components.

The third option was to create a central backbone into which all the existing ERP systems would connect. This option was dubbed the Enterprise Application Integration (EAI) approach. The EAI layer would manage two-way traffic between BAE Systems' procurement systems and Exostar, ensuring that the information was translated appropriately for each system.

Following extensive discussions, the third option was chosen because it provided the greatest benefit at low cost and minimal risk. This option was also considered to be more flexible and adaptable. One of the particular plus points was the potential to adapt the EAI strategy for other parts of the business. Not only would it be capable of unifying disparate ERP systems, it could equally be applied to enable other business processes that required streamlining, such as sales or HR, thereby supporting BAE Systems' longer-term business objectives.

A language for business

The evolution of programming solutions built around Internet technology has produced many benefits, not least the standardized user interface framework provided by the ubiquitous Web browser. The HTML (hypertext markup language) coding scheme defined for Web pages allows all kinds of information to be displayed by browsers and promises a high degree of consistency across different browser products and computer platforms. But while HTML has helped to simplify the creation of content, it remains merely a coding scheme for the visual layout of material. The items tagged in an HTML page have no business meaning. A piece of HTML may tell us, for example, that a word should be displayed in bold, but it cannot tell us that the displayed word denotes the price of the item placed alongside it.

Developers quickly realized that an analogue of HTML designed to incorporate the meaning of content as well as its styling would have a powerful effect on Web-based systems. If packages of content could also tell programs what their elements mean in business terms, then systems would be able to collaborate with each other without human intervention. Systems would be able to use common vocabularies, implemented as simple codes embedded in the data they describe, to work together.

The result is XML (extensible markup language). Developers use XML to create vocabularies that describe particular business areas, so that systems in the same business domain can communicate with each other. XML is also at the core of the development efforts of every major software vendor, ensuring a growing skills base and a broad commitment to its long-term use.

BAE Systems and CSC identified XML as the ideal solution for creating the EAI layer. Exostar provides a stable data structure that can be thought of as a target language. Each of the systems that needed to interface with Exostar spoke their own languages. But every system in this heterogeneous collection could be described thoroughly and accurately in XML. The team could then build XML adapters to pipe data between the different business languages.

A key benefit to this approach is that it has very little impact on legacy systems. As the name suggests, 'systems integration' usually demands that the systems being integrated each be modified in order to create a new, combined entity. This approach is disruptive, and highly risky. In the first place, every legacy system running in a business such as BAE Systems is there to perform a business purpose. Taking the system offline, or replanning its maintenance schedule, in order to integrate it with another system causes interruptions in service. Even system testing following integration will present some disruption to existing users.

Developers then face a potentially greater problem associated with invasive systems integration: the risk of introducing errors to the system during redevelopment. Most legacy systems fall into the category labelled 'if it ain't broke, don't fix it'. Legacy systems remain in organizations because they carry out tasks vital to the business. They are also usually complex systems that have been altered over many generations of development, to the point where developers may no longer be able to understand fully how they work. As layer upon layer of code builds up over the years, dependencies between parts of the system become harder to comprehend. These dependencies are often only discovered when attempts at maintenance or integration inadvertently break them, and the system begins to behave unexpectedly or erratically. Systems integration is not a task for the faint-hearted, and is understandably avoided in many parts of organizations.

Using XML adapters provides another means of getting systems to work together without tinkering with their internal workings. An XML adapter is designed to match the expected output and input of a target legacy system. It then works with that legacy system in a way that mimics what the legacy system is used to. The adapter acts rather like an antibody, attaching to the system through a communicating interface that matches the target. The opposite end of the adapter – in this case, where it 'speaks' to Exostar – matches the online exchange's defined inputs and outputs. By building an adapter for each target system, the entire portfolio of legacy systems can be connected to Exostar without any internal adjustments, loss of business service or an extended testing cycle. The outcome is more like systems collaboration than integration. The family of systems works together through the set of adapters, which encapsulate the required business logic. In a traditional systems integration project, the code dealing with communications with Exostar would be distributed among the legacy systems. The BAE Systems/CSC strategy enables much easier management of the systems portfolio going forward, since new adapters can be readily added to the set when needs arise.

From pilot to showcase

The team was highly aware that it needed to prove the business readiness of its solution if it was to win approval from senior management. Security was a key issue. The scale and confidentiality of BAE Systems' business meant that any failure to secure every aspect of the procurement process from loss, misdirection or capture would destroy the new solution's credibility. Consequently the team began by building a proof-of-concept system limited to one site. Transactions were limited to purchase orders and purchase order amendments, and transacted initially with a small group of selected suppliers.

Customer Support and Solutions (CS&S) Operations in the UK was selected as the pilot site. CS&S is dedicated to managing service delivery costs for all customer contracts. It is a global operation with service staff based in offices all over the world. The UK operation is situated on 30 sites and typically generates 23,000 transactions per year, rising to 65,000, through no less than 32 different procurement systems.

Risk was further reduced through the use of standard, validated management methodologies. BAE Systems' LifeCycle Management methodology was used alongside CSC's Catalyst™ approach to create and implement the solution, providing management control and quality assurance right the way from business case creation through to deployment and delivery to the support environment.

The team was aware that the project's success would rely on the cooperation of procurement staff both inside and outside BAE Systems. Although senior management could be bought in through demonstrable attention to issues of security and risk containment, those who use the systems everyday would be key to its delivering real benefits to the business. There was some initial resistance both from suppliers and BAE Systems staff, since the project changed the processes they were familiar with. CS&S staff were used to downloading purchase orders from their ERP system and e-mailing them to the supplier, then receiving responses to the orders by e-mail. Now they had to rely on a new system and new processes to transact orders with their suppliers.

This critical issue was overcome by running a number of workshops in the BAE Systems Solution Demonstration Facility. During the workshops both buyers and suppliers were able to try out the new system, executing a number of business case scenarios, reviewing the results and highlighting any issues that needed immediate attention.

Savings that count

The effect of connecting the first ERP system to Exostar radically changed the way the CS&S Operations department handled its procurement. The solution proved to be so successful and flexible that it was quickly deployed in several other BAE Systems business units. The roadmap for deploying the system throughout the global business is now in place.

Within CS&S Operations alone, the cost of sending orders to 6,000 suppliers was reduced by as much as £7 per transaction. This is expected to provide a return on investment of US $400,000 in the first three years, even before BAE started to calculate other benefits such as reduced cycle time and improved data quality.

The company's projected procurement savings of £20 million are impressive in themselves. However, BAE Systems has also acquired a platform for systems collaboration that will impact many crucial areas of its business. By removing the human translation of information between systems, and letting different systems share a common language via the EAI layer, BAE Systems has refitted the business for future expansion while attacking its operating cost base. The company's collaboration with CSC has also created the capability of collaboration for its many enterprise systems, and laid down a path to further, repeating bottom-line benefits.

Resolving the complex junction of a set of business applications such as BAE Systems' procurement systems is an undertaking that requires sensitive and expert handling. These kinds of systems integration projects are often best handled by external consultants, since they tend to bring the most up-to-date integration skills to the task. This is not to say that in-house staff are not equal to the task. But an external consultancy brings repeated experience of completing projects of similar scales and complexity, whereas for in-house staff an integration of this size and criticality might be a once-in-a-lifetime occurrence. The required technical skills, in this case those of XML, can be taught but their rapid application to the business environment cannot be assured. Organizations reduce their technology risk by using experienced help at such times.

CSC's position as a consulting partner also helped it perform a mediating role, ensuring that the organization's senior management were behind the project and that the right area was chosen for the pilot. The team's technical solution mediates among systems; its consulting style mediated among people.

CASE STUDY 9.3

A KNOWLEDGE PORTAL HELPS CLOSE THE DEPRIVATION GAP

The launch of a knowledge management portal to help regenerate the UK's most deprived neighbourhoods delivers guidance direct to users in the community.

The UK government's National Strategy for Neighbourhood Renewal aims to close the gap between deprived areas and the rest of the country within 10 years. Success depends on providing policy-makers, specialists in this field and community groups with ready answers to the question: 'What works where?' The National Strategy Action Plan called for development of a knowledge management system, which would be: 'a systematic and comprehensive guide to the information available on what works in tackling the various problems of deprived neighbourhoods. It will draw upon experience of what works, across England and beyond, and link into sources of evidence from other departments, outside bodies and regional, local and neighbourhood feedback.'

The Neighbourhood Renewal Unit (NRU) worked with PA Consulting Group to create a comprehensive, Web-based knowledge management portal to meet this need. The portal was developed using PA's Rapid Systems Development approach, which encouraged users to shape the portal and its content to their requirements. Despite a challenging development timescale of six months, the portal was implemented two weeks ahead of schedule.

Since its launch by Neighbourhood Renewal Minister Barbara Roche in October 2002, the site has received more than 350,000 hits. This level of traffic is well above the specified targets. Of the users surveyed 88 per cent have found the portal useful in the design and delivery of neighbourhood renewal programmes. This represents a step-change in user behaviour. As intended, neighbourhood renewal initiatives are now being based on evidence about 'what works', accessible from a single, authoritative source.

PA's Jim Knox says:

> What made this assignment so challenging was the wide range of users involved in neighbourhood renewal projects, from residents in deprived neighbourhoods to policemen, health and education professionals and policy civil servants. We had to find a common language for reaching all these groups, and helping them do their jobs better.

Inequalities in the quality of life

Over the past 20 years, hundreds of neighbourhoods throughout Britain have seen a wide gap open up between their residents' quality of life and that enjoyed by people elsewhere in the country. For example:

■ In the 10 per cent most deprived electoral wards, 44 per cent of people rely on means-tested benefits, compared with a national average of 22 per cent.
■ In the 10 per cent most deprived wards 43 per cent of all housing is not fit for habitation.
■ 40 per cent of the population live in the 88 most deprived local authority areas.

The National Strategy for Neighbourhood Renewal aims to close the gap between deprived areas and the rest of the UK by working with policy-makers, local agencies and community members to reduce levels of crime, unemployment, ill health and under-achievement. The government set up the NRU to lead the delivery of this agenda.

The NRU recognized that access to appropriate information was essential to deliver change. However, a departmental survey showed that only 11 per cent of people involved in delivering current neighbourhood renewal programmes were basing their design and delivery on evaluated evidence, such as studies of earlier initiatives. The same survey showed that 83 per cent would use such evidence if it were available.

Based on this survey and on similar findings from the government Policy Action Team 16 (PAT), the NRU identified an immediate need to develop an online knowledge management portal for the neighbourhood renewal community, giving access to evaluated evidence of not only 'what works' but also 'what does not work'. For example, the portal could share experience suggesting that CCTV initiatives to improve neighbourhood security need to be supported by other measures such as community wardens or 'alley gating'.

The NRU wanted all information to be delivered clearly and succinctly, so that it could be readily used by all kinds of people. The portal would include online networks of practitioners, policy and guidance documents, and case studies of projects that were either under way or completed.

The project called not only for skills in the design and development of knowledge systems, but also for familiarity with neighbourhood renewal activity in a large number of areas. The knowledge areas covered a complex mass of government policy, including housing, crime, employment, health and education. The team had to identify and address the key topical issues for each of these areas in order to make the site as relevant and usable as possible for its target users.

Designing the portal

The NRU/PA team made its first mark by agreeing and securing a brand for the portal: www.renewal.net. The team then set four goals – to:

■ clearly define the overall system requirements;
■ develop the www.renewal.net brand and imagery;
■ identify the overall look and feel of the site;
■ define an information model to support content classification and site navigation.

The new portal had to meet the needs of an unusually diverse user base, ranging from local residents to neighbourhood renewal practitioners. Users would therefore have varying degrees of IT literacy. PA used its rapid systems development (RSD) approach to drive out the optimal design. RSD is an iterative technique that involves users and other stakeholders in the design and development of a system from day one. RSD enabled the team to take into account the fact that renewal programmes had not historically made use of evaluated evidence. The technique ensured that users took ownership of the initiative from its inception. This was the only way to make sure that the portal included the content that users really needed, and that the users also modified their working practices to make use of that content.

The team's iterative approach also allowed it to prioritize development of the content to ensure that it matched the government's priority areas in housing and environment, health, education, worklessness and crime while designing both content and format to maximize usability of the site.

The team also had to formulate a strategy for capturing the vast amounts of content relating to neighbourhood renewal, and enabling further content to be added to the growing resource. Microsoft's SharePoint software was used as the platform for content management.

Over the six-month development life cycle, the team consulted more than 2,000 prospective users of the portal. The team held focus groups, workshops, brainstorming sessions, conferences and seminars. These consultations provided opportunities for reviewing and commenting on successive versions of the site, thereby helping to control the iterative progress of the project. The sessions also enabled the team to evaluate documents being developed for the site with the target audience.

Renewal.net's users include people from all walks of life, from senior civil servants and policy-makers to tenants within the UK's most deprived areas. Knox says that the diversity of the portal's users was a guiding factor in the team's design of the site:

> There are all sorts of people involved in partnerships to renew neighbourhoods, including members of the community and staff of statutory agencies like the local authority or police. Say they've identified a problem with abandoned cars. They can go to renewal.net, search on 'abandoned cars' and access half a dozen case studies on how the problem was tackled in other places.

The programme of consultation sessions also created visibility for the portal, and a demand for its services. The sessions allowed the team to promote the site widely prior to its official launch. On the supply side, the extensive discussions helped create a consensus on how the portal's information would be collected and displayed. This process included every government department concerned with neighbourhood renewal issues and policy.

Where suitable advice on renewal did already exist, it could be on any one of hundreds of Web sites and was therefore difficult to find. The team designed a content collection strategy that allowed users to identify and access existing policy and guidance documentation via a single contact point. In addition, templates were developed to ensure that new documents created specifically for the portal would be clear and easy to understand.

Much of the existing evidence consisted of complex, lengthy research studies. What users needed, however, was simple, punchy material written in plain English and straightforwardly answering the question 'What has worked and why?' The team arranged for the content to be rewritten to meet this need and conducted interactive user groups to confirm that the right note was being struck.

A critical part of developing new content involved recruiting the right team of authoritative contributors across the broad range of subject areas. Such a group had never been formed before. The project team organized coaching for these independent experts in writing effectively for the Web and for the portal's diverse audience. The launch content had to be developed in an aggressive timescale of four months and the activity required the team to create 250 documents from scratch. Each document was built around the needs of practitioners to make sure that the portal would provide short, readable and punchy documents, not long and inaccessible reports.

Collaboration across disciplines is very much a mark of successful neighbourhood renewal. The project demonstrated the benefits of this approach in microcosm by bringing together NRU and PA colleagues within the joint team. Bill Feinstein, Senior Knowledge Adviser at the NRU, says: 'I found it really valuable to be effectively part of the project team. I felt that we avoided many potential delays or wrong turnings by working in this way. The assignment has felt like a joint endeavour; the spirit has been collaborative.'

A recognizable, memorable brand helps to ensure that the site's material appeals to those leading neighbourhood renewal programmes. The team developed a distinctive brand identity in collaboration with users and with the Office of the Deputy Prime Minister's (ODPM) communications team.

A trip to renewal.net

Renewal.net is now the authoritative source of evaluated evidence of what has, and has not, worked in neighbourhood renewal. At the time of writing, there are 1,878 documents available on renewal.net, including 277 evidence-based case studies. The collection continues to grow as more evidence is collected and linked.

The site's layout is logical, uncluttered and devoid of distractions. A master section introduces neighbourhood renewal, including overviews, case studies, explanation of various policies, summaries of research findings, FAQs (frequently asked questions) and links to other relevant sites.

The team created a simple navigation structure to help users find information quickly within a complex web of government policy. Renewal.net addresses over 130 renewal issues, such as attracting investment in land and property, reducing domestic violence and reducing truancy, yet users can go straight to the area they need. The navigation structure helps to make sense of government policy, demonstrating how the various initiatives 'join up' to aid those involved in improving quality of life for communities.

New users can move to a 'how to' overview introducing people to bringing about change in their neighbourhoods. The material is full of proven ideas for getting things done including: how to build a partnership; how to define the problem; how to select a project; how to implement a project; how to monitor and evaluate; and how to influence mainstream programmes.

The portal includes a comprehensive 'jargon buster' covering the plethora of specialist terms used throughout the renewal sector, from 'active community unit' to 'working together learning together', complete with definitions and links to relevant sites. This resource in itself provides a handy primer for those getting to grips with the help available in neighbourhood renewal.

Users of the site can register for regular e-mail updates, detailing the latest additions to the site that are relevant to their particular interests. More than 500 users have registered to take advantage of this facility. The feedback from the user survey has demonstrated that this is an exceptionally valuable area of the site as it allows users to gain an understanding of new areas and how these reflect government policy priorities. Users can also access lists of upcoming events, searchable by region.

Elsewhere on the site, regional pages are being added gradually, so that users can quickly access documents relevant to their area. Entering 'parks' as a search term from the London regional page in February 2004 fetched 363 documents in total, with 15 highlighted as being specifically relevant to the London area. The full document set included a case study on Emerson Park Development Corporation in East St Louis, Illinois, an overview of vehicle crime, research into the design of English seaside towns and an event about engaging refugees and asylum seekers in service development.

While the portal's main function is the provision of authoritative data, the site also acts as a community resource via its discussion forums. Anyone can browse the forums, and those who register can also contribute. Forums are organized around the neighbourhood renewal themes of housing and environment, worklessness, education, crime, health and local economies, as well as by region, practitioner group and 'how to' topics. According to one user, renewal.net 'is an outstanding Web site, and an invaluable source of information for me.'

The portal's effects

Renewal.net was launched in October 2002 by Barbara Roche MP, the government minister responsible for neighbourhood renewal. In the three months following its launch, renewal.net was accessed around 530 times every working day, giving an overall total of around 35,000 sessions. During an average session users looked at five different pages, giving a total of around 176,000 page views. The visitor statistics are nearly 50 per cent more than the targets given in the project's business plan targets.

More importantly, a recent survey has shown that the site has dramatically changed user behaviour, with 86 per cent of users indicating that the site enables them to take a more evidence-based approach to the design and delivery of renewal projects. Prior to the development of the portal, only 11 per cent based their project decisions on evaluated evidence. The growing use of such evidence will increase the likelihood that renewal programmes will achieve their intended results, whether they are tackling violent crime or graffiti.

Renewal.net is also helping policy-makers to adopt an evidence-based approach. For example, criminal justice bodies have begun to take a more evidence-based approach to drug abuse, which has led them to create links with the education and health sectors. A formal ODPM evaluation of the project and portal is currently under way.

The concept of the Internet portal has developed from that of a consumer destination to a corporate management tool. The NRU has evolved the concept further, making the portal a tool of the community. The earliest portals attempted to concentrate useful services in strongly branded home pages, with the intention of driving large volumes of Internet traffic through those pages. Such commercial portals hoped to derive advertising revenues from the many millions of 'eyeballs' they believed would come to them first for all those people's Web needs. Most such portals failed because their brands and services could not deliver as much value as the comprehensive, optimized search engines such as Google or the authoritative news providers such as the BBC. In the enterprise sector, portals have been developed to guide users through the increasingly complex mass of documentation created for employee use. In many large organizations, corporate portals have replaced paper publication processes in areas such as employment policy or health and safety regulations.

The NRU has been able to exploit the development of portal sites and the underlying technologies that underpin them in order to serve a previously ill-supported, widespread population. Renewal.net does more than collect together trustworthy, usable information and make it accessible. The portal is also a major tool in the forging of a broadly based renewal community, providing it with structure, support and cohesion.

The project's sponsor, Barbara Roche MP, is clear on the project's fundamental aim of connecting experience with action: 'For the first time ever, evidence on how to improve health, housing and education; how to create jobs; and how to reduce crime, has been brought together in a clear and accessible form, targeted at those doing neighbourhood renewal on the ground.'

The NRU has commissioned evaluations of the site's impact on specific neighbourhood renewal programmes. In the meantime, anecdotal evidence suggests that this project is helping the NRU in its goal of eliminating the gap between Britain's most deprived areas and the rest of the country during the coming decade.

PA managed to combine relevant business sector experience in urban renewal with the technical skills necessary to get a complex portal up and running in a short time. The PA team's insistence on document usability and attention to the crafting of each piece of content by the right experts shows an insight into the enduring value of information: it is only when people can find, understand and be inspired by relevant information that they can take action and make the changes they seek, whether those changes are in the sphere of business, the community, or personal life. The lessons of what makes content work on the Web, and how Web sites can best be structured for a wide variety of uses, are derived from wide experience of creating solutions in a number of different settings, both commercial and public sector.

This broad knowledge of how content is sourced, refined and consumed for maximum value is a valuable commodity for those consultants who have acquired it in their work with clients. Just as those citizens and officials active in the neighbourhood renewal movement share their knowledge of what does and does not work, so the best consultancies act as a means of disseminating and applying best practice throughout the organizations with which they engage. In this case, PA combined a commitment to plain English communication with systems development excellence to prove that the most far-flung pieces of knowledge can be brought together, made to make sense, and empowered to make a difference to ordinary lives.

CASE STUDY 9.4

FLOW, STREAMS AND THE EROSION OF RESISTANCE

Implementing workflow and document management technologies has given one of the world's largest insurers a blueprint for creating change across the business.

Aon is among the world's largest insurance broking and risk management companies and its UK operation, with two London offices, is a specialist in highly complex insurance risks. The London Market has a long tradition of face-to-face interaction, which is a complex, time-consuming and expensive way of doing business. Automation is now catching up with the London Market, and players are beginning to modernize their business processes as the market abandons its reliance on paper mechanisms. The overall evolution of the market is governed by its progress in enabling electronic transactions. However, individual players can make important steps towards a paper-free environment by reassessing their internal processes. By addressing their internal needs they can make savings and create flexibility, while making themselves better prepared for the dawning era of inter-company electronic trading.

In 1998, Aon Limited decided that its long-term future lay in greater electronic trading with its business partners. Electronic trading would demand more efficient ways of exchanging information, both within the market and within the company itself. The company realized that the change to electronic trading would put great strain on the company's systems, business processes and staff.

The move to electronic trading would clearly need a new system to improve the company's handling of both insurance content and transactions. Aon began a four-year partnership with Impact Plus to deliver an environment that would yield savings in its business processes and make the company ready for the online business regime emerging in its industry. Impact Plus's Graham Whitehead says:

> The way they were looking at it was that they wanted stepping stones to electronic trading. They wanted tools that would allow them to understand where in the renewal process a particular risk was, what correspondence they had received from a client in relation to a particular risk or set of risks, and to get a clear picture of their risk processing responsibilities.

The team began by building a seven-year business case setting out the value of introducing document management systems, workflow technology and new ways of working to go along with the new support systems. Over a period of three months, Aon and Impact Plus staff worked together on the business case to gain a thorough understanding of the way the company worked. To ensure ownership within the business, the business case was discussed at every level within Aon Limited, and was then presented to executives from Aon's headquarters in Chicago.

The key to the business case's approval in 1999 was its focus on automation as a lever for greater control of the business. New systems would help achieve a far greater level of process consistency across the business, while improving customer service by providing fast access to client information. Savings would be made by better managing the escalating amounts of paper documents and e-mails being sent, received and duplicated. At the same time, improvements to the company's systems would allow it to embrace industry initiatives on Regulatory Compliance and the exchange of important information among industry participants. It all adds up to the largest project Aon Limited had ever undertaken at that time, and which is on target to save the company tens of millions of pounds while readying it for improved competitiveness in the evolving insurance industry. Achieving the project's goals will give Aon a level of efficiency and organizational flexibility not found in any of its competitors.

Commonality and differences

Though document management and workflow systems will improve the productivity and flexibility of any information-intensive organization that adopts the technologies, these are not simple generic solutions that can be successfully applied to businesses in a random fashion. While the broad benefits of generic applications such as word processors or Web browsers make them relatively straightforward purchases for the organization, workflow in particular strikes right to the heart of what the business does, and how it does what it does.

Workflow systems formalize and support the processing of packages of information within multi-disciplinary environments. Workflow is the white-collar world's equivalent to process automation via conveyor belts and specialist workstations. In a typical workflow system, sets of information such as funding applications are captured electronically on their entry into the organization. Documents that arrive in paper form are scanned and stored as digital images, and may also be converted into computer-readable text using optical character recognition (OCR) techniques. Incoming documents are categorized and tagged, much as traditional paper-based files are created.

But since a workflow system lives in a networked environment, electronic files can be sent immediately for the attention of the staff members that need to work on them next.

Workflow systems allow document collections to be routed in sequence or in parallel, depending on the underlying business process designed into the system. So, for example, our funding application might be routed to three individuals in sequence so that each can check different aspects of the application for completion of sections, adherence to the rules of the scheme and supporting documentation. If the application passes these three stages, it may then be passed simultaneously to the members of a decision-making board for their approval. The workflow system marks the changing status of each case it deals with as work is done on the case. The system therefore acts as a combined library, document control mechanism and progress-chaser.

While some technologists have attempted to develop generic workflow processes for many business domains, including insurance, these have rarely met with success. One reason is that even the best generic system requires tailoring to its individual target business environments. Tailoring the generic system entails researching the business processes of the target organization, just as creating a system from scratch would do. The task of adapting a generic framework to particular environments often has no cost or time advantage compared with starting with a blank canvas.

Another reason why generic workflow processes meet scepticism lies in every organization's firm belief in its own uniqueness. Companies understandably believe that their success to date indicates their competence: they have grown their own businesses, and see their processes as an organic part of the success they have achieved. Furthermore, the mechanics of competition suggest that success can be related, if perhaps only obscurely, to the manifest differences found in each player's approach to business. It is seldom possible for management to point to a particular aspect of the organization's operations and associate it with business dominance, and when such an identification is made the focus is often on a novel, standalone system imported from outside the organization or developed in-house as the dream of a single motivated individual. In traditional white-collar environments such as the insurance industry, where inputs, outputs and value-adding processes are all composed of information, the connection between process design and business performance is especially hard to trace. The result is a paradox for managers tasked with creating change: people tend to believe in workflow as a concept, but believe equally strongly that it cannot be applied in their own environments.

Phil Tyson, Aon's Programme Director for the project, recognizes that these beliefs are intimately related to the company's business domain: 'The highly specialized area of insurance in which we operate has a 300-year heritage of doing business face to face and a track record for resisting change; we knew that the cultural hurdles would be significant.'

Aon is a good example of the problem of turning from the generic to the particular, since the company exhibited all the variety of its industry within its own walls. Each business unit performed similar functions, but each was convinced it worked differently, and that the differences among divisions were essential. The team found that the practical consequence of Aon's evolved habits were complex processes involving much shuffling and shuttling of paperwork between teams, and a heavy photocopying bill. In order to add a new insurance policy to the various systems in the relevant business units, a key contractual document had to be photocopied at least six times. The team also noted that years of inertia has helped make the current inefficiencies appear normal, and created a reluctant attitude to change. If technology was to be a business enabler at Aon, the business environment would also need to be addressed to ensure that the technology solution 'took'.

Twin tracks to change

The Aon/Impact Plus team ran a vendor selection process to find and engage the right technology partners. Tenders were invited from selected consortia and the responses scored against pre-agreed criteria. Reference visits were then made to large reference installations around the world in order to see the various types of solution in action. A winning consortium was chosen based on its knowledge of the London Market and the proven quality of its product set. This consortium was made up of FileNET, a leading provider of content management and workflow tools, and systems integrator August Group. The team then turned to the task of creating the changes in culture and working practice it had identified as crucial to the project's success.

The team invented a two-pronged approach to the project. One stream of activity would concentrate on IT delivery, or 'getting the technology ready for the business', as the team defined it. A second, parallel stream would work on internal change, 'getting the business ready for the technology'. This approach was based on Impact Plus's Programme and Change Management (PCM) technique.

The members of the business readiness stream worked closely with Aon staff to prepare the 11 business units for the coming electronic revolution. The workstream created 'change teams' in each business unit, meeting on a weekly basis to plan the phased introduction of new working practices. The change teams were supported by cross-departmental analysts, who were able to identify and communicate similarities and differences among the different Aon teams. There were over 2,500 people in the business units, each specializing in different areas such as aviation, shipping and financial services. All these staff believed that their working practices were necessarily unique. The team was able to show them that many of their processes were very similar and that, with some redesign, they could benefit from following common processes.

Getting people to recognize similarities in processes can be difficult to achieve; but once those involved have begun to represent common processes, they can rapidly move to the opposite extreme and begin to search for 'the one, complete system' that will work for everyone. The team knew that this is a misleading path. According to Whitehead: 'The typical route is to define processes very tightly, but that way it gets too complicated. Our view was: we've got the experts, but the administration tasks are holding them back. Let's let them take their decisions, rather than try to put all their expertise in the system.'

In other words, the team's guiding principle was to target the mechanisms of the work, not the expertise behind the work. The aim was to remove paper, not brains. The project's clear respect for the value added by the staff was a major aspect in its success. Requirements for the system were gathered diligently from everyone involved. Each view of the system's requirements was captured, documented, shared and challenged.

The business change workstream

The team set out five goals for the business change workstream:

- Create a carefully phased, low-risk introduction of the system to the business.
- Establish clear ownership of the new way of working by each of the business units.
- Create a well-planned change process.
- Ensure that common business processes are followed by all the business units.
- Establish a clear focus on achieving the benefits within each business unit.

In order to phase in the new system, the project team worked with each change team to understand the business unit's trading cycle, the pattern of peaks and troughs in its workload and the competitive pressures it was experiencing and predicted for the future. Project activities could then be planned to fit into the business cycle, minimizing the impact on the continuation of normal business. The team also set up a dedicated 'familiarization' area so that change teams could get hands-on experience of the system as it developed. The familiarization facility allowed staff to explore and discuss different ways of using the system, and to choose those that would generate the highest level of benefit. Tyson says: 'Feedback from the familiarization sessions proved that this approach reduced the risk associated with going live and helped greatly in removing the uncertainty and even fear associated with the new system.'

Early access to systems helps to show staff that what is being built is intended to be relevant to their duties and preferences. This kind of exposure also helps trigger ideas about better ways of working, redundant procedures or areas of ambiguity. From the point of view of a system's functionality, many people find it hard to specify what they want a system to do in the abstract, but are very capable of critiquing a working prototype and using their reaction as a springboard to defining their requirements. This experience also demonstrates to those staff involved that they are genuinely in control of the development, and that the business benefits of the system really do form its top priority.

Ownership of the project by the business units was designed into the project's delivery by the creation of the change teams. Each change team grew steadily in capability and confidence to a point where it became wholly responsible and accountable for delivering the necessary change within its own area of the business. The change team, rather than the project team, became the first port of call for queries from staff within a business unit. Change teams also took ownership of the communications exercises linked to the roll out of the system.

The business units had only minimal experience of working with formal project planning tools and were initially unconvinced that change could be delivered successfully. Staff views were informed by the prevailing belief that technology had failed to deliver against its promises throughout the industry. In order to reassure each business unit about the organization's determination to achieve its goals, pragmatic and detailed project plans were created, based on a common template created by the project team. Each plan showed the key deliverables and milestones for the unit in a single page. This concise presentation focused the business change activity around specific goals and outcomes, and demonstrated that the project was under control.

The team was also able to identify parts of the business processes that were common to all 11 business units and where common workflows could be followed. These processes were then automated using the FileNET workflow tool, and became the core of the new system.

Highly visible planning, ownership and process modelling activities demonstrated the team's commitment to readying the business for a step-change in performance. All of these activities had also to be coordinated with a clear focus on achieving the business benefits determined by the project's business case. Widespread and regular discussions about benefit realization therefore started early on in the project. Each business unit was made aware of the timescales and level of benefit expected for its area.

Organizations always experience a reduction in productivity as users get to grips with a new system, but the team did not want the changeover to undermine the realization of the project's business goals. The project team therefore guided each change team in quantifying the scale and duration of the expected dip in productivity, and helped each business unit to plan activities to minimize the impact.

The change teams ensured a gradual and orderly transfer of ownership from the project team to the business. This approach also allowed Aon to keep the project team to a small size. The new flexibility and capability for change proved critical, in the aftermath of 11 September 2001. The attacks on the World Trade Center led to some of the toughest trading conditions ever experienced in the London Market and the change teams played a vital role in ensuring that, despite the extremely complex business environment, the implementation continued to progress through this difficult period.

The systems stream

The design and build of the new system took 18 months, with new releases of software and working practices issued at regular intervals. By delivering the system and its working context incrementally and in lockstep, the team was able to transition the business in an open and coherent manner, with improvements to functionality arriving in discrete and digestible portions. This strategy echoes the 'stepping stones' philosophy underlying the project.

Among the key criteria for the project's success was the reliability of the systems it delivered. Aon staff pointed out that when their existing systems were unavailable, they could revert to a paper back-up. But under the new plan, which involved a wholesale shift to electronic files, if the system went down they 'might as well go home'.

The team therefore designed a highly resilient system with a standby server and a disaster recovery system at an alternative location, to ensure that users would have near-uninterrupted access. The standby system can be brought online within 20 minutes if a component in the main production system fails. The disaster-recovery server can be made available within a few hours, should a disaster affect the first two systems. The system architecture has been designed to allow for automatic and instantaneous switching between any of the three systems in the future, should the need arise. This is an example of planned replication, undertaken to ensure resilience. Aon used to replicate procedures because it had no better way of performing its business processes. Now it has standardized its business processes, but replicated their support mechanisms to ensure continuity of delivery.

To date, the computer system and associated new ways of working have been rolled out to more than 2,500 users. The business now has automated processes that are fully compliant with industry regulations and business standards, and open to audit. More efficient ways of handling correspondence and policy-related documentation have been installed, and all users have access to common, well-understood business processes. The company has achieved end-to-end automation of new business, administration, claims and accounts processes. It now has a single repository into which all documentation – including e-mails – can be filed and to which everyone has access. Links to Aon's policy documentation and correspondence production system, central processing system and e-mail system are in place. The new systems environment also includes a single authoritative reference list of client organizations, replacing a plethora of previous databases. Populating the new client database involved purging the company's aggregated records of some 30,000 redundant entries.

Going forward

Change projects measured in years inevitably have to roll with the punches delivered by unpredicted changes in their external environments. This project had to endure a great challenge to its programme when the terrorist attacks of September 11 led to the rapid re-engineering of the company's very industry. The challenges of electronic trading in its market and inertia in its organization were dwarfed by a sudden change in the insurance industry's posture in the face of increased global terrorism. However, the commercial effect of the disaster was an upturn in premium trends. The industry's cost-cutting attitude switched to one of growth. A key implication for Aon of the industry's change in direction was a shift in emphasis from reducing staff to retaining them, and their valuable expertise. This project is therefore delivering on its business case in a different format from that originally envisaged. The business benefits are being measured in terms of improved service, quality and capacity rather than cost reduction. Another way of looking at this change of emphasis is to say that the project has allowed Aon to direct its investment towards growth at the required time.

Impact Plus introduced a key principle into its work with Aon: the twin-track approach to change. The claim that 'technology must serve the business' is often made by consultants but undermined by single-minded attention to the installation of systems, and an unthinking disregard for the working environment in which those systems will function. Impact Plus was careful to create equally weighted streams of activity aimed at creating the best possible climate for the introduction of the new systems. The firm was also determined to give equal billing to the new ways of working that would surround the new support functions, so that the human dimension of the change never fell from view. By pursuing their twin-track approach, Impact Plus proved that, in business, parallel lines can indeed converge on a successful implementation.

'Implementation' is another keyword to associate with this project and Impact Plus's general approach to its work. The firm has a strong belief in implementation, not just ideas. For this team, workflow is a lens through which processes can be examined and corrected. It is detailed, nuts-and-bolts work that does not respond to grand gestures or sweeping visions. This attitude gives the consultancy a highly practical take on its own capabilities. For example, looking back on the project, Impact Plus's Graham Whitehead finds one aspect he might do differently, if he could turn the clock back: 'We could have done more role play – more scenarios. We ran scenarios in the familiarization environment, but that was well into development. For example, "client" can mean different things to different people, and we found out through scenarios that we needed a richer definition for it.'

The lasting effect within Aon is the recognition that change is possible, and liberating. This project has given the company a blueprint for making change, based on a dual-stream approach to technology development and business readiness. It is an approach that is now being used on other projects within Aon as the company continues to respond to its evolving business environment.

References

Friedman, M and Boorstin, D J (1951) How to Plan and Pay for the Safe and Adequate Highways We Need, in *Roads in a Market Economy*, G Roth (1996) pp 223–45, Avebury Technical, Aldershot

Goldratt, E M (1994) *Theory of Constraints*, North River Press, Croton-on-Hudson, New York

Kunde, J (1999) *Corporate Religion*, Financial Times Prentice Hall, London

Williams, D and Parr, T (2004) *Enterprise Programme Management*, Palgrave Macmillan, London

Index